Reading Hong Kong, Reading Ourselves

Edited by
Janel CURRY
Paul HANSTEDT

City University of Hong Kong Press

©2014 City University of Hong Kong

All rights reserved. No part of this publication may be reproduced, stored in a retrieval system, or transmitted, in any form or by any means, electronic, mechanical, photocopying, recording, Internet or otherwise, without the prior written permission of the City University of Hong Kong Press.

ISBN: 978-962-937-235-4

Published by
    City University of Hong Kong Press
    Tat Chee Avenue
    Kowloon, Hong Kong
    Website: www.cityu.edu.hk/upress
    E-mail: upress@cityu.edu.hk

Printed in Hong Kong

Reading Hong Kong, Reading Ourselves

Contents

Preface *ix*

Introduction *xiii*

Stage One: Initial Encounters

1 Eating Hong Kong:
   The Experiences of a Food Lover and Nutritional Scientist
   Hedley FREAKE 2

2 Street Level Sociology in Hong Kong
   David JAFFEE 24

3 Philosophy in the Streets: Walking in Hong Kong
   Gray KOCHHAR-LINDGREN 44

Stage Two: Seeing

4 Hong Kong: Cultural Transformation of the Public Sphere
   Tricia FLANAGAN 66

5 The Other Side of the Postcard:
   Navigating Linguistic Landscapes in Hong Kong
   Jackie Jia LOU 90

6   Discovering Hong Kong through Movement
       Elizabeth HUEBNER   112

Stage Three: The Search to Find and Understand the "Authentic" Other

7   Reflections on Geography, Hong Kong, and Beyond
       Janel CURRY   140

8   The Colonial Past in Hong Kong's Present
       David A. CAMPION   162

9   Hamlet in Hong Kong
       Joseph CHANEY   188

10   Are You in the Safe Zone?
       Cultural Sensitization and Religion for a Teaching Traveler
       Ivette VARGAS-O'BRYAN   210

Stage Four: Learning and Communicating in Place

11   How Good Am I? Self Evaluation in an Examination Culture
       Christopher DENEEN   230

12 Reflections on Learning and Teaching in Hong Kong
     Susan GANO-PHILLIPS   *250*

13 Rhetoric and the Art of Mid-Level Administration in Hong Kong
     Paul HANSTEDT   *272*

Stage Five: Cross-cultural Movements

14 Seeing/Doing Chinese History from Two Sides:
     Hong Kong and the United States
     David PONG   *286*

Postscript   *309*

Contributors   *313*

Preface

When I came in 1988 to live in Hong Kong, I read Jan Morris's new book, *Hong Kong*, as a treasure of discovery. The coming handover from Britain to China in 1997 was much in the air. Her easy descriptions of people and places created vivid moments of a city living on the cusp between its British colonial past and its Chinese mainland future. Her book shaped my experience of my new home. I returned to her chapters like returning to favorite neighborhoods. She clearly loved Hong Kong, and so did I.

Thirty years later I read *City Between Worlds: My Hong Kong* by Leo Ou-fan Lee. I marveled at how Leo Lee could show me how to re-see the city and its neighborhoods that I had long come to assume was home. Leo Lee's sense of history, literature and film, converging from East and West, built up layers of new meaning in his roamings and readings of buildings, streets and the flow of people in intricate, fluid, urban spaces. Lee's book re-enchanted Hong Kong for me. He led me to new conversations with the city I had stopped seeing as new.

Books about cities can open pathways to discover new places, and familiar places anew. This collection of fresh essays by fourteen reflective visitors about living in and learning from Hong Kong is chock full of discoveries for the new visitor to Hong Kong, and for the old hand who wishes to see his familiar city anew.

A great global city reshapes and renews itself. This morphing takes place not only in its physical landscape and features of infrastructure, but in the experiences it offers to sojourners who come and stay awhile. Visitors bring new ways of looking, questioning and appreciating the life of its people and institutions. This book of fourteen essays reveals the life of Hong Kong through their diverse academic disciplines of seeing, inquiring and expressing what they discover.

These fourteen "flaneurs," each ambling about different sections of the city, share their insights in finely-honed, first-person prose. A "flaneur" is someone who walks unhurriedly through an urban landscape, following serendipitous promptings, and gazing at whatever presents itself for reflection. Each of these fourteen flaneur frames reveals the same city in surprisingly different ways. This is a tribute to its two editors, a geographer (Curry) and a literature scholar (Hanstedt). All the writers knew one another through their work at different Hong Kong universities on the Fulbright Hong Kong General Education project (2008–2012). We are grateful to Mr. Po Chung who made gifts to the universities to host these academic guests and absorb their ideas about general education in the new four-year curriculum. A delightful spin-off from this project, this book exemplifies what general eduction can be: bringing many unique perspectives into focus to allow us to understand a common theme in depth. In this case, the theme is Hong Kong.

Reading Hong Kong, Reading Ourselves emerged from the regular sharing of their myriad encounters with Hong Kong life and society.

This helps to give the book a coherence, and a strong measure of fun as they learned the byways and back streets of their new city. One can imagine their many evenings of restaurant meals and rich storytelling that later firmed into the chapters of this book. In subtle ways, the writers refer to one another across their narratives, welcoming their complementary contributions to the whole.

Reading Hong Kong shows how subjective a city is. The thoughtful visitor brings his or her own ways of seeing into play when knowing a place layer by layer, for the first time. The deeper the observer penetrates and discovers the inner patterns of Hong Kong life, the more we come to know, as if in a cultural mirror, the author and sojourner of each essay. Each is making their own Hong Kong. But as they all touch in some way on underlying truths about life in our city, we smile with recognition. The city is like a text one reads and deciphers, linking one's sense of other cities with one's present experiences of this city in this moment of time. In reading the city, the reader discovers not only what is "out there" in the ever moving surround of Hong Kong's urban life, but also what is inside oneself as newcomer and as from another city and culture. Each essay writer brings to this creative book his or her education, personality, temperament, and home place of contrast. But little is predictable given the amazing serendipity of the way a place and person interact to create a mutual identity, if only for a day, a month, a year, and if you are lucky, even a lifetime.

Hong Kong is a much visited place. Over 50 million people, many from mainland China, stream through its hotels, restaurants and shopping malls each year. That is eight times our local population. We are told many more will visit our city in the future. That is a lot of first impressions! We sense well-worn stereotypes about Hong Kong from this happy, chamber-of-commerce viewpoint. But Hong Kong may be at risk of not just being "over-run" by visitors, but also "over-seen" without being understood by our guests. Hence the value of the few visitors who take their time here, go to unexpected places, ask funny questions, and by imagination think carefully what it might be like to be a Hong Kong person. Their ideas are small mirrors in which we might catch a new glimpse of ourselves as Hong Kong people. They do us a favor.

During thirteen years from 2000 as head of the Hong Kong America Center, I have had the pleasure of welcoming and orienting many young scholars and students who came to live, teach, and study in Hong Kong's universities. I encouraged each exchange visitor to discover their own Hong Kong and find ways to give voice and language to these experiences. A city is an endless running collection of commentaries about itself through such visitors who aim to get under the skin of the city. Let us reciprocate the hospitality that the people of this city have shown us through well-considered story-telling. That is what we have here. I commend this book to your reading of Hong Kong and, like these authors, your reading of yourselves in the process.

Glenn SHIVE PhD
United Board for Christian Higher Education in Asia

Introduction

Reading Hong Kong, Reading Ourselves builds on the growing interest of using "place" as text while providing a model of deepening cross-cultural encounters. The book, while focused on Hong Kong, serves as a model for reading "place" through the lenses of a range of disciplines, with each chapter exploring Hong Kong through a different perspective. The chapters, written by scholars whose disciplines range from English literature (Hamlet in Hong Kong) to nutritional science (Eating Hong Kong), are tightly bound through their common task of reflecting on their encounters with this place as disciplinary scholars. Each chapter is written in a personal and experiential style, but is also grounded in several key concepts from the individual disciplines that shaped the author's perceptions and encounters. The manuscript is also tightly held together in its goal of communicating a range of frameworks through which we can explore and read a place. Thus the book provides a starting point for approaching the learning of a new context—a way to begin to know what questions to ask.

The idea for this book arose out of the context of a four year Fulbright project, directed by the Hong Kong American Center, that placed scholars from a broad range of disciplines in individual Hong Kong universities to aid in the development of general education programs. As one of these Fulbright scholars, in the second of the four years, I soon realized that each of the Fulbright scholars was personally encountering Hong Kong through their own disciplinary lenses! This led to us realizing that the fullness of cross-cultural encounters might be able to be taught through providing a new model of seeing a place through these various lenses.

The majority of the contributors to this volume are US citizens who participated in the Fulbright program. But the group also reflects the diversity of the United States. One is a British-born scientist and another is originally from China, having been raised in Hong Kong but having spent his academic career in the United States. Added to this mix were others we encountered in Hong Kong who were from elsewhere but are now in academic positions in Hong Kong—a Chinese linguist who did her graduate studies in the United States, an Australian artist, and an American professor with a Chinese spouse. The cross-boundary mobility of the group of authors is in itself reflective of the growing experiences of the present generation and more so of the reality of life for the next generation. In fact many of us sought out these experiences in order to help prepare our children for a lifetime of crossing cultural boundaries, as well as better prepare our students at home in the United States.

With this goal in mind, this book has several major audiences. First, the book is meant to serve as a model for students going abroad, enhancing their skills of observation. The number of students who travel overseas from the United States in order to study has now reached one million a year. Secondly, the book is meant to also serve the growing number of interdisciplinary freshman or capstone undergraduate seminars. One of the key approaches to such courses has been to focus on a city from a variety of perspectives. This text, then, provides a concrete but rich cross-cultural example of this approach, one that provides a model for courses that are going to explore any variety of places. Thirdly, the book is targeted at providing a roadmap for undergraduates who are going abroad for internships as well as the increasing number of people in business who spend significant time overseas. It provides a starting point for approaching the learning of a new context—a way to begin to know what questions to ask. And finally, we hope this book will also be of interest to the general educated travel audience.

The book is organized in the same way that we encounter a new place. The first section of the book is on "Initial Encounters." When we first arrive we are often overwhelmed and confronted with the changes around us, bringing to the forefront everyday aspects of our own cultures that we had taken for granted—food and cooking, the unwritten rules of informal interactions amongst people, and our common streetscapes.

After we learn to become more comfortable in our surroundings, moving beyond initial encounters, we begin to start to "see" what is there and make more distinctions and differentiations. The second section focuses on this "seeing" which often involves paying more attention to the visual cues around us including language and public space. But it also includes our early attempts to find ways to be with others in this new culture, in spite of the linguistic and cultural barriers.

The third section of this book reflects the next stage of longer-term cross-cultural encounters—the search to understand what we are seeing and experiencing. We call this section "The Search to Find and Understand the 'Authentic' Other" because we find that our understanding changes daily and that there are many cultures and interpretations rather than just one. While the search to understand never really ends, it does drive us toward the need to see the place in the larger context of history, global interactions, and broader philosophical categories.

The fourth section, "Learning and Communicating in Place," includes chapters that begin to deal with how we actually develop ways to live and work within this other culture. Ultimately, when studying or working abroad, you become a participant in the culture. Understanding cultural cues and developing effective strategies for being active participants in institutions become necessary. As anyone will tell you who has attended a university abroad or had children in K-12 educational systems in other countries, education systems are particularly reflective of institutional and cultural values.

Introduction

The final essay in this book is by David Pong. David was born in China, raised in Hong Kong, went to university in Britain, spent his academic career in the United States teaching Chinese history, and as a Fulbright scholar worked with universities in Hong Kong on their general education courses on Chinese civilization. He embodies a life of crossing cultural boundaries: teaching American students about China at the University of Delaware, and sharing approaches on how we teach American history in the United States with Hong Kong colleagues who are faced with the task of communicating the complexities of Chinese civilization to their students who come from a variety of backgrounds. His essay reflects on the generosity of many who helped him in this journey, the opportunities that he has been given, and the strategies he employed in order to not just survive, but thrive in various contexts.

All the contributors to this book are scholars who are inherently interdisciplinary, curious, generalists, educators, and communicators. They speak from their disciplines, but also their hearts in these essays. And in giving this book its title, *Reading Hong Kong, Reading Ourselves*, they all affirm what anyone who has lived abroad knows: living abroad not only changes each of us, but ultimately leads us to a greater understanding of our own cultures, homes, and selves.

Janel CURRY

Stage One
Initial Encounters

Chapter 1

Eating Hong Kong:
The Experiences of a Food Lover and Nutritional Scientist

Hedley FREAKE

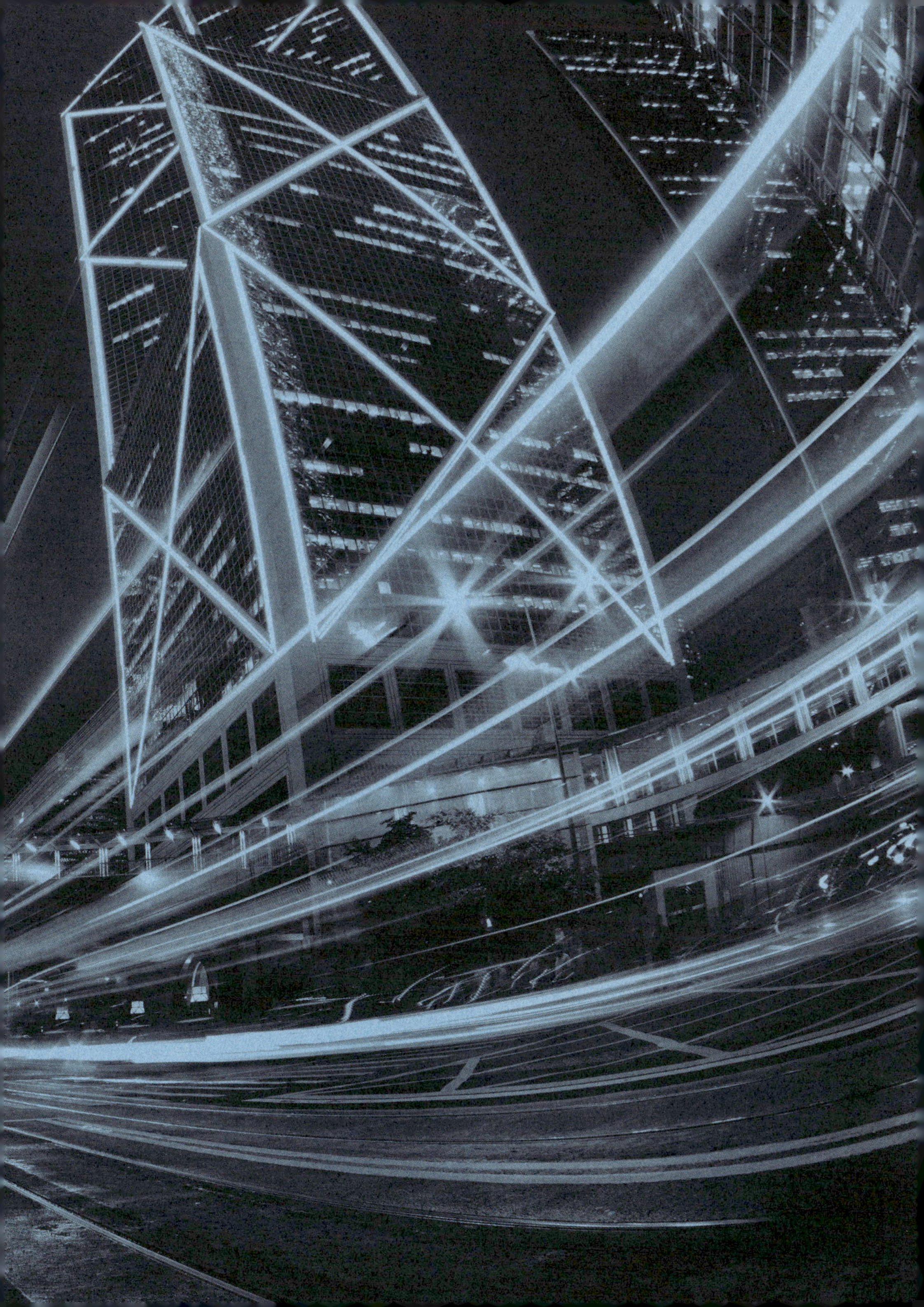

Food has always been an important part of my life. It probably started with being breast fed but I usually date it to when I was about 12 or 13 and I became deputy cook to my mother. She started working outside the home and I was responsible for preparing lunch for those who were around. I am the sixth of eight children, although I think by that time some of the older ones were elsewhere. The food was simple and straightforward and British, but I developed a feel and an understanding for it that was unusual for somebody of that age. Living in Ghana, West Africa for a year when I was 18 expanded enormously my concept of what food might be and then in my early twenties I spent three or four years working as a chef and a baker in a variety of restaurants. That led to the pursuit of a degree in nutrition, followed a PhD and a trail that culminated as a professor of nutrition. But while my nutritional biochemistry laboratory became an important part of my life, it never totally supplanted my kitchen.

My appointment in Hong Kong was centered at Hong Kong Polytechnic University (PolyU), which is situated in the heart of Kowloon, one of the most densely populated parts of the world. I taught an introductory nutritional biochemistry course, focused on the nutrients and their function in the body and similar to courses I teach in the United States. But one of the reasons that I love nutrition as a discipline is its breadth. It considers everything from the molecular details of nutrient function inside cells to why people choose to eat the way that they do. Although in the classroom I was dealing with the biochemical, I knew that in the larger world of Hong Kong I would have the opportunity to conduct nutritional investigations of a more applied and experiential kind. I would get to eat Hong Kong.

Wonderful Worlds of Whampoa

I lived with my family in an apartment in the Wonderful Worlds of Whampoa, a high-density planned development close to PolyU, built mostly in the 1980s. It contains about 75 15-storey tower blocks, all similar to each other. They were laid out in clusters, in a pretty thoughtful way that facilitated interaction between the occupants. The wonder of the place came from all the malls and other facilities that were incorporated. There was Fashion World, Treasure World, Home World, Pebble World and then of course the ship—a full sized passenger liner, made out of concrete and sitting in six inches of water. This alluded to the shipyard past of this neighborhood, which had been built on reclaimed land. The ship contained restaurants and a department store. Just across the street was Gourmet Place, a four-storey building above the bus station, with lots of good restaurants and a movie theater. There was even a bowling alley in the basement.

So, these wonderful worlds were what we got to call home. There were very few westerners living in Whampoa and none in our block. We looked out over Victoria Harbour, though in an easterly direction and so not directly towards Hong Kong Island. We had about 750 square feet for the four of us and our kitchen was maybe 10 x 8 feet. This is very typical for Hong Kong; we were living a middle class Chinese existence. A notable feature of this kitchen was the lack of an oven, though again that was quite usual by Hong Kong standards. We cooked on a two-burner gas stove, which we supplemented with a rice cooker (usual) and a microwave oven (less usual). We also got a small toaster oven that my sons pressed into service to make pizza and chocolate chip cookies when those cravings developed.

Those unusual situations aside, the set up of this kitchen points to immediate differences between the Western and Chinese styles of cooking. My mother would not have known how to cope with just two burners. Her standard meal structure was meat, potatoes and vegetables, which required three burners or two burners and an oven. For anything beyond the basic, very often all four burners and the oven were called into play. Chinese style cooking is heavily wok-dependent and calls for cooking dishes sequentially and quickly in that wok. Given the rice cooker, you could probably get away with a single burner stove a lot of the time. The other big difference, though I think this relates more to the overall size of the apartments rather than the availability of cooking facilities, is the extent to which people eat out. We made a number of good friends in Hong Kong, but when we were invited to eat with them, it almost always meant going out to a restaurant rather than going to their home.

1. Eating Hong Kong: The Experiences of a Food Lover and Nutritional Scientist

Whampoa's Home World contained a supermarket, called ParknShop, ironically named because very few people drove there. It was designed as a place for one-stop shopping, basically the same as might be found in the United States though there were also significant differences. It was smaller and much more congested and carried a wide range of Western and Eastern foods. The supermarket was very convenient, being less than a five-minute walk from our apartment. As a Westerner, it would be entirely possible to live in Hong Kong and shop at the supermarkets and buy familiar foods, albeit some of them at great expense because they had been imported from afar. But more interesting was to go a little further and visit the wet market. One of the recurring themes of Hong Kong is the conjunction of British Colonial and Chinese influences, and wet markets are an interesting example of this. Every neighborhood has a municipally owned market building that sells predominantly food, though clothes and other household goods are also to be found. Our local one had the public library on an upper floor. The organizational structure always seemed to be the same. The ground floor contained vegetables, flowers, fish and tofu. Upstairs was meat, poultry and fruit and then above that places where cooked food could be bought. The vegetable stalls would look pretty familiar to a Westerner, though some of the produce would be unfamiliar, with endless varieties of greens and strange roots. Communicating prices and amounts was a challenge that could usually be surmounted.

For some reason, most of the fruit was sold at stalls and small shop fronts in the street neighboring the wet market, rather than inside the market itself. Many of these places seemed to be open all hours. A wide variety of fruits were on sale, from the very familiar and always available (apples and oranges) to the exotic and seasonal

Fresh fish stall at the wet market

(durian and lychees). Canned lychees are easy to find around the world but, of course, cannot compare to the fresh version. I have never seen canned durian, although I did come across durian-flavored chocolate in Hong Kong. It is an ugly, large and rough and thick-skinned fruit, which to my nose also had an ugly smell. There were sulfurous odors overlaying the more typical fruit fragrances. The flesh is white and creamy. It gets creamier and more strongly flavored as it ripens. When I indicated interest in tasting some, my friends advised me to try less ripe "starter durian." It was acceptable, but did not encourage me to move on to the more advanced levels.

The manner of selling seafood is probably what gives wet markets their name. Freshness is such an important consideration for Chinese people when it comes to food, so to the extent possible, seafood is bought live. This part of the wet market is a constant flow of water and bubbling oxygen. The finfish are almost all unfamiliar and even those fluently bilingual are hard put to give English names to what is available. The shellfish are more recognizable, with lots of clams, crabs, scallops and shrimp. When we bought finfish, they would kill, gut and scale them for us, although the head would inevitably be left on. Shrimp were sometimes in water and sometimes on ice, but they would just be scooped into a bag, weighed and handed over. They would then dance around in the bag as they warmed up on the way home. Preparation therefore involved killing in addition to cooking them. This was easy enough, if unpleasant, if they were to be boiled, and actually familiar to those who have dealt with lobster. But often, I would want to stir fry them. Apart from the ethics of consigning them live to the wok, (although I wonder how different it is from boiling water, beyond the fact that we have to watch) I did not want the legs and shells. So I became quite adept at beheading them with a cleaver. This is but one example of the consequences of being closer to your food supply and not buying everything ready to cook if not ready to eat.

Being closer to the food supply is an ongoing theme when it comes to contrasting Hong Kong food with US food. That is ironic given the ultra-urban nature of Hong Kong. The vegetables in the wet market come predominantly from the People's Republic of China, less than an hour away. Some come from rural parts of the New Territories of the Hong Kong Special Administrative Region, although those farmers find it hard to compete with the mainland. Interestingly, a number of the local farmers are starting to produce organic food as a means to better compete with their neighbors to the north, an approach that has become quite common for small farmers in the United States.

Much of the fish is still sold live but fewer of the chickens. Traditionally, no self-respecting consumer would dream of buying chicken wrapped in plastic and every wet market would have rows and rows of caged live birds. But bird flu and SARS caused the Hong Kong government to attempt to centralize the slaughter of poultry and keep live birds out of the wet markets. They were largely successful and many of the cages are now empty, though live birds are still available for the purists.

The chickens share the second floor of the wet market with the butchers. While beef is to be found, the predominant meat by far is pork. There are no live pigs to be seen, but clearly what is on sale there is not long dead. This is good because there is a complete lack of refrigeration, despite the sub-tropical temperatures. I am not sure what happens to the unsold meat at the end of the day. There are lots of pork chops to be sold, but of course there are many other parts of the pig and they are all on sale too. Well, I say all, but I never saw brains, which may be the tissue about which I would have most concern. There were lots of intestines and trotters and ears.

It has long interested me where people put the dividing line between what they consider food and not food. One part of this is which species of animal and plant are included, but then another is which parts of those species people actually consume. The peoples of southern China are notoriously liberal on both fronts. We heard a number of sayings related to this, for example that people would eat anything with four legs that was not a table. If food and/or protein are in limited supply then the definition of what constitutes food tends to get expanded. You can introduce whole new species, but more commonly for meat it means using all parts of the animal. Why just eat the muscle when you have all the organs available? I

1. Eating Hong Kong: The Experiences of a Food Lover and Nutritional Scientist

was in the market in Mai Chau (in Vietnam rather than China) and saw very little of the kind of meat that Westerners are accustomed to, and a whole lot more liver, intestines, lungs, skin and feet. There weren't any English speakers around so I couldn't discover whether the muscle meat had been sold earlier in the day, or, as I suspect, was being marketed in more prosperous areas.

Even buying chicken at the supermarket in Hong Kong had its differences. I bought cut up chicken pieces, wrapped in familiar plastic at our local supermarket. When I tipped them into the pan, the expected wing and breast and leg were there, but then so were a couple of feet, as well as a "parson's nose," essentially the chicken butt. I cooked it all up happily, although one of my sons commented that the actual meat was rather sparse. But then he was not in a good mood because he had just spent two hours unsuccessfully searching for tortillas. He had a hankering for tacos, which was destined to remain unfulfilled.

From time to time I would have lunch with a historian colleague from PolyU. Once aware of my interest in testing food boundaries, he started taking me to places well-suited for such experiences. With respect to animal parts, this culminated with a trip out to Yuen Long in the New Territories to a restaurant that specialized in bovine sexual organs. Unusually, this trip also involved the rest of my family, including my oldest son who was visiting from the United States. We ordered up a large bowl of the sexual organ stew and proceeded to investigate what it contained. The penis and sliced testicles were quite obvious. I would recommend the former over the latter, mostly for textural reasons. Testicles are not muscular and kind of mealy. With the help of the menu and some translation, we also identified scrotum and what translated to "female happy parts," probably uterus. The whole was rather tasty, rich and savory. But the social experience was probably more interesting than the gastronomic. The traditional Chinese view is that eating particular parts of an animal will assist the health and vigor of the corresponding parts in the consumer. Thus sexual organ stew might normally be ordered quietly and consumed privately in a back corner of the restaurant by men with concerns for their virility. At some point during our far-from-quiet lunch, I looked up and noticed how much the other customers were enjoying the sight of this bunch of white men taking great and public delight in eating sexual parts.

Moving from diversity of parts to diversity of species, frogs and turtles were standard fare in the wet markets. I never saw snakes there but they were available in Hong Kong. Some restaurants would house cages of snakes ready for customer collection and cooking. We visited a snake store in Shuen Wan, an old neighborhood on Hong Kong Island. One wall was covered with wooden cabinets with lots of hinged drop down doors; each marked with the Chinese character meaning poison. Behind these doors was a rich variety of live, poisonous snakes. The people running the store were very relaxed about opening the doors and pulling out their merchandise. They were snake wholesalers, selling to local medicine shops and restaurants. Snake is a hot food in Chinese terms, meaning that it produces heat in the body and should be eaten at cold times of year. It was late spring when I was at that store and so past the peak of snake eating. Therefore they did not have any ready-to-eat snake delicacies. They did have various snake pharmaceutical products available, including rather attractive looking snakes pickled in alcohol. The shape of a food is also important from the Chinese perspective. Therefore snakes are also thought to be good for male

1. Eating Hong Kong: The Experiences of a Food Lover and Nutritional Scientist

virility. Luckily, there was one restaurant nearby still serving snake off-season and so we went there for lunch. There was actually only one snake item on the menu—snake soup with shark fin and abalone. It would not have been my first choice for a snake dish. It was good but unremarkable. It had many ingredients and figuring out what was snake and what was something else was tricky. The shark fin and abalone made it relatively expensive and neither one of those would make my list of favorite foods.

The most bizarre foods we ate were not in southern China, but rather in Beijing. We visited a market there well known for its interesting food. Some things we could recognize, but others were a mystery. We were fortunate in finding one of the stall owners who spoke a little English and he was very happy to proudly show us all he had available. So we started at his stall and selected silkworm larvae, scorpion, dog meat and sheep penis. Does that sound like a tasty meal or what! The sheep penis was the surprise on the menu, but there they were, anatomically unmistakable, butterflied and threaded onto a stick. In case, this wasn't enough to identify the organ, the vendor made several gestures that really drove the point home. Actually, everything at that stall was sold threaded onto a stick, so that we would never have known the dog was dog if we had not been told. It tasted like chicken, of course, but looked more like little pieces of pork. We wondered about the scorpion tail and whether the venom would survive the cooking process. We ended up breaking off the very tip, just in case.

The method of cooking at this stall was the same in all cases—throw them in the deep fryer, an approach that I appreciated from a food safety standpoint. It rendered everything small and crunchy. So, if you want to know what a scorpion tastes like, I could tell you it is similar to silk worm larvae and both are very crunchy, without having a lot of other flavor. The sheep penis was perhaps a little tougher than other cuts of lamb.

Next we tried a starfish. Surprisingly, that was only shallow fried and it was the only disappointment of the day. The outside was fairly tough and fibrous and only a little crunchy. Inside it was softer, definitely nautical tasting, but not particularly appetizing. It was the only thing that we didn't actually finish. We moved on to grasshopper and centipede. The grasshopper would definitely get my vote out of those two. Once the centipede had been deep fried, it was difficult to get it off its stick—or even to tell it apart from its stick. The grasshoppers, on the other hand, better maintained their integrity and provided one of the most pleasant crunches of the meal.

Serving dog meat is not legal in Hong Kong. When I ate it in Beijing, it was without too much thought, mixed in as it was with other exotic fare. I was brought in direct contact with the reality of considering dogs as food in the town of Yangshuo, near Guilin in the south of China. This is actually a very touristy area, with the River Li and its beautiful limestone karsts that are memorialized in many Chinese paintings. I always liked to get to the food markets in these places and this one was easy to find, in a large single storey building just off the main street. There was a sign close to the entrance, interestingly in English as well as Chinese, advertising a restaurant serving dog meat. And there, buried in the back of the market, alongside the live chickens and ducks and rabbits, were the dogs. I first caught sight of one whose throat had just been slit and was bleeding out. That was right next to several cages with light colored mongrel dogs. We had been told that people think light furred dogs taste better than dark colored ones. This seems unlikely, but who knows? It was certainly upsetting to see a dog with its throat slit, though I am not sure whether it would have been any different for me if it had been a sheep or a pig. Getting that close to the reality of being a meat eater is never easy, but is really a logical consequence of that food choice.

My PolyU colleague delighted in pushing the boundaries of what I would eat. He finally found my limit with stinky tofu. This is essentially tofu or soybean curd that has been left to rot. The normally benign tofu is marinated in a fermented brine for some length of time. Ingredients and time vary with the vendor. Shops that sell stinky tofu can easily be recognized by their distinctive odor, that of rotting protein. They tend to be take out only, probably because sitting in such a place would be akin to dining with a skunk. We therefore decided to get stinky tofu as an appetizer, and then go on somewhere else for lunch itself. This plan was agreed upon and then the day before my friend came to me suggesting I might like to change the date. As part of his attempts to become a good Buddhist, his practice was to avoid meat on the 1st and 15th day of each month and our date was for the 15th. I said that vegetarian food was fine with me and so there was no need to change.

Our gastronomic excursions always had locales and this one was to occur in East Mongkok, an older part of Kowloon. When my friend was younger, he had gone there regularly to buy pet fish. There are lots and lots of small stores selling innumerable, magically colored varieties of fish, plus all the required accoutrements. It is a relatively run-down neighborhood and so perfect for good cheap restaurants. We decided that, since it was the 15th and many people would be avoiding meat, we should go to the vegetarian restaurant first before it got too crowded. Unfortunately, when we got there, we discovered that the restaurant had changed and was now heavily centered on meat. We elected to move on to a second choice, which focused on food from Yunnan Province. But that also no longer existed. This is not an uncommon occurrence in Hong Kong, where restaurants open and close with great rapidity. So we crossed the road to eat at a dumpling restaurant.

It turned out that it was part of a chain, a Chinese variety of fast food. They had about five different kinds of dumplings that could be sold boiled or fried. The idea was to select one or two kinds of dumpling and combine it with one of five kinds of soup. It was very simple and formulaic, but very tasty also. I had hot and sour soup for the first time in Hong Kong. All of the dumplings had meat in them, but my friend had decided that he had met his religious obligations by searching out the other restaurants. He could not be blamed for the fact that they no longer existed and he was being forced to eat dumplings containing meat.

There were several elements of this dumpling restaurant that interested me and can be contrasted with US fast food. First, one of the employees was sitting there, busily stuffing and folding dumplings. We asked her where the wrappers came from and found they were made at their central facility. In the United States, everything would be made at the central facility and delivered frozen to the outlet. Here, labor was sufficiently cheap that the assembly work was done in the store itself. Then the serving dishes, plates, bowls everything were real china or plastic, nothing disposable. It's often difficult even to get a napkin in a restaurant in Hong Kong, but that's another story. The chopsticks, spoons and small bowls were kept in drawers within the tables, from which the customers would help themselves.

Having finished lunch proper, it was time to search out the stinky tofu restaurant. Part of me was hoping that it would have met the same fate as the other restaurants we had originally intended to visit, but soon I could tell that was not the case. The unmistakable odor became apparent amidst all the other street smells from about a block away. It grew stronger and stronger until we reached the storefront. It seemed like they had a variety of things available, including sausages and animal parts, but we were single-minded. For HK$6 (less than a US$1) I got a brown paper bag containing a two-inch cube of the magic stuff on a stick. It had been deep-fried a toasty golden brown. By this time, we had started to become accustomed to the smell. Texturally, this food is good. A nice crunch to the outside, with soft and creamy inner parts. Unfortunately it tasted just like it smelled and as I started to eat it, the taste and smell combined synergistically in a rather unpleasant way. Fortunately there were several condiments available, both sweet and savory. I found that the hot sauce was pretty effective for masking the flavor, though it could not override the smell. My friend assured me that I was not required to finish the whole thing. I heartily agreed and jettisoned the larger half of it in a handy garbage can.

I asked why people ate it; did it have some perceived medicinal benefit? I was told no, it was just that some people liked to live on the wild side. Stinky tofu is outside of normal behavior and consumed by people who like to be a little outrageous. Other people denied that and said that they truly enjoyed the flavor. I think that must be the case, because otherwise it would not be so widely available. I have a broad definition of food, but stinky tofu was a little much for me. The soft inside part was full of gas bubbles from active fermentation. No wonder the smell was so powerful. I wondered which bacteria were responsible and hoped that they had all been killed by the frying process.

We had agreed that this was to be a three-part luncheon adventure so now we went in search of Chinese dessert. My colleague was looking for another spot remembered from his childhood and he found it, with a little directional help from some street vendors, —the Yee Shun Milk Company. I had seen these places before, though never been in. Their windows are filled with dishes of various puddings or custards. Milk-based puddings did not seem very Chinese to me, but apparently these restaurants, which originated in Macau, have been around a long time. They definitely represent a fusion between East and West. The menu also included fried eggs and sausage and sandwiches. But we were after dessert. We both got steamed milk, flavored with ginger. I thought of it as something you might be fed in a British convalescent home. Very nutritious with all those milk and egg proteins but easy to get down. It was softly set, nicely flavored and not too sweet; the perfect antidote to stinky tofu.

As I mentioned before, people eat out a lot in Hong Kong and I bet there are more restaurants per square mile than anywhere else in the world. All shades and varieties are available ranging from innumerable, very cheap cafes to very ritzy and expensive restaurants, equivalent to any in the world and beyond my means. Real estate is very expensive and so restaurants can be found on any floor of a building, not just the ground floor storefronts. You can get excellent food in shopping malls. On one occasion, we wanted dessert late in the evening after going to a movie. The theater was about a 10-minute walk from a big ritzy mall so that was where we headed. The mall, Langham Place, is architecturally very interesting. It is spread over 12 floors and has some wonderful open areas that allow you to

1. Eating Hong Kong: The Experiences of a Food Lover and Nutritional Scientist

look down through most of those floors. Clearly not very "green," since it must take a lot of energy to cool that volume of air. It also has some very long escalators, which means that you can get up 12 floors in three flights. Anyway, to get back to the food, we were in search of dessert, but also noticed the crowds of people, at 10:30 p.m., sitting and eating dinner. There were lots of different kinds of food and all of it looked good. Actually, I am sure there must have been a McDonalds there also, so perhaps there were exceptions. We ended up at a Japanese/Western fusion restaurant on the 11th floor and enjoyed delicious and unusual desserts. The mall did start to close around 11:00 p.m., much later, of course, than those in most US cities.

There are other aspects of the culture of eating in Hong Kong that differ greatly from the west. Initially, people were surprised and pleased by our prowess at using chopsticks. I have long enjoyed using them. I think it does take a little more skill and attention than using a fork but this is good for the eating experience. It also has implications for what is to be eaten. You cannot eat a steak with chopsticks alone, but you can eat a whole fish, and actually chopsticks are very good for separating the meat from the bones. But preparing food to be cooked in a Chinese style often involves lots of chopping—the cleaver is a central tool in the kitchen—and this makes sense when it is to be eaten with chopsticks. Those less skilled with chopsticks are helped by the fact that creating a mess is not a problem. There can often be a lot of debris associated with Chinese food, all the bones and cartilage for example, and this spills over from the plates onto the cloth. Waiters serving tea will often slosh it around with gay abandon.

Chinese restaurants favor round tables for larger groups, in

19

Eating Chinese dim sum with chopsticks

contrast to the long rectangular banquet tables found in the west. This emphasizes equality since there is no obvious head to the table. It also makes it less important who occupies the adjacent seats, since you get access to everybody around the table. Chinese restaurants tend to be very noisy as people engage in loud conversations across their tables. Talking quietly to your immediate neighbor would be considered impolite because you would be excluding others from the conversation.

Food is going to be shared. Often, one person will take responsibility for choosing it and the dishes will be delivered to the center of the table for people to help themselves. However, at least in more formal or traditional settings, it is not just a free for all. Those

1. Eating Hong Kong: The Experiences of a Food Lover and Nutritional Scientist

with seniority either from age or position would be expected to start each dish, though this might take the form of serving an honored guest. Children might be expected to wait until others have helped themselves, but at the same time adults would be serving food to the young ones and making sure they got enough. One person may order and frequently one person will pay for the group. Publicly calculating the cost per diner and each contributing would be considered gauche, though sometimes people will argue with each other over the right to pay the bill.

Chinese people think about food in many dimensions. Nutrient content may not be one of them, at least traditionally, though effects on health are regularly considered. Several dimensions have already been mentioned, for example, freshness, shape and the ability to generate heating or cooling effects in the body. Color, taste and smell are also important. In the United States, medicines come from pharmaceutical plants, but in China, traditionally they come from plants and animals. One of my sons got sick while in Hong Kong with a sore throat and laryngitis. He decided to see what traditional Chinese medicine would do for him. We were with one of my Hong Kong colleagues and he volunteered to facilitate the process. First was finding a practitioner. There are plenty of them around, with little shops around the neighborhoods, but we wanted to make sure we found a good one. We chose one that I pass frequently on the way to and from work and there is always a line of people, sitting on stools in the store, waiting to see the doctor. My son took his place in line and slowly progressed to the front. The doctor felt various energy points and asked several questions before prescribing a concoction that was to be taken for four days. It would not be ready until the evening, and in fact we had to go back for each of

Reading Hong Kong, Reading Ourselves

The traditional Chinese medicine store

the next four evenings to pick up a 10 oz paper cup that was filled with the medicine. I don't know the ingredients (barks, leaves, roots, animal parts, etc.), but it was black and thick and smelled sort of like licorice, but worse. The taste was extremely bad—very bitter, the sort of thing you might give somebody if you wanted them to throw up. I just took a small sip to see what it was like but Duncan was supposed to consume the entire 10 oz. Many people in Hong Kong told us subsequently that they have switched to western medicine because they cannot deal with the taste of these remedies. My son did his best, and by the fourth day got down about half of it, but I think he has had his fill of Chinese medicine.

Did it do any good? Hard to say, because he was not that sick and would have got better anyway. My Chinese colleague's point of view was interesting. He said that experiencing the bitterness was inherent to the cure. The suffering endured was part of the price to be paid to get the benefit of health. Personally, I stuck to food as food, not as medicine. The richness and variety to be found, just from a gastronomic perspective is truly outstanding.

This essay is entitled "Eating Hong Kong." There is clearly another one to be written that would be called "Drinking Hong Kong." Perhaps because of my English roots, tea is an important part of my family's culture. We spent a lot of time exploring the tea culture of Hong Kong and other parts of China. Much could be written about that, as well as its contrast with the Starbuck's coffee culture, and then just the simple issue of whether water should be drunk hot or cold. That will all have to wait for another time.

Chapter 2
Street Level Sociology in Hong Kong

David JAFFEE

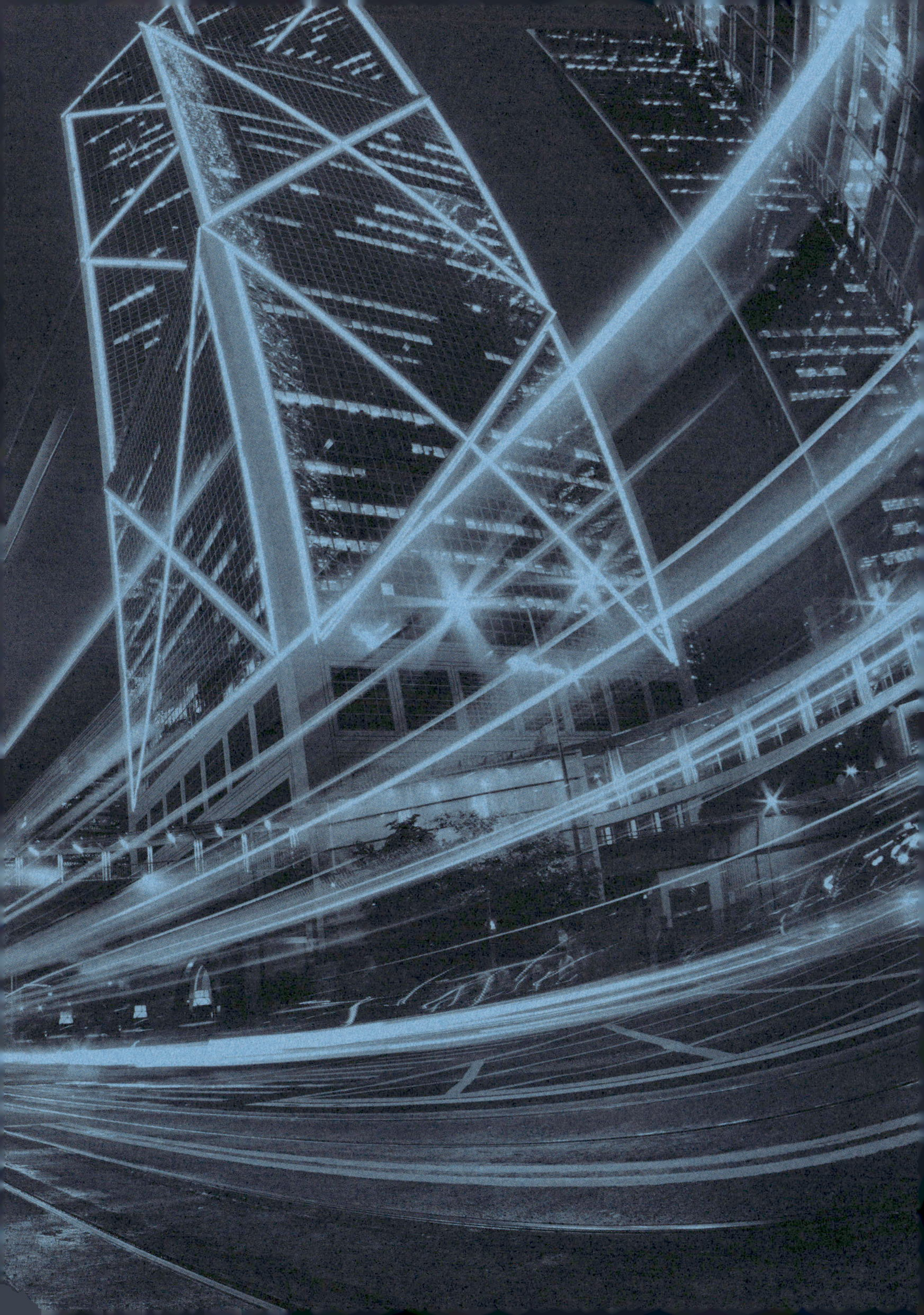

Introduction: Sociological Observation in Hong Kong

We sociologists claim special powers of vision—we possess a lens through which we can see and make sense of the world differently than others. The social sensitivity and analytical framework of sociology contributes to a heightened interest and awareness of one's social surroundings. However, when people travel to distant countries, and find themselves amidst foreign cultures, I like to think that they too become sociologists, at least in the amateur sense, and also become more observant and socially curious. It is axiomatic to say that when situated in a different or foreign environment one becomes more finely attuned to and interested in interpreting the surrounding circumstances, arrangements, and forms of public behavior; and that the outsider is able to see things that the insider takes for granted.

Spending a year in Hong Kong allowed me to put the sociological enterprise into practice as I spent many hours walking around the city, traveling on public transportation, eating and drinking in many different types of establishments, and simply taking in what the city had to offer. From a sociological perspective, what I found most fascinating were the forms of public behavior of the native population, the way social life was organized and structured, both physically and socially at the street level, and the messages communicated through commercial and public signage. I was afforded many hours of natural and unobtrusive observation of social life in a wide range of settings. From my analyses I would arrive at various interpretations and conclusions, some of which may prove to be quite erroneous.

Conducting such analyses while visiting a different country can be a tricky business. After all, sociology is the quintessential "critical" discipline. It makes critical statements about social arrangements and seeks to uncover not just the obvious and transparent ("manifest") but the less obvious ("latent") purpose, function, and implications of these arrangements. However, to spend time in another country making critical statements can often be interpreted as a form of ethnocentrism, or in my case the work of just another "ugly American;" one who is unable to transcend his own national cultural baggage and accept different social patterns and cultures. For this reason, and by default, most social scientists would start from a position of "cultural relativism"—that what is observed in another country should be understood and analyzed not against some absolute standard but in the context of that particular country's culture and history. This is good advice for the traveler. But cultural relativism only takes one so far, and it often precludes critical analysis in favor of an unexamined acceptance of everything as "just the way it is." This would hardly be an acceptable way for a sociologist to diagnose and analyze American society. One might reasonably say that American culture produces this or that form of social behavior. But one would also, as a sociologist, want to consider the forms of social behavior in the context of the larger social good or its contribution to social pathologies.

All this is meant to say that I am faced with the delicate task of observing, describing, and identifying different and perhaps unique Hong Kong social characteristics, while also trying to understand them but not making judgments about them. This is very difficult. Another challenge is the issue of observation and objectivity.

Georg Simmel, a 19th and early 20th century German sociologist, wrote about the special status of the "stranger" and the ability to engage in quasi-objectivity: "The stranger is thus being discussed here, not in the sense often touched upon in the past, as the wanderer who comes today and goes tomorrow, but rather as the person who comes today and stays tomorrow .... Another expression of this constellation lies in the objectivity of the stranger. He is not radically committed to the unique ingredients and peculiar tendencies of the group, and therefore approaches them with the specific attitude of 'objectivity' .... Objectivity may also be defined as freedom: the objective individual is bound by no commitments which could prejudice his perception, understanding, and evaluation of the given ... he is freer practically and theoretically; he surveys conditions with less prejudice; his criteria for them are more general and more objective ideals; he is not tied down in his action by habit, piety, and precedent." While Simmel conceded that this might be something of an exaggeration, I found these words comforting as I made my observations and inferences about local habits.

Some have also argued that untainted, and perhaps more objective analysis is possible from solo travel and observation. Paul Theroux, the novelist and travel writer, makes a point of noting that he always travels alone. He recommends this practice to avoid second-hand impressions, based on the unsolicited perceptions and comments of traveling companions, which can mediate and filter the raw sensory stimuli. When alone, according to Theroux, you can also immerse yourself in the cultural, physical, and social surroundings without the distraction of concern for the comfort of others. As it turned out, during my year in Hong Kong I was separated from my family, and my travels about Hong Kong were almost invariably conducted solo.

2. Street Level Sociology in Hong Kong

I often wonder if I would have been as sensitive to certain behavioral patterns if I was accompanied by a companion and thus distracted by conversation.

Taking the insights of Simmel and Theroux, I might best describe my status in Hong Kong as the "lone stranger." Simmel's use of the term stranger is significant. Rather than "visitor" or "guest" it denotes a form of alienation from the local population. I would argue that it was not just self-imposed but also reinforced in my navigations through the streets of Hong Kong. There were a number of factors contributing to this status. Before arriving in Hong Kong I made two assumptions. First, I assumed that there would be many Caucasian residents, expats, or "*gweilos*," as they are known, among the population; second, that most people would be able to communicate in English. Both of these assumptions proved fallacious. I often found myself as the only gweilo on the street, in a neighborhood, or in a restaurant (particularly in Kowloon, the area of Hong Kong where I lived). Thus, while strangerhood (as a condition of being an outsider and the "other" in terms of physical characteristics) is a common status throughout Hong Kong, it is more common for gweilos in some places than others. Regarding my assumption about language—it turned out that most people in Hong Kong do not speak English and, if they do, it is not American-style English or is relatively underdeveloped so that communication was a much more significant challenge than I had anticipated.

I should note that while in Hong Kong I made no effort to learn Cantonese (apart from a couple pat phrases), which is the dominant form of Chinese language spoken in Hong Kong. Cantonese is a very difficult language and I realized early on that if I had devoted myself to learning how to communicate, it would have precluded reading and studying other (I thought more interesting) things about Hong Kong and China. In short, the opportunity costs were too great. The intonations and inflections and accent points of the language are critical and subtle. For example, when I thought I had learned how to say "good morning," my students told me I was actually saying "get dressed." This might explain the less than positive reaction I received from the cleaning women I greeted one morning in my office. I decided if my attempt to learn and use the language produced even greater misunderstanding, I should be content with the state of total illiteracy.

Behavior in Public Places and "Uncivil Indifference"

The most significant observation I made doing street-level sociology concerns the behavior of Hong Kongers in public places. At many times and in many places—streets, neighborhoods, restaurants —I was the only Caucasian and I was conspicuous by my physical features. Therefore, I expected that people would acknowledge my existence, say hello, greet me, make eye contact, nod, etc. or engage in some other form of symbolic interaction. However this never or rarely happened. Even when I tried to make eye contact, nod, or smile there was never any response or sense of recognition. This was the single aspect of Hong Kong public behavior I found the most interesting and, in my effort to understand it and explain it, it provoked a renewed appreciation for the work of sociologists such as Georg Simmel and Erving Goffman.

Goffman prefaced his classic work, *Behavior in Public Places*, with a plea for street-level sociology to become a special domain for sociological inquiry "... for the rules of conduct in streets, parks, restaurants, theaters, shops, dance floors, meeting halls, and other gathering places of any community tell us a great deal about its most diffuse forms of social organization ... The study of ordinary human traffic and the patterning of ordinary social contacts has been little considered."(pp. 3–4)

Goffman provided me with a foundational sociological tool to make sense of the unresponsive public behavior of Hong Kongers. He developed the concept of "civil inattention" to describe the most socially acceptable behavior of co-present strangers in public places; "one gives to another enough visual notice to demonstrate that one appreciates that the other is present (and that one admits openly to having seen him), while at the next moment withdrawing one's attention from him so as to express that he does not constitute a target or special curiosity or design." The classic locations for such public behavior are the subway or the elevator. The point is that it is socially unacceptable, or "uncivil," to stare at strangers in these kinds of public settings. (However, as a sociologist I routinely violate this norm for the sake of street-level sociological research.)

In my initial analysis of life in Hong Kong, I decided that the civil inattention of the subway and elevator (the "lift" in Hong Kong based on British phraseology), two places I spent a great deal of time in Hong Kong (moving horizontally and vertically), was a form of behavior that Hong Kongers simply transported and generalized to all interpersonal interaction on the street, the walkway, the mall, the restaurant, etc. However, the longer I was in Hong Kong, and the more experiences I had of being entirely ignored and unacknowledged in a wide range of settings, the more I believed that the behavior was something slightly different than Goffman describes. In many cases I did not detect even the "visual notice to demonstrate that one appreciates that the other is present."

Inevitably, this led me to wonder about the "civility" of this behavior. I decided to describe it more critically as "uncivil indifference." I should add that it did not apply exclusively to me as a physically distinct foreigner, but to the way Hong Kongers seemed to non-interact with all public strangers. While the behavior of sealing oneself off from and ignoring others is often seen as a particular adaptation to urban life, I would argue that it takes an accentuated form in Hong Kong. My conversations with others provided additional confirmation of this impression. However, in using the term "uncivil" I am also crossing the dangerous line between description and evaluation.

In what sense was it uncivil? Here I need to engage in some comparative analysis. Many Americans would ask me, while I was in Hong Kong, "Are the people friendly? "Are they nice?" Based on the behavior that I have described (public behavior among strangers) I would reply "no," Hong Kongers are not "friendly" or "nice"—but then add a very important qualifier—at least not in the way Americans interpret the meaning of these words. People do not say hello and for the most part they do not smile. In elaborating further, and trying to avoid being too culturally imperialistic, absolutist, or ethnocentric, I would go on to say that for Americans, on the other hand, being friendly is often a loud, boisterous, animated but typically superficial affair. This is not the way Hong Kongers conduct themselves, so such an expectation would make no sense. However, as a sociologist I would say that the lack of any gesture toward others in the form of mutual acknowledgement and greeting is a socially unhealthy sign in any society or community. Some have used the term "social capital" to describe levels of trust and reciprocity among individuals. Many have written about the decline in "social capital" in the United States and within communities as measured by the strength of human relationships, connections, and interactions outside the home.

There are also certainly aspects of Hong Kong behavior that people would regard as quite civil. For example, people in Hong Kong seem exceptionally tolerant, patient, orderly, and self-controlled. There is no overt hostility, anger, or violence exhibited toward others. In fact, there seems to be an unusual absence of public displays of emotion. People form lines and queue-up in an orderly fashion; there is no pushing or shoving. In this sense, there is a high level of civility. Further, once you have met and become an acquaintance, people will greet you with a smile and ask how you are doing.

Having said all that, there is still something I would regard as anti-social about the "uncivil indifference" I have identified. One small way it manifests itself is in the failure to hold open the door for the person following behind you. This rarely happens in Hong Kong, and almost all Westerners I spoke with made note of this fact. When I practiced this form of social etiquette there was either a look of surprise from the person behind me, or more commonly it was ignored and unacknowledged. I also noticed that it was not "paid forward" (or backward) in the person holding the door for the next person following behind them. For this particular act there was an absence of what is referred to as "generalized reciprocity." Under the regime of uncivil indifference, however, it is perfectly logical. Since there are no other people present to acknowledge—they are invisible—there is no reason to hold open the door. This type of "everyday incivility" may not even be regarded as uncivil by the standards of pedestrian life in Hong Kong. I need to acknowledge that I have imposed this judgmental label based on my own culturally proscribed experiences.

Another example was the absence of assistance. There were dozens of times when I would be standing at a crowded and congested street-corner peering at my Hong Kong map. But never—not once—during the entire time I spent in Hong Kong did anyone ask me what I was looking for, whether I was lost, or if I needed directions. If I tried to communicate a need for assistance by looking around at the passing pedestrians, hoping someone might make eye contact, it was equally futile. In fact, people seemed determined to avert my gaze.

As noted about civil inattention, in Hong Kong I often received little visual acknowledgement. As a sociologist I had never given much thought to this aspect of human behavior and interaction but I was now in a different place and I was becoming sensitized to the most subtle facets of social life, and how very small things can have much larger implications. It led me back, again, to Simmel and Goffman, who both identified eye contact as significant for the intensity of engagement in public places. Simmel wrote that "Among the individual sensory organs, the eye is destined for a completely unique sociological achievement: the connection and interaction of individuals that lies in the act of individuals looking at one another. This is perhaps the most direct and the purist interaction that exists .... The eye reveals to the other the soul that he or she seeks to reveal. Since this obviously occurs only during the direct look from one eye into another, the most complete reciprocity in the entire sphere of human relationships is achieved here."

Goffman, building on Simmel and applying it to public places, argued that "Eye-to-eye looks, then, play a special role in the communication life of the community, ritually establishing an avowed openness to verbal statements and a rightfully heightened mutual relevance of acts." If one is determined to avoid all interactions with strangers, the eyes become a strategic device. Goffman provided me with yet another tool to make sense of my surroundings for he saw eye contact as the initiation and invitation for "face engagement" involving "two or more participants in a situation joining each other openly in maintaining a single focus of cognitive and visual attention." If that is the case, and eye contact is to be avoided in Hong Kong, might this be because one also wants to avoid the "face engagement?" This may be due to the fear of having to converse with another, and in my case that would involve the use of English, or establishing a relationship that could involve obligations. As noted, for Americans the face engagement is entered into more casually and frequently, and this is why Americans might describe themselves as more "friendly." For Hong Kongers, and maybe Asians more generally, the face engagement carries with it greater obligations, responsibilities, and risks. But does visual avoidance also weaken the civil social fabric? Or, as Goffman concluded about eye contact, "a heightened sense of moral responsibility for one's acts also seems to develop." Research on eye contact also indicates, as one might expect, that its frequency diminishes as one moves from the small community to the large urban center as a result of increasing information overload and social impersonality.

I have found it quite interesting to ask Hong Kong residents about the reasons why people seem to behave in the ways I have described here. I should mention that no one has ever refuted my observations about Hong Kong street behavior. In my conversations with Hong Kong residents about my observations, people have offered a range of explanations. They are offered, and in some cases asserted, as if undisputed truths. Of course there is no way to empirically adjudicate among the competing and complementary attributions. But the various explanations are as sociologically interesting as the behavior itself. One common explanation is stress, overwork, and fatigue. This is no doubt the state of the masses in Hong Kong, but I am not entirely convinced that it explains the lack of affect and civil symbolic interaction. After all, the Filipina population in Hong Kong is also exploited, overworked, and socially subordinated but they also are more likely to smile and acknowledge other people. Another explanation is the fear to engage with a stranger, particularly a Caucasian, given the potential communication difficulty. This seems quite plausible. Another is the general lack of trust of any other who might, if they initiate an engagement, have ulterior motives or take advantage of them. It is interesting people would be so distrustful given the low crime rate in Hong Kong and the high level of street safety in almost any place in the city and territory (but more on trust below). The unwillingness to offer assistance, according to some, is based on a fear of being wrong. This issue comes up in a number of different contexts from the inability to get clear answers from people in stores to the reluctance of students to participate in class. Another broader explanation—Hong Kong is a very competitive society with a focus on school success, getting a good job, keeping the job, and making money. Children are raised in this competitive environment from birth and the net result is a social fabric characterized by low levels of interpersonal trust. Finally, there is the role of Chinese culture as some, usually academics, attributed the behavior to the culture of unemotional stoicism and aspects of Confucianism. For the latter the "Doctrine of the Mean" prescribes moderation, rectitude, objectivity, sincerity, honesty and propriety. It discourages extreme or reckless forms of behavior. Thus, people are reserved and do not want to draw attention to themselves or cross social boundaries.

In exploring Confucianism explanations further, I discovered that the strength of interpersonal trust varies depending on the party in question. Research has found that in societies influenced by Confucianism there are high levels of interpersonal particular trust (with family and friends) but with low levels of interpersonal generalized trust (out-group members and strangers). Much of what I observed can be related, perhaps, to a generalized distrust, and even fear, of strangers. This explanation is consistent with what one of my students told me when I asked him why people don't respond to a hello or nod when passing on the street. He said "people will think you are either strange, crazy, or wanting to take advantage of them." One study I came across categorized Hong Kong among "low-trust" countries, while another, based on surveys of the population, reported low levels of trust of other members of the society.

All of this is consistent with the one and only unsolicited form of interaction initiated by a Hong Konger, usually on the subway or street, which occurred several times during my stay. There would be a tap on my shoulder followed by the person pointing at one of the pockets in my backpack that was slightly unzipped. No verbal communication was required. I originally thought this caution odd, considering the low levels of street crime in Hong Kong, but in this larger social context it was a civil gesture, but one that also communicated the larger sense of generalized distrust.

Hong Kong as a Vertical City

I have used the term "street-level" to denote the casual, everyday, mundane, and public aspects of Hong Kong life. However, of all the cities in the world, this may be the wrong language to use. This is because Hong Kong is known as a vertical city. So much of what happens in Hong Kong occurs above (or below) the street level on the elevated walkways and above the ground floor (G/F). There are so many tall buildings, with so many floors, that in Hong Kong the designation of first floor (1/F) cannot be wasted on the first level, but is reserved for the first elevated level. When people think they are on the second floor, they are on the first floor. I have never spent so much time riding escalators or elevators ("lifts" in Hong Kong). This is because, unlike any place else, many commercial establishments—cafes, restaurants, retail stores—are above the street level. Under these conditions, looking up is as important as looking from side to side.

In Hong Kong land is scarce and expensive. Therefore, housing developers build as high as possible to maximize the return on their property investments. These factors contribute to the population density of 6,349 per square kilometer, the 4th densest among the world's territories. I did not know any Hong Kong resident who lived on the ground floor. More people live above the 14th floor in Hong Kong than any other place in the world. Not only are living spaces often located at stratospheric heights—and housing costs astronomical—they are also notoriously small and cramped (average residential dwelling under 500 square feet).

These patterns of the built environment in Hong Kong have enormous implications for almost all aspects of life. The pulse of the political economy and the identification of the ruling class find their source in the sale and control of real estate property. For street-level observation, small dwelling size and high population density translate into highly congested public spaces. It seems as if no one ever goes home in Hong Kong. The streets and malls and restaurants are always bustling and crowded. Because living space is tight, the home is not a place for extended relaxation or entertainment. There are no McMansions, "cribs," or backyards. Therefore, people spend leisure time outside the home in the air-conditioned comfort of the unlimited number of shopping malls and plazas.

Billboards and Definitions of Desire and Beauty

One thing you will see in Hong Kong no matter the direction you gaze is commercial advertisements for various products. There appears to be no commercial billboard restrictions in Hong Kong. They are placed anywhere you might rest your eyes while you are waiting for a subway train or riding an escalator. Observing these billboards, I concluded that there must be a huge market for wristwatches in Hong Kong, as either cause or consequence, of the excessive number of wristwatch advertisements. They are on the largest illuminated billboards in the most upscale commercial districts of Hong Kong. These showcased timepieces are so extravagant and expensive that they can't simply be called a "watch"—these are "chronometers." Several internationally famous entertainment figures adorn these displays including, unexpectedly, Nicolas Cage, whose image has haunted me throughout my travels about Hong Kong.

What and how things are advertised helps to decode a society's cultural fashions and definitions of desire. Walking through the upscale shopping malls, of which there seems to be more than could possibly be economically sustained in one city, you cannot help to notice the large number of cosmetics shops and huge facial images of very white, and often very Western-looking, women. Almost every one of these cosmetics shops is promoting a whitening agent. The message is clear—the whiter the better. The ads say it all: "The most powerful whitening serum ever," "Empower your radiance with a flash of pure white light," "Let there be light," "Cyberwhite brilliant perfection." There is nothing subtle about this blatant exhibition of what sociologists call "colorism" on full display throughout Hong Kong. After seeing these images, I discovered that the skin-whitening market in Asia is worth a reported US$18 billion. The social preference for obtaining and retaining whiteness also explains why women carry umbrellas during the summer which I mistakenly assumed was to protect from cancer-producing ultraviolet rays.

Thin Hong Kong

There are no obese people in Hong Kong. This may sound like a gross overgeneralization but after spending a year observing the local population I can make the claim with a great deal of confidence. That is, I never saw any US-style massively obese people in Hong Kong, and very few that I would even describe as "chubby." The only time I would spot an unusually large person, they would turn out to be a Westerner from the United States, United Kingdom, or Australia. Assuming I did not have a biased sample (obese people are less likely to walk outside, use public transportation, etc.), what is the explanation for thin Hong Kong?

It is not due to a lack of eating. One thing that will strike visitors is the sacred ritual of lunch that entails almost every working person leaving their office at exactly the strike of 12:30 for an hour and a half. If you work above ground you will have to wait in a queue at the elevator at 12:30, only to wait in another line at every and any lunch-serving establishment.

It was Gordon Gekko, in the film *Wall Street*, who proclaimed that "lunch is for wimps." In Hong Kong there is no such sentiment. In fact, stockbrokers are accustomed to a long and leisurely two hour lunch. Thus, the proposal to change the starting time (to noon), and reduce the length of the lunch hour to one hour, in order to bring the Hong Kong bourse in line with global trading hours, was met with massive opposition. As one broker was quoted in the local paper "Chinese people take meals very seriously. While the Westerners can have sandwiches every day, we want soup and several cooked dishes to share." It has been observed that Hong Kong residents eat out in restaurants more often than any other population in the world.

So, if food intake does not explain the slender bodies of the Hong Kong population, it must be due to genetics, diet, exercise or likely some combination of these. Since there is a massive literature emerging on rising obesity levels in China (see the book, *Fat China*), thinness is not an inevitable genetic fate. But there does seem to be evidence that obesity among the Chinese takes a different body form than it does in the United States. And if obesity is rising in Hong Kong, the phrase "it's all relative" must be applied because the United States is light years ahead on gross national girth.

Diet has always been regarded as a major source of Chinese health. The menu here is heavy on soup, vegetables, fish, chicken, pork, along with rice and soybeans. When people eat out they have

41

thousands of restaurants to choose from and these are small and medium size operations that are located everywhere in Hong Kong serving traditional Cantonese fare. People tend to share dishes rather than consume a single entry solo. While fast food is available, it is not on every street corner and it does not seem to be as widely consumed. People drink tea rather than soda. However, there are a large number of bakeries selling various buns and desserts.

In terms of exercise, though people eat out a lot, they will likely have to walk some distance to get to the restaurant. Hong Kongers do a lot of walking to bus stops, public transportation stations, etc. Most people do not drive or own cars. I believe the walking culture is a major contributor to the relatively lean population.

As noted, all of this may be changing as Western dietary habits and less physical activity, along with greater stress, creep into the lifestyle. It seems that in China it takes less increased obesity to produce correspondingly high increases in diabetes. Diabetes in China has now reached epidemic levels.

Spending a year in Hong Kong has been one of the greatest privileges of my academic career. Living in a vibrant city with a world-class public transportation system, where one does not have to drive a car or worry about street safety, afforded me the unique opportunity to explore a large part of Hong Kong on foot. As a visitor from a different national culture, and as a sociologist, I tried to pay attention to the world around me and the different forms of behavior, the built environment, and the cultural messages. These observations further stimulated my interest in the unique patterns of social organization in different societies and the range of explanations for these variations.

2. Street Level Sociology in Hong Kong

I suspect if I stayed in Hong Kong for two or three more years my perceptions would change and what was most salient at the beginning—for example interpersonal behavior in public places—would recede to the background and be replaced by other observations. But it is likely these would also entail further critical analysis. Sociologists are not known for being community cheerleaders, boosters, or members of the Chamber of Commerce. The reflex is to uncover the social problems, dysfunctions, latent tendencies, social pathologies, inequities and injustices that plague all societies. Sociologists are in search of the darker side of social life—and we never fail to find it.

Chapter 3
Philosophy in the Streets: Walking in Hong Kong

Gray KOCHHAR-LINDGREN

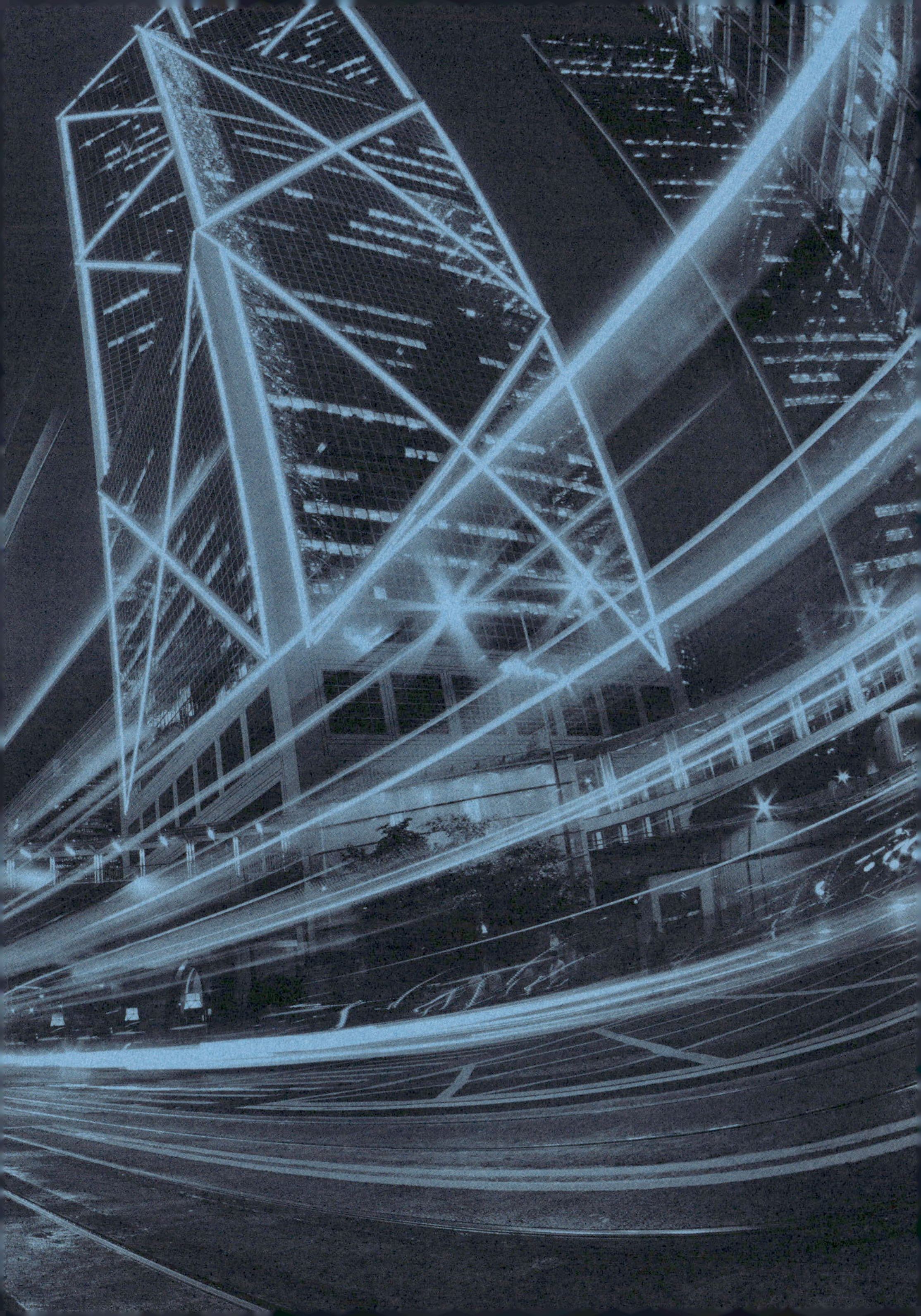

Only thoughts reached by walking have value.

Friedrich Nietzsche

City streets lead us to a deep experience of thinking as we amble along sidewalks, tarry by food stands, sit outside at a café, or hustle through the traffic from one side of the street to the other. We are always alone and always flowing along with others. How do the reflective surfaces of puddles, glass buildings, and cameras operate? What about the pleasure and pain of crowded streets replete with a combination of readable and unreadable signs? How do architecture, advertising, strangers, eating, and shopping affect our thinking as it works to establish itself to accompany the rhythm of walking? Philosophy and walking, then, belong together as they conjoin thought with urban experience. There are, of course, formal pathways toward this conjunction—one could follow the flâneur through Baudelaire and Benjamin; urban theorists such as Simmel, Jacobs, Lefebvre, Harvey, and Soja; or the phenomenologies of Heidegger, Merleau-Ponty, or Casey—but the place to begin is always on the streets.

I love walking through Hong Kong, on both sides of Victoria Harbor; up Nathan Road and into Mong Kok and the Temple Street Night Market or to the delectable Spicy Crab; through the Whampoa Garden with its huge concrete ship; along Canton Road with its glittering shops next to the Ocean Terminal; through the old enclosed Walled City with its echoes of Triad violence; and, after an MTR and bus ride, along the paths through the sweltering green trails of the New Territories. But for our journey today, I will stay close to home and only wander along some of the streets of Hong Kong Island

3. Philosophy in the Streets: Walking in Hong Kong

Central District is the main business district of Hong Kong

itself from Kennedy Town on the western tip of the island, up along Victoria Road as it overlooks the Lamma Channel, and then back down through Hollywood Road, Wellington Street, or Lyndhurst Terrace in the Central district. There will be other days for other routes and each street, in any case, resonates with all the others.

The Cemetery on Victoria Road

The Chung Yeung Festival, also called the Double Ninth, is one of the ritual days that Hong Kongers visit the graves of their ancestors, wiping the dust and grime of the year off the engraved stones that mark the place of the dust of the remains of those whom they have loved. This is the site of mourning, perhaps the accompaniment to each and every one of our memories, since memory always carries with it the lingering effects, as affect and image, of the "it was." Since, for each of us, experience is cracked along an infinite number of fault-lines, all of our hearts are broken. What we do with that brokenness is one of the essential questions. It is fitting that Chung Yeung occurs in the Fall when even here in the subtropics the weather breaks on the rack of time. It is a bit cooler now, and, thanks be unto Tin Hau, the Goddess of the Sea, that the humidity has fallen off a bit. The winds, too, are shifting from arriving in the city from the South China Sea and are beginning to be primarily from the northern mass of the mainland. This will bring hazy clouds of particulates and pollution—Hong Kong's pollution problem is becoming more and more severe—but, for now, the birds are chirping and tiny red blossoms are appearing. This feels like a kind of new life, this autumnal pulsing of time, but it is related, as usual, to a passing as well. Whidbey Island, my home on the North American side of the Pacific Rim, is wet and cloudy by this time of year, but in both places, separated by so many differences, there are yellowed leaves curled on the ground.

The men, women, and children arrive in buses, mini-buses, and taxis, coming from the island, Kowloon, the New Territories, and beyond to stand at gravesites, wipe the dirt away with clean water and enact the ceremonious rituals that honor the ones who have passed but are nonetheless present for the visitors. As I walk from Sha Wan Drive along Victoria Road, the cemetery spreads out on the steep hillsides on both sides of the road. The mountain rises to the right; the Lamma Channel and the outlying islands spread out to the left. Each gravesite marks a hole in the world that will never be filled but each gap also evokes memories not only of each individual, all that we'll never know, but also of ancient China, Egypt, the Neolithic, and the earliest funerary rituals of Cro-Magnon and our lost cousins, the Neanderthals. This marks the presence of the human. A butterfly, blue along the wing-edges, shimmers in the dappled sun as it flits among the greenery and then flutteringly soars up among the buildings in what must be a strange combination of disorientation and ecstasy. With an exquisite elegance it floats along the micro-currents of air in its hidden vortices, arabesques, and velvet pockets.

Everyone buys bouquets of flowers splashed with whites, reds, and yellows and carries them gently to the plinths of the graves. Flowers, the perennial symbol of new life, of the blossoming of life alongside, and perhaps out of, death. Roses, narcissi, white lilies, chrysanthemums, red poppies, and asphodels sacred to the goddess of the underworld. Architecturally, the grave is reminiscent of a house or a temple which holds the spirit of the ancestors, loved and feared, served and supplicated.

I take my daily walk past the huge cemetery built along Victoria Road—and stretching up to Pok Fu Lam—with row after row of grave markers covering a great bowl scooped out by nature and by great earth-digging cranes. From the road, whether driving or walking, I can make out the black-and-white photographs of people attached to the gravestones peering out at me from an instant of their lives now long ago vanished, looking at me from the place of death with a calm and dignified gaze.

When they were alive, they were looking into the camera as if toward the face of death and now that gaze is reversed, looking, as it were, backwards. They are looking from their past into my future at the moment of the present. As if from a sheer blank wall and an absolute unknowability. There is no knowledge here, but there is nevertheless an encounter across worlds. Death is an "X" alongside all human representability, a presumably existing something that exerts causality on the close side of phenomenality where we stand and speak with one another.

One middle-aged man bows to the black-and-white photograph of his mother. For a long while he stands, in his simple black trousers and creased white shirt, in a firm but relaxed posture, looking intently at the image of his mother's face. He does not look away, nor does she. Then he bows, slowly and with decorum. Three times. I, in turn, bow toward him, slightly and inconspicuously, and continue my walk along Victoria Road, past the shirtless flower dealer and past the Home for Coffins, toward Sandy Bay, where I will loop down toward the sea.

Hollywood Road, Wellington Street, and the Man Mo Temple

Wandering down Hollywood Road in mid-morning while waiting for my fitting appointment with Ranooni Bespoke Tailor, I find this time of day gorgeous, soft with sunlight and full of both restfulness and possibility. The day is here, and good, and the day is yet to come. Other parts of the city are already in full swing as I take the minibus down past Dragon Faith Realty and Joy Ocean Massage. Any business might be an opening to the other world, and the principles of the other world, always present in this world, apply here as well. Wind and Water. The Dragon. Here on Hollywood, though, we're

3. Philosophy in the Streets: Walking in Hong Kong

still at that quiet moment before the shop doors clatter up to reveal the storefront windows and keys turn in the locks as proprietors step inside to rearrange the desk, to straighten out exhibits before the wandering shoppers begin to arrive.

This moment of balance and of the unfolding, like a fan, of the instant that becomes the fullness of the day, is exhilarating, but calmly so. It is the moment of being-poised-for when each word of that phrase is pregnant with what might come. The buildings visible from the street are lit by the slanted sun but are also still emerging from the long shadows. There are dilapidated housing units with grime covered radiators, long strips of peeling gray paint, rusted air conditioners, and drying

Hollywood Road runs between Central and Sheung Wan

laundry. The tiny balconies, balconies in name only, are reflected by the shining new office buildings and condominiums of steel—is it still steel?—and glass.

There are many moments in Hong Kong when one sees reflections on every side, as reflections reflect reflections. The taxi stand on Pedder Street is a particularly illuminating spot for these reflections. It's a delightful, slightly frightening, and extremely provocative moment for thought. The simulacra produce other simulacra as I look on and become enfolded in the reflections. The crumbling living quarters and the new offices bespeak different histories, economies, politics, and architectural dreams. Function and form; form and function.

The streets are becoming a bit busier, but not much, not yet. All of these people in Central, myself included of course, have been preceded and will be succeeded by a host of strangers. Hong Kong is an image of both the hectic rush of capitalism and the haecceity of every human life. Everything comes and goes; everything leaves within itself a space of replaceability. This is what facilitates the dynamism of this place, the very possibility of motion, and maintains the essence of the human as the site of the trans- and the meta-.

I enjoy lunch at the Lebanese Café on Wyndham Terrace before wandering down to the Man Mo Temple. At the Café there is the usual and lovely Middle Eastern music, old photographs of Lebanon (whether they are "authentic" I have no idea), a rather garish color-scheme on the walls, and a tacky painting of a wealthy woman. Red, green, and clear glass form the little lamp shades. The lunch of hummus, sujuk, pita, and Coke is excellent, filling. In Lebanon, governments are coming and going with the ongoing investigation

3. Philosophy in the Streets: Walking in Hong Kong

People offering incense to deities in the Man Mo Temple

of the assassination of Rafi Hariri by the UN Dispute Tribunal. But everywhere in the world are Lebanese restaurants, food being the easiest port of entry for all the diasporas spreading around the globe along flight paths and freight paths.

I pay the bill, then wander around the corner and take the short hike down Hollywood. The Man Mo Temple is next to Ladder Street—one of those delightful steep cliffs of stairs that lead from one level of the city to the next—and just up from Shun Tak on the harbor. It's quiet so far, Sunday morning or a Friday afternoon, with soft light suffusing the city and the Temple is part of this repose. Places like the Man Mo exude a kind of serenity, even in the midst of megalopolises.

Reading Hong Kong, Reading Ourselves

Money changes hands—from human to human and from human to the gods—constantly, but it is not, not exactly, "business" in the same manner as across the street or down the road since a narrowly defined "profit" is not the goal of the exchange. As everywhere, there is a wish for prosperity, virtue, and happiness, a better life all around, and there are gifts given toward that end. Here, with every exchange, there is also an act of gratitude, a "thank-you" travels with every joss stick, bow, or exchange of coins.

Man Mo is smack in the middle of high-rise Hong Kong, but an older city, an older opening toward the earth, is also preserved here, held in reserve. A steady stream of visitors, locals and tourists, move in and out of the Temple, lighting incense and purchasing Hell Money to toss into the burning oven just outside the doors, which, like the Ming Tombs outside Beijing, are marked with a high threshold. Ghosts, thank goodness, can't jump. Inside, it's full of fragrant smoke of all the coils and sticks of burning incense. Perhaps the gods thrive on the number of offerings and the thickness of the smoke?

Young and old, male and female are lighting the sticks and bowing to the many gods, with Man and Mo—the god of literature and the god of war who are occupying the same space—at the center of the action. Stepping outside and around the corner from the main altar is a smaller enclave with an altar, a room full of boxes with texts and photographs—perhaps they hold the ashes of the ancestors?—a fortune-teller, who can also work in English, and a souvenir shop. I buy a small statuette of Kwan Yin, Goddess of Mercy, and nod in the direction of the fortune-teller, who, perhaps, I will visit the next time I visit the Temple.

The exterior decorations are still vivid, though much of the roofline has been charred or removed. There are discontinuities along the architectural line of transmission, and apparently it's not the type of thing to renovate with new replacement materials. There is something appealing about this lack of upkeep—the brokenness of history that nonetheless supports an active relationship between the living, the dead, the gods, and the city. The world is red-hot incense with its ash drifting in invisible clouds across the harbor.

Then it's back to Segafredo's on Wellington Street I go: Une caffé per amico! I had hoped to run by ReCycle to pick up a few gifts, but after walking down Caine to Elgin, the shop turned out to be closed. I'm now giving both sides of Wellington Street equal attention, since I so often hang out at Pacific Coffee, with its posters of Europe, across the street. I consider a lovely warm ham and cheese baguette with a latte in a smooth porcelain black cup accompanied by a small round biscuit.

Leaving Segafredo's for the bustle of Wellington Street, I head down toward Sheung Wan, passing the ornate frieze of red, gold, and green set into the front of one of the buildings. It looks like a representation of the zodiac, but I'm not sure. Most of the signs in this city I cannot read and many I can read only parts of. The emerging into consciousness of the frieze, however, also suggests another phenomenon concerning my capacity to see, to observe, to take note of, and to understand.

It's as if I have an inherent limit to the amount of stimulus I can absorb and retain—and the neuroscientists could certainly tell us something about this—for I very often have the experience here in Hong Kong that something new, yet something I must have retinally seen many times, becomes part of my awareness. I have a physiological unconsciousness that must be constantly streaming along but only at times imagine itself as consciousness. I walk along Wellington Street, with this complex amalgamation of British, Chinese, European and material histories, and "Wellington Street" becomes a constantly shifting phantasmagoria of perception. Some things come into view while others vanish out of sight. I continue, of course, to imagine them there after I have walked around the corner; I continue to imagine the other side of the street and my destination in Sheung Wan.

"Wellington Street," like any other street name, is neither a stabilized neutral place "in" which people and cabs and carts come and go nor is it a jumble of disconnected particles of stimuli or qualia. It is an inextricably connected play, a constant dance that exhibits both patterns, consistencies, names-and-images, as well as a capability for incessant change in which one moment bows graciously and gives way to the next.

The Travelator

The Travelator cuts across a number of the city's districts. It is a quarter mile long escalator, the longest in the world, which runs from down in Central up along Shelly Street to the Mid-Levels, passing through the bar and restaurant district of SoHo as it goes. (The name "SoHo" itself travels smoothly between New York, London, and Hong Kong, bringing with it the aura of the bohemian and urban chic.) Traveling down during the morning commute and back up after 10:00 a.m., the travelator becomes extraordinarily handy in the subtropical humidity that blankets these hills and mountains.

3. Philosophy in the Streets: Walking in Hong Kong

It opens up a whole set of commercial possibilities for those who otherwise wouldn't bother with, or couldn't physically handle, the vertical angles. It must have been a massive engineering feat, one that accompanies the MTR lines blasted from underground, the tunnels from one side of the island to the other, from the Hong Kong to the Kowloon side of the harbor, and the reclaimed foundations for the soaring skyscrapers and new piers. Hong Kong is a built environment par excellence.

A moving sidewalk: an oxymoron. Stand still and move along: the acting out of a paradox. This isn't Zeno's paradox, however, for one easily reaches the top of the escalator and the O Café without any intellectual gymnastics or knowledge of the limits in calculus at all. Zeno, of course, never had any trouble arriving at the market in Elea or at Parmenides's house either. One foot in front of the other, or, simply stand still and lets the elevator whisk one up the hill. Zeno just thought it all; thought it odd that objects, like an arrow, can move through ever smaller units of space that can always be divided and sub-divided, infinitely. How does movement occur if such is the case? The ordinary world is not as it appears. The simplest "fact"—we can get from a to b—is infinitely complex. The thought-world and sense-world might be at odds?

One can step off the escalator at Lyndhurst Terrace or Hollywood Road without any problem at all. The Peak Bar or Red or Cicada—with their luscious steak mint dish—is easy to reach for a drink or dinner. Buying a pork bun at 7-11 or ordering a falafel to go are not challenging undertakings that take much thought. Refuting Zeno is not necessary for the daily round to work and pragmatism tops idealism every time we want a pork bun.

Logic itself is like the travelator, carving its way up and down the hillsides; it is the system of the MTR and tunnels burrowing under the earth and water. Through making correct distinctions, cuts in being, and through the correct application of rules, we are enabled to travel toward the Peak, accumulating shiny nuggets of truth to hold in our palms as we go. The ridge becomes steeper, sharper, in the bright sunstruck day. One step at a time, but everything is linked and the timed steps are set into motion together. The logician, of course, cannot just enjoy the ride to the top of SoHo and get off for a cup of coffee at Café O. He must know how the travelator works—that will be called "technology"—and toward what it runs, in the end. This will be called "teleology" and will have metaphysical implications, regardless of what the logician thinks about metaphysics. But, as for us, we'll hop off and get an iced coffee before continuing our wanderings.

Kennedy Town

This morning I hopped on the 56 outside the flat on Sha Wan and rode down Victoria Road, overlooking the Channel, flat under the chilly winter sun, to Kennedy Town for a haircut on Catchicat Street (where we also have our laundry done at Cooper's, get our keys cut, and eat at an Indian restaurant). For these services, I pop my head in the door and mimic snipping my hair as I put on a questioning expression. English and Cantonese don't help, but the body language in the right context does. The questions are known ahead of time and almost no meaning needs to be generated. Snip? Yes. Sit. Money. The End. That's the narrative line, prescribed by social habit and the pragmatic ready-to-hand knowledge of how to get along in the world

3. Philosophy in the Streets: Walking in Hong Kong

in which hair, customary fashion, scissors, money, and chair coalesce into "haircut."

Since thinking is the art of interrupting the prescribed, of veering off unexpectedly into another direction, in the direction of the other, not much philosophy goes on here. There is, of course, a lot of that chitchat, if one knows Cantonese, that is so essential to oil and polish the social body called Kennedy Town, Hong Kong, Catchicat Street, and it is always interesting to discover how people talk about the scale of place to which they feel most attached. Philosophy is also a tiny step to the side or to the back in order to reflect upon chitchat, so there is a bit of that. More importantly, there is an aquarium.

The aquarium is full of brilliantly colored red, blue, and golden fish with gossamer fins light as summer sails that luff along in a light breeze as they undulate as if weightless. Strollers on the street gaze in at the fish in wonder, not really paying attention to the function of the shop, while I sneak a peek when I can while being snipped by the barber, a middle aged man with gray streaks beginning to appear in his black hair. Gazing into the fish tank as if it's another world, people on both sides catch their own reflections and whatever is behind them, though vaguely, as they watch the graceful underwater floating of the bright-scaled fish.

I am down in Kennedy Town picking up the laundry at Cooper's, which boasts a freshly painted sign. Today I walked down from the flat—it takes about an hour—along Victoria Road, the sea and sky a bright blue today, for a change. It is quite warm as well; a delightful winter's day. It is good, as always, to be in Kennedy Town with its lack of pretension. Lunch was done, shopping for the most part finished, so the streets were relatively quiet as everyone went about their Sunday afternoon business.

Walking around the block, I noticed, really for the first time, how many hole-in-the-wall restaurants there are. Simple tables and chairs, few decorations, the menus only in Cantonese. They are all delicious, I'm sure, as this is where the locals eat, tumbling out of their tiny packed flats to do *Tai Chi* in the park or to ramble through the streets. There are plenty of western eateries here as well—the ZigZag Café, the Italian specialty shop, McDonald's—but most of Kenndy Town is local business in both food and otherwise: the barber, the butcher, the fish market, the keymaker, the laundry. Peoples' workaday lives exhibit such a sense of dignity.

I have no idea where the majority of Kennedy Town's inhabitants work, whether most are local or many head down to other sections of the city (although it does get very crowded on the buses during rush hour, so many are headed elsewhere on the island or over to Kowloon). The massive container ships are all plying the waterways today: MOL, Maersk, Evergreen, China Lines: a steady stream of seaborne traffic. The ships are piled higher with containers than back in August, a good sign of increasing trade. The MSC ship headed back out to sea from the harbor at the moment is filled to the brim from aft to stern with only the highest level of the bridge visible.

Kennedy Town, named after a British governor and not the American president, is a place worth watching exactly along these lines. When next I'm in Hong Kong, there will be new luxury high rises, new eateries, a new MTR station. We'll see how Cooper's, the shop that sells incense and paper grave-goods, Mr. Ho's foot reflexology shop on Hau Wo, the little sidewalk altars that grace the streets, and the hole-in-the-wall noodle shops do when they face the blistering force of world finance coming to their doorsteps. It will be a throw of the dice.

The World City

Hong Kong loves to speak of itself as a "World City"—and it certainly is—but all of these "worlds" that converge in Hong Kong are not congruent or symmetrical. They sidle up to each other, cast their eyes this way and that; touch each other in a back alley, a mall, or a massage shop; idly eye each other in the IFC elevators; or walk by each other indifferently as they jostle across Queensway or Nathan Road. Goods of all sorts, some visible and some not, are streaming around within the city and then out across all sorts of boundaries. A world city, perhaps, is defined by the amount, intensity, and variegation of its traffic.

And all this talk of "World Cities" is not new. Already in the 19th Century, Berlin was talked of as a *Weltstadt* and certainly others have fit into that category of being the center of an increased density of worldwide connections, wealth, and creative productivity across multiple sectors. At this point in history, all the major cities are becoming capitalist world cities, especially with the state-sponsored capitalisms of Moscow and Beijing beginning to deepen their holds. They are not metropoles in the old colonialist sense, standing at the center of relatively well-established empires, but they do exert a similar magnetism for finance, jobs, and innovation, as they become multilayered nodes in the network of globalized traffic.

Like all the capitalist world cities, Hong Kong is under constant de- and re-construction. It's always (un)building itself, both vertically and horizontally, though there are more limits for the latter, given the geography. Tunnels, subways, skyscrapers, expansion into the green zones, land reclamation. It's all here, all close at hand. An experiment in social and physical design. Hong Kong is a series of reflecting surfaces, a series of linguistic improvisations in Cantonese, Putonghua, English, French, German, Tagalog, Malay, Italian, German, and a concatenation of dialects, which I am completely ignorant of.

We are not any longer the classical *flâneur* idling in front of the huge glass show-windows of the new department stores, *les grands magasins* of an earlier century, but always caught in the grit and smog of the crisscrossed lines of power, are traveling along electronic webs (though not without obstacles and surveillance from all over the world and from far above the earth) as we stroll about Hong Kong with our mobile-devices vibrating.

The thought of Hong Kong with its swarms of people moving like a river, like a glacier, like a cloud along the sidewalks, streets, up and down the escalators, and along the pedestrian passageways both above and below the ground. The city is an immense excavation of the earth, a displacement that has uprooted the contours of the land with its hosts of other populations. The city is a slow, steady explosion that creates a furrowed wound in the earth in order to establish its own apparent order. This is the finite order of human habitation.

Hong Kong is a space that has been blasted from the earth. It fills Victoria Harbor; it creates an artificial island for the construction of Chek Lap Kok, Hong Kong's airport; it paves and wires the earth for the construction of a platform for digital and genomic mutation, with the hope of fame, wealth, and immortality humming faintly in the background.

What does it mean, then, to think on our feet? It means that we're quick to see connections and to adapt to new situations; it means that we're attending to the world as fully as possible as we wander through familiar or strange city streets trying to find a train station, a coffee, a book, a painting, a lover, or simply just to wander and see what we see. It means we fall in love with the street scenes, the tilt of grooved pavement, the grit that blows about in the wind that sweeps in from the ocean or down from the Peak. It means that we need our feet to be in motion in order to learn the practices that teach us to think.

Stage Two
Seeing

Chapter 4

Hong Kong: Cultural Transformation of the Public Sphere

Tricia FLANAGAN

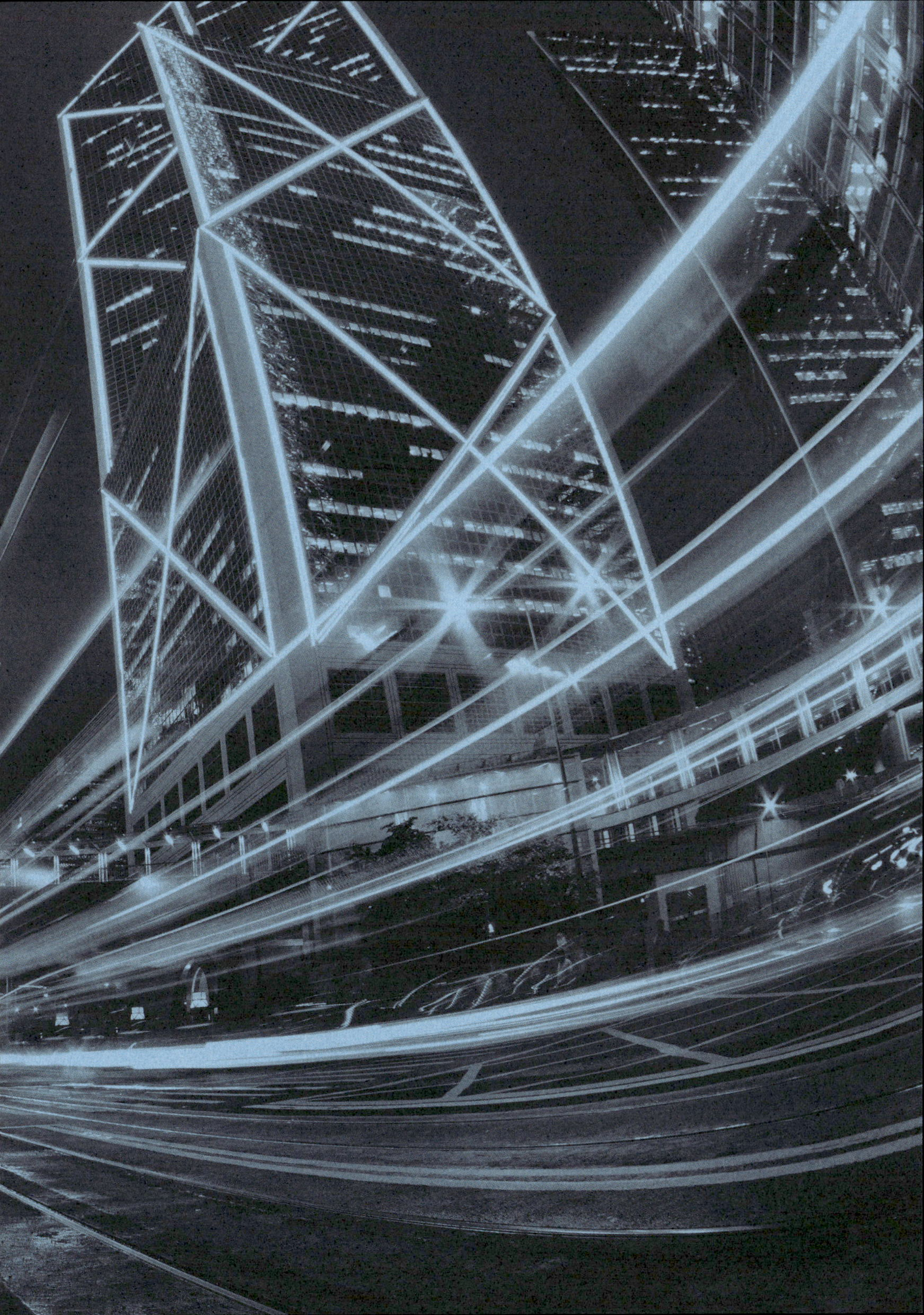

Art reveals a great deal about both the people who make it and the period when it is made. Public art in particular reveals much about the society and communities from which it emerges. Public art by definition is art that communicates with a public audience. The term has also come to mean art that seeks alternative routes to engage the audience apart from the art gallery. It can also be called "urban art" or "public sculpture." Art in public space takes into account the location and conditions surrounding it, revealing yet more about a place. How a society defines what is considered public has much to do with what it considers private. As an artist who works in public space, I am fascinated by the zone that exists between public and private spheres, a zone or space that shifts under the pressure of politics, religion and even fashion trends. It is in these unresolved spaces that I locate my art practice.

Public space in Hong Kong is unique due to its combination of high population density, rugged physical setting and subtropical climate, its history of being a British colony but now part of mainland China, and its economy based on international commerce and finance. It is a vertical city, built in tight valleys where skyscrapers are dwarfed by the mountains around them. The manner in which people use space appears strange to an outsider. Underwear is hung out to dry in the streets, people do their morning exercises on public footpaths, and every Sunday domestic helpers occupy the public space of city squares and parks, and transform them into personal domestic space. This is normal to the locals, but I see the city from the perspective of an artist who sees public space as the medium for social sculptures, public interventions, implantations, attributions or offerings.

4. Hong Kong: Cultural Transformation of the Public Sphere

Hong Kong 2007

My time in Hong Kong began almost by surprise and with no preparation virtually. I was offered a job and having only a short time to consider the offer, I consulted the only book about doing business in Asia in my local library. The book included items such as learning the common courtesies, such as giving and receiving things with two hands. However, one point stood out. It was a remark about Westerners' habit of structuring time. When planning for the future, in an Asian way of thinking, one accepts that the future will bring things not expected when conceiving the plan. Since most of my life had been spent chasing time, this concept was a welcome change of perspective. Entering Asia without language skills or knowledge of Chinese culture, I could not understand or control what was going on around me, so why not accept and enjoy the unpredictable?

In my six years of arts education I learned little about Asia. Seven years of postgraduate research focused on public art reflected the hegemony of my Eurocentric Western education and revealed little about the Asian condition. Therefore, what is written here has no claim to be an authority on the subject. This is not an apology but rather an acknowledgement of being written from ignorance, and therefore this text does not seek to preach the truth but reflect my encounter with Hong Kong with my eyes wide open as I searched to discover some truth.

Hong Kong residents have witnessed incredibly fast and drastic changes in their living environment. Within living memory, in fact within just two generations, the New Territories has evolved from open fields to high rise buildings. The population explosion means that the post 1980s generation experience space in a completely different way than their parents did.

Electronic City/Network City

The urban transit system is fully automated with the Octopus card, a transport card that uses Radio Frequency Identification (RFID) technology to control masses of bodies in motion every day. The city operates like a river system: everything flows down from the mountains into the convulsing mass of the metropolis. The heavy rail network Mass Transit Railway (MTR) runs with the strength of the Bosporus and its tidal flows marked by every peak hour. The tributaries feeding this river system are massive networks of green and red mini-buses. At high tide the peak hour congestion pushes the infrastructure to its limit, but it may be incorrect to refer to this swollen river as a crowd, if a crowd is something that dissipates.

The density of this body of people waxes and wanes, ebbs and flows, but never dissipates. It is simply an experience of high-density population.

Space is a precious commodity here. People are fairly orderly and wait in queues. At railway stations they stand between painted lines, with arrows indicating the direction of movement in or out of the train. Guards patrol the platform and keep people behind yellow safety lines. To stop the crowds spilling onto the tracks at peak times, many city stations have sliding glass doors to provide a second barrier. But once the doors open, it gets chaotic as people cram and squash each other trying to get themselves into the train. The guards blow whistles and yell at people to stay back, but often the double set of doors, on the trains and then the platforms, open and shut several times while handbags and protruding limbs are wiggled and juggled into place to allow the doors to close.

Arriving at a busy station, even if you wish to stay on the train, you may get sucked out with the crowds and have to get on again. It is a bit like getting in and out of the surf; you need to anticipate where the flow is moving and then work with it. You need to let yourself flow out with the wave and then float in again as the surge runs back. If you fight it you just get exhausted, like trying to swim against a rip current in the ocean.

You don't need a car in Hong Kong. In fact, finding a place to park would be frustrating and expensive so most people use public transport. The transport network is the mediator of people's movement and experience of the city.

The trains are still packed at 11 o'clock at night, filled with tired faces on their way home from work. If not sleeping, almost everyone

Reading Hong Kong, Reading Ourselves

Hong Kong 2007

is gazing at a portable screen. They look busy and professional, but often when you look over their shoulder they are playing games, from complex animated worlds to Tetris on a cheap cell phone. People don't look at each other or make conversation.

Hong Kong people are well dressed. They wear tailored suits when it is swelteringly hot outside. In the Central Business District (CBD), it is an art to get between home and work while staying in air-conditioned passageways.

Vertical City

Physical places are shaped by geography, weather, time and politics. Hong Kong sits like a shiny gateway to Mainland China that is convulsing with industry pumping out products to the world. Hong Kong is the glossy front cover, a well-oiled machine that is in permanent hyper drive.

Located amongst mountain peaks, the city has been forced to grow up rather than out. This is Hong Kong's public space. I was used to navigation in open plan cities, a skill that is useless when transit is in a maze of inter-connected shopping centers. Here you need to read signs and follow the flow of people. Street traffic and pedestrian traffic take different routes. Business cards often supplement the person's address with the closest MTR station and the exit number. Then you follow the signs and just pop up from the maze of underground/overground labyrinths that connect all of Hong Kong's CBD.

In Hong Kong, it seems that architecture has been inverted. Although there are many landmark buildings and unique façades that make up the cityscape, on a human scale the awareness of being inside any particular building is eroded as I move seamlessly in an endless mesh of interconnected interiors. It is often hard to know whether I am below or above ground, and floor plans are more like network maps, or to use another natural metaphor—a rhizome.

In response to this experience of the city I conceived a public artwork. "Transit textiles" (2009) illuminates and maps the geospatial interrelations and personal connections that are made (and lost) as we move through a physical urban space. My artistic intervention accentuates movement: the passages we make when we move through the public and the private, the local and the global, between centrality and marginality, and amid the personal and the commercial environments that exist in urban spaces.

The project artifacts are the result of a combined geospatial and cultural analysis of the city. Transit Textiles' focus is on one of Hong Kong's cultural hubs—the Academy of Visual Arts. This project was a catalyst for civic participation, bringing together eight artists from various backgrounds and disciplines, engaging them as they moved through the city. And by way of art practice and audience

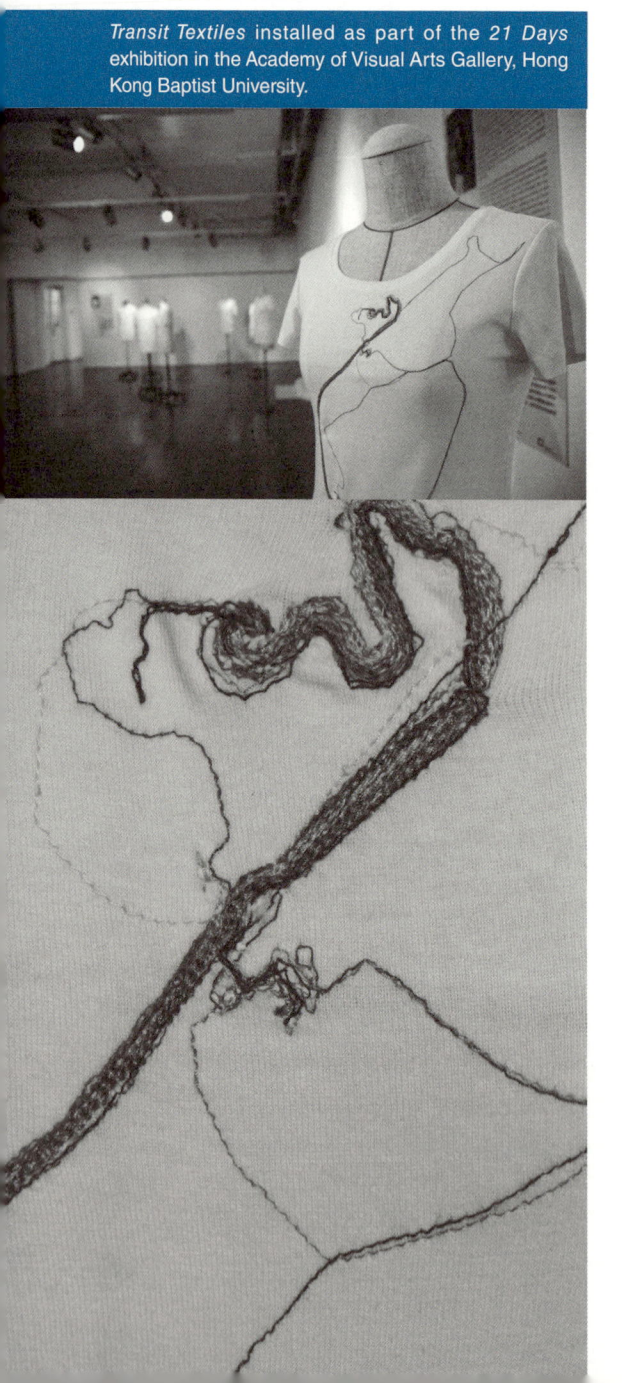

Transit Textiles installed as part of the *21 Days* exhibition in the Academy of Visual Arts Gallery, Hong Kong Baptist University.

participation, the data is mapped memorializing the traces made from daily routines into keepsakes of the city. The mapping reveals the personal, yet public and collective, experiences of the city. These movements are then realized in textile form.

For almost all cultures, textile or cloth is the substance that we begin with (birth) and end with (death). Fabric is a significant substance for all. We use a daily set of cloths to cover and wrap the body. We use cloths in domestic environments, and for special occasions. But it is the most ordinary textiles that are in most demand at times of need or distress. This is when we get out a blanket (or a canopy) that becomes our sacred cloth and a second skin.

Wearable textile maps are created according to data accumulated over 21 days—making the art both organic and emergent yet structured. The "wearables" become evidence of the activity, coming into being on the street I engaged with participants while embroidering the results. By means of stitching the artist maps the networks of movement into the cloth, creating patterns that evoke the free flow of the individual in public space. The maps reveal something about the characters of the participants. Each one is unique, yet it is clearly recognizable as part of the series—like an organic logotype.

The distinction between hardware and software is blurring as everything becomes embedded in technology. American writer and urbanist, Adam Greenfield, calls this "Everywear." Intelligent environments enable just about everything to be customized, fostering individualism in ways we could not imagine in the past. The boundary between public and private is evolving. What does private mean in a world where data on sites like Facebook can make public the intimate details of one's "private" life?

We are less connected to public spaces and places. The cell phone is one device that enables this boundary creation. Through our cell phones we keep close and connected to the people and spaces from our private lives—those we already know—rather than connected to those who are around us in the city landscape. "Transit Textiles" maps and connects people who are unfamiliar with each other, yet are all familiar with the space of the city. In doing so the project also elucidates and examines "boundaries"—we as artists are working though our boundaries of culture and language—but we are also asking people to reflect on their own boundaries of space and place.

Contemporary citizens in fast-moving economies reveal a great deal about the changing dynamic of cultural life. Mobile individuals who move through a city create boundaries to manage their interchanges in the urban landscape. Contemporary cities are mediated spaces. The reputation of a city is an advertorial and marketed space. It is a structured space. It is an environment that we "buy" ourselves into. This project is an attempt to probe these boundaries and re-personalize the space. This is a public art project that helps citizens to transition from structure to a reflexive position in the modern urban space. The "nomadic data stitching station" can be put wherever a power source is available. Like a busker, I can carry what I need to set up and engage with participants by locating myself in the flow of traffic. Information gathered is sewn directly onto the cloth, embroidered into network maps. The resulting artworks are then given to the participants.

As mentioned in the introduction, public art by definition is art that communicates with a public audience. Projects like "Transit Textiles" are examples of alternative ways to reach an audience outside the art gallery. But we can also learn about Hong Kong by looking at traditional public sculptures.

Hong Kong is teeming with public art. Corporate towers and government offices buy objects from renowned sculptors to ornament their lobbies. You will find Henry Moore, J. Seward Johnston jr., Larry Bell, Van Lau, Freeman Lau, Rosanna Li and Danny Lee among others. Traditional monuments and urban sculptures act as physical anchor points in this digital city, where every surface appears to flicker with light—an ever-changing electronic billboard overloaded with signage, all competing to catch the public gaze. Among the neon and LED messages, traditional monuments are dwarfed by skyscrapers or overlooked in daily life. We could call them invisible monuments—they lay quietly waiting to be discovered.

4. Hong Kong: Cultural Transformation of the Public Sphere

Historical City

The colonial days of the British Empire are still evident. Government signs remain in English and Chinese and the city's parks are full of colonial monuments, like paperweights holding down fading memories. Queen Victoria sits stoically in Victoria Park, a park that sits on Victoria harbor—territory that is no longer her domain. On Sundays she is inundated with migrant workers who collectively turn the public space of the park into an outdoor lounge. Every possible open space in the city is carpeted with flattened cardboard boxes and rugs that delineate the public space into a kind of chaotic floor plan. Through this floor plan, walking tracks organically emerge, written across the squares and parks by people who need to transit these spaces. The patchwork floor plan of "rooms" that are created is populated primarily by Filipino

Statue of Queen Victoria, Raggi, Italy. Cast in London in 1890, installed in Hong Kong in 1896, moved to its current location in Victoria Park, Causeway Bay in 1955 (2011).

Reading Hong Kong, Reading Ourselves

Domestic helpers on Sunday in Victoria Park (2011)

women who play cards, do each other's hair, paint their nails, eat, drink, sleep and relax. They have little privacy in their jobs as domestic helpers, working long hours and living in tiny rooms at the back of people's apartments. Their rooms are usually just big enough for a bed. Sunday is their only day off and this is why what I see appears so intimate; it is the only time they can relax and be themselves.

Queen Victoria sits silently watching over the re-colonization of the park, and the subversion of public space into private domestic space. If the monument could speak the migrant workers would surely sympathize with her. For as stoic and stable as she appears she has endured much. The statue of Queen Victoria was cast in a foundry in London in 1890 and was originally erected in front of the Hong Kong and Shanghai Bank to commemorate the diamond jubilee of her reign in 1896. Due to metal shortages during World War II she was shipped to Japan, where she sat in the Sakurajima Arsenal in Osaka until she was recovered in 1946. Raoul Bigazzi, a local Hong Kong sculptor, undertook restoration work in 1952 and carefully erased the physical traces of this unpleasant history. In 1955 the sculpture, in her former glory, was placed in her current location in Victoria Park.

Monuments, both Chinese and colonial, document the city's history and can be found all around Hong Kong Island, Kowloon and the New Territories. Typically they are great hunks of heavy and expensive materials, like the granite and copper monolith commemorating the 1997 return of Hong Kong to China that sits outside the Hong Kong Convention and Exhibition Center in Wan Chai. They reveal much about the place and the times in which they were built.

But now back to the here and now. Public art like public space in Hong Kong has evolved. Empty public spaces are no longer viewed as voids waiting to be given meaning by placing monuments in them. Spaces are acknowledged as being full of history and influenced by their surroundings. Public space is perceived more broadly to include domains such as virtual space, and public art reflecting these changes engages in new forms of media that are not only physical.

What little public space is still available in Hong Kong needs to be left alone, reserved for temporary projects. If not the city will lose the capacity to react, to accommodate creativity and to embrace change as it happens. Cities like Berlin and Melbourne are dynamic places that foster creativity because they are dotted with pockets or voids that signal potential. If everything is built up, in the time it takes to tear down and rebuild the creative energy will go elsewhere.

Political Space

Public Art projects become the catalyst for public engagement, transforming public spaces into areas for dialogue, generating new ideas and altering public perspectives. Over the past ten years communities in Hong Kong have become politically active in voicing their concerns and have often adopted strategies led by artists, or arts organizations such as Woofer Ten (Shanghai Street Art Space) and Local Action. Benchmark public art projects grew out of the fight to preserve the Star Ferry and Queen's Pier in 2006 and 2007. Their focus was on the public's right to have a say in the development and preservation of the city. The controversy arose for many reasons (bad planning, lack of public consultation, growing interest in collective memory, etc.) and the protests drew a larger and noisier group than ever before. Some of the first to gather were artists who would create public art or engage in performances as a form of protest.

Hong Kong, when it was under British rule, always felt an obligation to speak out about injustice in Mainland China. Victoria Park marks the start of the annual 4th of June Tiananmen Square Memorial march to the government headquarters in the Central district. It began in 1989, when up to one million Hong Kong residents took to the streets for an outpouring of public concern over the events taking place in Tiananmen Square in Beijing. This event along with the 1 July march, on the date of the handover of Hong Kong from British to Chinese rule, are widely cited as illustrative of the increasingly politically active post-80s generation in Hong Kong. Of course the history of public demonstrations can actually be traced further back to the workers' rights movement in the colonial era.

The post-80s generation in Hong Kong has grown to be politically active and the momentum could be said to have begun through public art projects such as those described above. More recently (2010/11), artists were heavily involved in the protests in the New Territories to save Choi Yuen Village from being demolished for a planned railway line, which sparked a debate about whether to permit alternative lifestyles in Hong Kong.

In Kwun Tong, where old residential areas were sold to developers, a public art project by artist and activist Anson Mak is preserving the local heritage in a unique way. Mak set up a multimedia platform in 2009 to capture, archive and disseminate the images and sounds of Kwun Tong. The project (www.kwuntongculture.hk) documents the transformation of the community over 12 years until the redevelopment is complete. In this case the created public forum becomes the site for public art.

As a public artist, I am always fascinated by the tension between the intention that exists in a space and how the space is used: the difference between the way a space was designed to be used and the way the public actually uses it. Equally interesting is the way individuals and communities relate to, and are created by, both the built and the natural environment.

Hong Kong is the highest density city in the developed world, and public space is scarce. This public space is controlled largely by private corporations and monitored by the state. In the period we refer to as modern in the art world, the institution known as the art gallery took control of the art world, removing it from the common space of everyday communities, deciding what is good and what is bad. The pecking order today is clearly curated by the auction houses, where value is equated in economic terms to dollar values. In Hong Kong it is shopping centers that monopolize space and the new curators are the corporations who own them. They make their decisions based on entertainment value; art becomes a spectacle for the consumer.

Addressing this issue artist Benny Lau infiltrates consumer space and thinking in his public art project "The Changing Machine." His vending machine is wheeled into public areas in the shopping center and sits inconspicuously amongst other vending machines. Instead of offering soft drinks or bottled water it displays issue-specific artworks. The intention is not so much to provide a public artwork for appreciation, but rather to encourage people to experience giving rather than taking; to enable the public to raise concerns and participate in changing their own environment; to provide a platform for local groups to promote pressing issues and to act as a mobile gallery for local artists and designers.

Space is extremely limited in Hong Kong. There is not enough space to bury the dead. If you die here cremation is the only option. Space is so expensive that students live with their parents in single room apartments or in shared dormitories. Emerging young artists Leo Lai and Kenji Lau have produced poignant public art works in response to this issue.

In his project, 1 sq. ft, Leo Lai explores the relationship between expense and value as he questions the ideology of owning a flat in Hong Kong. The price of property in Hong Kong is among the highest in the world. He constructed a Perspex box and invited property owners to inhabit the box for a portrait photo taken on their property. The title of each photograph reflected the price per square foot of the property.

Kenji Lau has responded to the lack of space by creating a wearable public artwork that is styled from donated garments and is designed for nomadic living. The bustle of the outfit is a wearable wardrobe and the head-piece doubles as a sleeping bag. This is a micro-utopic vision that portrays his generation's desire for independence while maintaining the post-1980s devotion to the chic appearance of Hong Kong youth.

Private Spaces

From public spaces to private spaces this essay would not be complete without a peek into the most private domain of modern life: the toilet. As with many other spaces in Hong Kong the public toilet is a mysterious place that poses many questions for the uninitiated foreigner.

One image from the series 1 sq. ft. (Photo: Leo Lai)

There are two kinds of toilet culture in the world: sitters and squatters. Just as there is a clear divide in eating customs between people who use chopsticks, cutlery, or fingers, the so-called Westerners are sitters and the rest of the world squatters. There seems to be no rational

Wearables by Kenji Lau for the *Utopia* exhibition, Koo Ming Kwon Exhibition Gallery, Kowloon Tong. (Photo: Kenji Lau, 2011)

explanation to this preference in posture. Canadian-American architect and writer, Witold Rybczynski, in his book about home, considers this issue in relation to comfort. He suggests possible answers that are interesting but not conclusive. For example, in cold countries a natural response to cold floors would be to create seats above them. This seems plausible if we consider that most "squatters" are from the tropics, but the Koreans and Japanese live in cold climates. Another problem is that the origins of seating are found in warm climate cultures—the Mesopotamians, the Egyptians and the Greeks.

Regardless of why, it is true that neither culture feels comfortable in the position of the other. Traditional toilets in Hong Kong are squat toilets, which explains why Western style toilets sometimes have footprints on the seat. Often the toilet paper is outside the cubicle so you must collect some on your way in, or better still, carry a packet of tissues with you just in case. The flush mechanism may be either a foot pedal or a button. Plus, remember to empty your pockets before squatting, as it is no fun retrieving your possessions if they fall out.

In public toilets you often find people doing their dishes or filling water bottles or kettles. When space is expensive, not every flat or

4. Hong Kong: Cultural Transformation of the Public Sphere

shop has its own bathroom. Many apartments don't have a kitchen or much storage space and so people tend to buy food daily and eat out often. Luckily, as labor is cheap, food is relatively inexpensive—if you eat where the locals do. Under the towering housing estates you can usually find many small restaurants. Fo Tan's local bus interchange for example, is taken over every evening by the many small restaurants surrounding it, and becomes a large outdoor eatery. (The Fo Tan Dai Pai Dong).

Squat toilets in Hong Kong (2007)

Peripatetic Places

Since the handover to China in 1997, Hong Kong has been under the "One Coutry, Two Systems," which means one country with two political systems. The final public art project described here involves an investigation into the peripatetic zone that is created between two hegemonies, a place inhabited by people in transit whose lives are lived between the two spaces. These are people transiting the border daily or weekly. Who can and who cannot go is heavily controlled, but with the right papers it is possible to work or study and live between the two.

85

Selvage Stories, exhibited as part of the 7th Triennale Internationale Des Arts Textiles Contemporains de Tournai—5 Continents Woven World, Brussels 2011. (Photo: Aurelie Chadaine, 2011)

The public artwork "Selvage stories" (2011) is an analogue wearable navigation kit for "monadic" travelers living between borders or nation state ideologies. Etymologically "Selvage" stems from late Middle English as an alteration of "self" + "edge." The installation articulates stories collected from peripatetic individuals such as nomads, migrants, immigrants, expatriates, post colonials, or other transient people.

This dialogue began between Hong Kong and Mainland China and then expanded to engage voices from people all over the world discussing border issues. After working closely with participants, art objects are created and presented back to the community in the form of an installation. Visitors to the exhibition

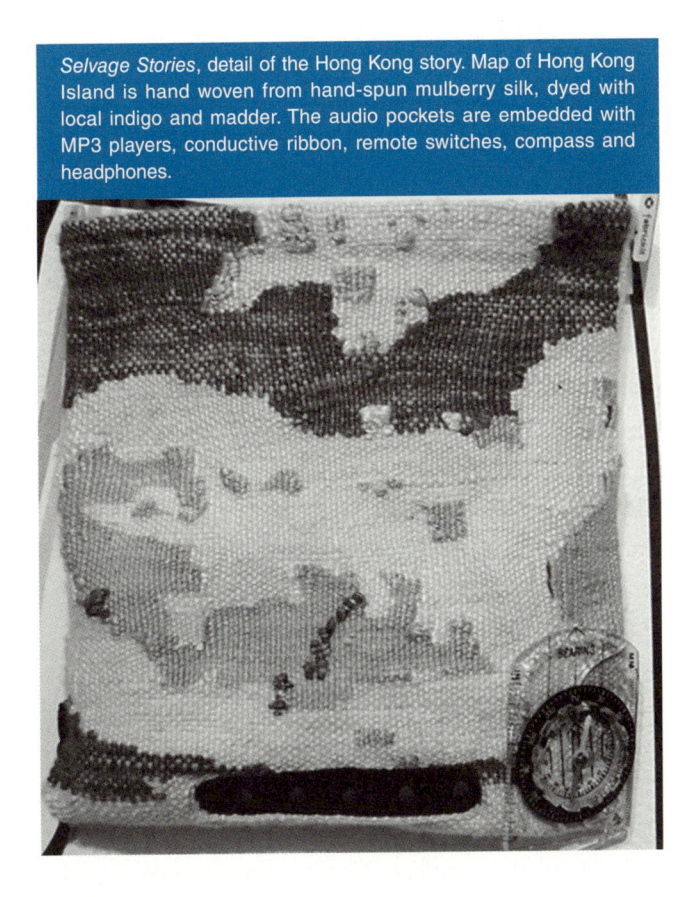

4. Hong Kong: Cultural Transformation of the Public Sphere

Selvage Stories, detail of the Hong Kong story. Map of Hong Kong Island is hand woven from hand-spun mulberry silk, dyed with local indigo and madder. The audio pockets are embedded with MP3 players, conductive ribbon, remote switches, compass and headphones.

encounter an esthetic fusion of tradition and technology in a series of audio stories and wearable maps crafted from native fibers and dyed with natural dye stuffs collected from the region that the maps depict.

Two maps are woven for each location: topography and transport system. Technology is embedded into these ethnographic textiles (A compass, a power adapter, a rechargeable SIM card, a rechargeable

RFID transport card and an MP3 player with headphones). The maps form a series of pockets that are interchangeable on a base skirt. The skirt stands on a dressmaker's dummy as a substitute for anonymous travelers.

Viewers interact with the installation by putting on the headphones and listening to stories of locals while viewing the linked maps. For example: Dembi from Inner Mongolia talks about his nomadic life and his time as a guard patrolling the Mongolia/China border; Herr Litzrot from former East Berlin reflects on his culture before and after communism; David, an American historian, reiterates the global development and origins of the notion of nation states; and Alan, a British immigrant to Australia, tells tales of unspoken borders of class in the hierarchical England of his youth. Momo describes what it is like living in contemporary Hong Kong and the effect of "One Coutry, Two Systems." She discusses the trade between mainland China and Hong Kong over the Shenzhen border. Each system offers opportunities to the other. In the past, middle class mainlanders would come to Hong Kong to buy quality goods they could not get at home, like baby milk formula. Apple Macintosh sales were the largest outside of the United States because mainlanders would buy them here to avoid fakes. Hong Kong people's quality of life was promoted by their access to cheap products over the border in Shenzhen. There was a booming enterprise of people who made a business of carrying goods over the border. But today Hong Kong people feel that their quality of life is threatened by the mainlanders' crossborder purchases. "Selvage stories" takes stories from the margins and embeds these texts into textiles.

Giorgio Agamben, an Italian Continental philosopher, once said, "The refugee should be considered for what he is, that is, nothing less than a border concept." In the age of globalism this idea is worth reflecting on, particularly in the case of Hong Kong with its long history as a trading port. It has always been a place where cultures collide and new ones emerge. In the past Hong Kong was heralded as the place where East meets West. Now as the new middle class mainland Chinese come across the border, Hong Kong is a place where two Asian systems reunite. The strength of the project is that it engages people at street level, it takes esthetics and fuses it with political agency. It enables a dialogue to take place in which cross-cultural perspectives are heard equally. The idea is not to present any one answer as fact or truth, but to stimulate thoughtful discussion by revealing each to the other.

Selvage Stories, detail of the Hong Kong story. Map of Hong Kong's Mass Transit Rail (MTR) system is hand woven from handspun mulberry silk, dyed with local plant dyes. The pocket holds a rechargeable RFID transport card.

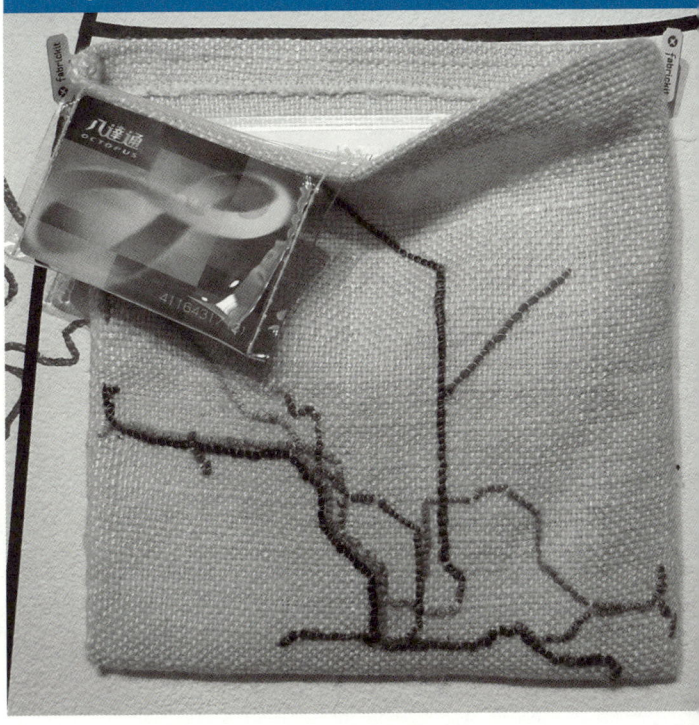

Chapter 5
The Other Side of the Postcard: Navigating Linguistic Landscapes in Hong Kong

Jackie Jia LOU

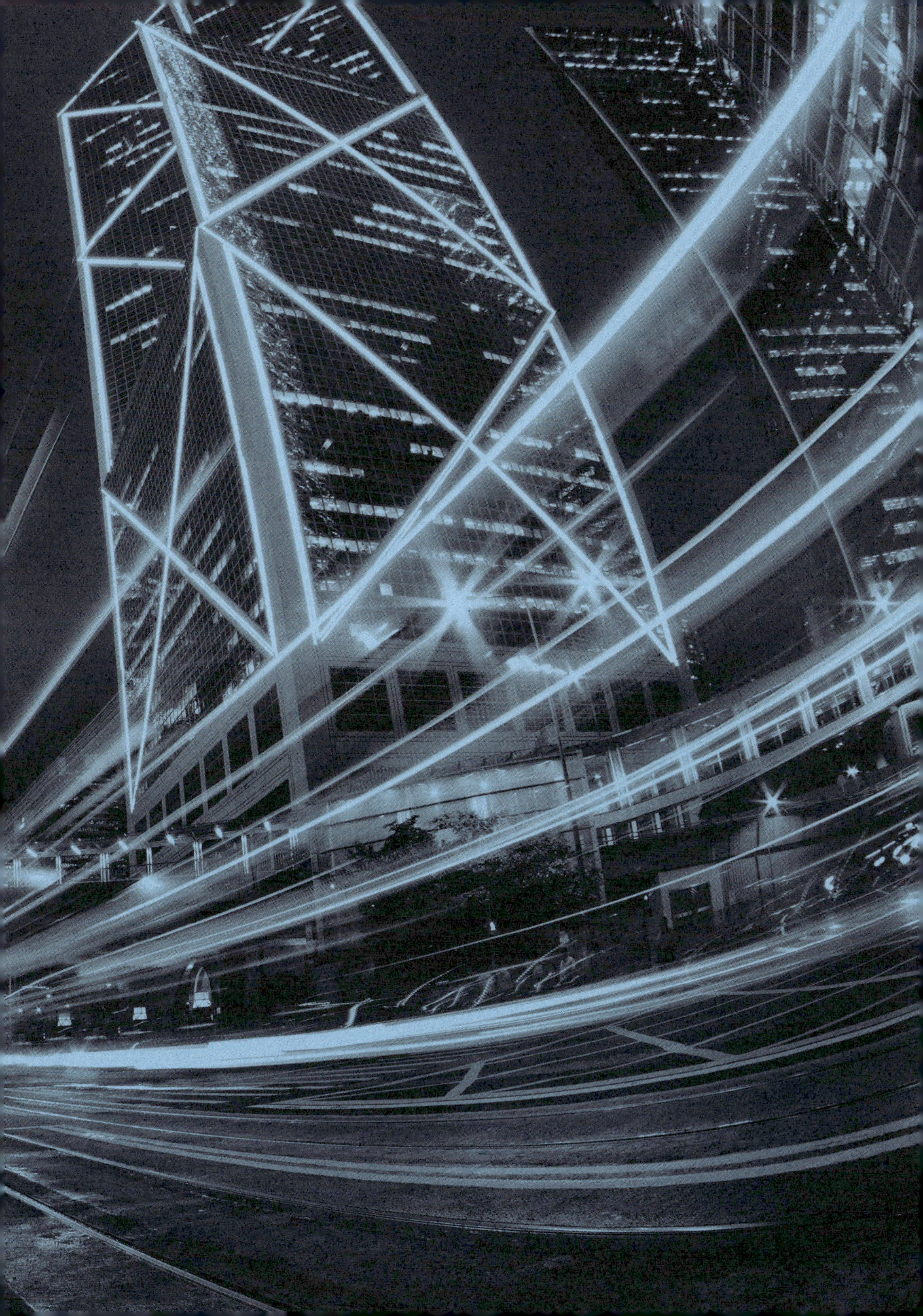

On a hot summer day in August 2000, a T99 train was about to depart from Shanghai Railway Station for Hong Kong. On board were twenty some college sophomores selected from two top universities in Shanghai—Fudan University and Shanghai Jiaotong University—to complete their undergraduate studies at City University of Hong Kong. They were the second batch of an experimental program to see whether students from mainland China could adapt to the tertiary education system in Hong Kong and contribute to its competitiveness. Every year from 1999 to 2001, about 200 students from mainland China were selected and distributed among four Hong Kong universities. The train started to pull away from the station. Through the window, I saw, among the many parents and relatives who were still waiting on the platform, my mom wiping off the tears that had been gathering in her eyes since we had left home. Suddenly, one of the students rushed towards the door, waving and wailing goodbye to her parents. Her melodramatic actions induced some restrained chuckles inside the cars and would remain a comic episode in our collective memory for many years to come. At the same time I wondered if those of us who appeared nonchalant about leaving home were not simply hiding our melancholy in happy chatter and poker games, which entertained us during the 24-hour journey. None of us was quite sure what to expect then. Although it had already been three years since the handover, individual travels to Hong Kong remained closed to mainlanders. Hong Kong, in some ways, still felt like a distant, mysterious, foreign place, which existed in kung fu movies, canto-pop songs, and stories that overseas relatives brought back.

Thanks to the media stereotypes of its violent street battles and triad societies, my family, particularly my grandmother, initially opposed my decision to study in Hong Kong, which they concluded was a dangerous place for a young girl to live alone. However, for me, this sense of danger and risk only added to the appeal of freedom. Above all, I was attracted to the notion of attending lectures and completing all of my assignments in English. English was always my strongest subject, and I was under the impression that we were selected not simply based on the total scores achieved in the national College Entrance Exams but more crucially on our English language proficiency, as demonstrated in prizes won in competitions such as English for Sciences, face-to-face interviews in English with representatives from City University of Hong Kong, and optional TOEFL scores. At that time, the best secondary school students went to Peking University, Tsinghua University, Fudan University or Shanghai Jiaotong University, but the best of the best went to Harvard, Stanford, or liberal arts colleges like Smith or Wellesley. Thus, linguistically speaking, studying in Hong Kong sounded almost as good as studying in the United States. I was excited but also apprehensive about the prospect of studying in an all-English environment. I remember I wondered aloud to my college roommates in Fudan: Would I be able to compete with my future Hong Kong classmates who would already have had six years or more of English as medium of instruction (EMI)? Would I even be able to understand the lectures? Such was the simplistic postcard image of Hong Kong that I carried in my head before I arrived—a fully bilingual city, with everyone from toddlers to the elderly switching between English and Cantonese at ease and universities operating in English, the more educated tongue. This misconception of Hong Kong's linguistic situation would influence many choices that I made during the subsequent three years of study at City University of Hong Kong and, to a large extent, shape the space of my activities, which would in turn reinforce my limited perception of the city's linguistic landscape.

This postcard image remained intact until I began my postgraduate study in sociolinguistics at Georgetown University, where I gained a deeper and more critical understanding of the relationships between language and ideology, language and identity, language and politics, and language and place. My studies and also first-hand experiences of these issues in the United States enabled me to reflect upon my initial biased encounter with Hong Kong's linguistic landscape and made it possible for me to see beyond the postcard image during the second encounter when I returned to my alma mater as an assistant professor nine years later.

Hong Kong's Linguistic Landscape: First Encounter

My first encounter with Hong Kong's linguistic landscape was a bilingual one, even somewhat stubbornly so. When the train pulled into Hung Hom Station, I was amazed to see all the signs were in both Traditional Chinese and English. As Simplified Chinese is the script that has been used in mainland China for the past half a century, Traditional Chinese had the same effect as English in creating a sense of foreignness about Hong Kong. The same could be said about auditory aspects of the linguistic landscape. In 2000, the announcements on the Mass Transit Railway (MTR) were in Cantonese and English, both foreign tongues to me. While I could read Traditional Chinese without much difficulty, I could comprehend far less Cantonese than English. I remember, during my first year of

5. The Other Side of the Postcard: Navigating Linguistic Landscapes in Hong Kong

Bilingual sign on MTR

study at City University of Hong Kong, whispers around me in the library did not distract me at all as I could not understand a word.

I was not very motivated to learn Cantonese, either. Expecting Hong Kong to be bilingual, English alone seemed to suffice and somehow more important than the local dialect. In the orientation program for mainland students organized by the university, we sat in a circle and were asked to introduce ourselves briefly and our newly chosen Christian names (according to the organizer, every student in Hong Kong had a Christian name, which would make it easier for expatriate professors to pronounce and remember). We had in fact been informed of this before our arrival, and after much deliberation, I picked "Jackie," after the cellist Jacqueline Du Pré, and also because it sounds close to my Chinese first name "Jia." Other students chose

95

names such as Anita, Alfred, Lynda, and Phil. Instead of suggesting Britishness or Americaness, for us, these English names were essential for survival in Hong Kong.

Academically, in line with my expectation, all of my lectures, assignments, and presentations were in English. Even during group project meetings where most of my Hong Kong classmates used Cantonese, I was exempt from using it, as switching to English or even Putonghua would be easier for both sides. It also turned out that my worry about my English language proficiency was unfounded. While my spoken English was less fluent than some of my classmates, my written English, especially grammar, was well above the class average. After appearing on the Dean's List, I found myself accepting invitations from the top students in the class to join their project groups, many of whom were either American- or Canadian-born Chinese or graduated from international or prestigious EMI secondary schools in Hong Kong. This gave me more opportunities to practice spoken English even during group discussions which unfortunately on the other hand made it even less necessary for me to learn Cantonese.

At that time, City University of Hong Kong did not have any student dorms, so all of the local students commuted. The students from mainland China, including some postgraduate students, lived in the Jockey Club House, with other international exchange students from the United States, Australia, France, Holland, Norway, Singapore, and all over the world. English was naturally the lingua franca for us to communicate with each other.

This international but in fact monolingual English linguistic environment also extended to the shopping mall adjacent to the university campus. Jokingly known as the "white zone" of the university, the shopping mall, Festival Walk, is tailored to the affluent neighborhood where it is located and the upper-middle class in Hong Kong. There, I found mainly international brands such as United Colors of Benetton, Calvin Klein, Agnes B., Chanel, Esprit, Marks & Spencer, Page One (the designer bookstore), and Pacific Coffee (the designer coffee shop). Chinese writing was hard to find in the shop signs in Festival Walk. Thus, the first time I walked into Pacific Coffee, I ordered a cup of latte in English without even thinking about it. Plus, my fellow Shanghai students and I observed, after a few trials and errors, that if the shop assistants did not understand our Cantonese, we would, in general, receive better customer service if we switched to English rather than Putonghua. Of course, this rule of thumb does not seem to apply any more in present day Hong Kong, with mainland tourists shoveling Louis Vuitton handbags off the shelves in luxury boutiques.

Before I describe my second encounter with Hong Kong's linguistic landscape, however, I should acknowledge that my first encounter could only represent some, but by no means, the majority of mainland students' experiences with languages in Hong Kong. With the goal of starting their professional careers in Hong Kong after graduation, many of the mainland students identified with the Cantonese-speaking culture in Hong Kong much more than I did. They followed Cantonese soap operas on TV and listened to Canto Pop. When they had group project meetings with local classmates in the common room, I heard them using Cantonese for the discussion. As a result, within half a year, their Cantonese was much more fluent than mine. Correlated with their high language proficiency in Cantonese, their activity spaces also seemed wider than my own. They ventured out of Kowloon Tong to shop in the wet market in the nearby Nam Shan Estate or Ladies' market in Mong Kok, where visually Chinese writing also predominates over the linguistic landscape. Ten years later, some of these students from Shanghai have become permanent residents of Hong Kong and even hold HKSAR (Hong Kong Special Administration Region) passports. They are also settled linguistically. At the multinational companies, where most of them work, written communications still takes place in English, but they interact with colleagues in Cantonese.

Looking back, it seems that under the wrap of the bilingual landscape on the surface, Hong Kong is actually two cities; one in English and the other in Cantonese. They sometimes intersect, but most of the time they are separate. Two individuals can even be within the same physical space but inhabit two entirely different linguistic and cultural worlds, and their lives run parallel to each other most of the time. This separation was even evident among a small group of mainland Chinese students, as we were gradually socialized into different spheres of the city. In my case, however, I never became fully incorporated into either world. After spending three years in Hong Kong, I left for Washington, DC to pursue a doctoral degree in linguistics at Georgetown University. During my six years of postgraduate studies and research, the relationship between language, identity, and place was a constant theme that intrigued me academically. The first lesson that I learned in sociolinguistics is that no language is inherently superior than another. The facts that the United States does not have an official language policy, standard American English does not exist, and many linguists oppose the so-called "English Only" movement were astounding revelations to me. I consequently started to question my own bias towards English as the default and more useful language in an international city like Hong Kong, and the ideology behind it. I also learned that even the classification of a linguistic variety, such as African American English, as a language or dialect is not simply a scientific exercise but imbued with ideology. I realized Cantonese (and even my own mother tongue, Shanghainese) is not simply a dialect of Chinese but a legitimate language on its own, and began to appreciate more the role that the Cantonese language plays in the expression and construction of Hong Kong identity. Moreover, a sociolinguist, especially a discourse analyst, is trained to see the social world as constructed through language, not the least of which is the idea of a socially and discursively constructed "place." In my dissertation research on Washington, DC Chinatown, for example, I gained a critical understanding of the chasm between a unified, multilingual appearance and a more fragmented linguistic reality, and how the former was employed as a symbolic resource to construct the idealized ethnic neighborhood. Thus, by the time I accepted the job offer as an assistant professor at CityU, the postcard image that I had in my mind six years earlier about a bilingual Hong Kong had been shattered to pieces. I was determined to practice speaking Cantonese more and to familiarize myself with different parts of the city so as to experience the "real" Hong Kong.

Hong Kong's Linguistic Landscape: Second Encounter

Ma On Shan, New Territories

The first step I took towards this goal was to live outside Kowloon Tong, the area where CityU is located. I also intentionally avoided

Hong Kong Island, where the rent is almost twice as expensive as in Kowloon and where expatriates tend to concentrate. In the end, I found an apartment in a newly developed area of Ma On Shan, a district in the New Territories, called Tai Shui Hang. It is a narrow strip of land between Shing Mun River, which turns eastward into Tolo Harbor, and the mountain Ma On Shan, named after its saddle-shaped peaks. The area, which once only had a fishing village (Tai Shui Hang Village), now had a MTR station (Tai Shui Hang), a public housing estate (Kam Tai Court), and several private housing estates bearing names such as Mountain Shore, Sausalito, and Ocean View. My apartment is in a relatively smaller, two-block estate called La Costa. All of these buildings have bilingual signs on the front gates. However, as the reader might have already noticed, the Romanized names of the MTR station (Tai Shui Hang) and the public housing estates (Kam Tai Court) are phonetic transcriptions of the original Cantonese names. In other words, they are the sounds of Cantonese place-names transcribed in the Roman alphabet, instead of English translations. The private housing estates, however, have different Chinese and English (or I should say European to be more accurate) names. La Costa is 嘉華星濤灣 (literally, Carnival Star and Swell Bay); Ocean View is 海典灣 (Ocean Classic Bay); Mountain Shore is 曉峯灣畔 (Dawn Peak Bay Shore).

Except for the names of these residential estates, the regulatory signage in the MTR station, and road signs, the linguistic landscape in my neighborhood can be described as largely monolingual Chinese. In my estate, La Costa, the more durable signs, for example, "Management Office" and "Gym," are in both Chinese and English. The elevators announce the floors in Cantonese first and then English (Yah Ng Lau, 25th Floor). Notices from the Management Office

5. The Other Side of the Postcard: Navigating Linguistic Landscapes in Hong Kong

regarding maintenance issues such as temporary suspension of flushing water are also bilingual, but the English translation is often full of errors. In general, the more temporary the signs are, the more likely that they are going to be in written Chinese only. For instance, the estate's club house offers a wide range of classes and workshops for children in the summer, which are announced on a colorful billboard placed in the lobby. All the descriptions are in traditional Chinese writing with the exception of the word "Hip Hop" in the name of a hip hop dance class for kids. Indeed, there seems to be little need for English signs in the estate. Most of the residents are local Hong Kong Chinese. In the past two years of living here, I have seen about five westerners in my building. The same pattern can be extended to the neighborhood in general. On the waterfront promenade, the map and permanently installed signs showing directions are bilingual, following the convention of official public signage in Hong Kong. Signs that are posted ad hoc, e.g., "fresh paint" or homemade flyers advertising properties for sale, are in Chinese only.

"Fresh Paint:" An ad hoc sign in Ma On Shan

As I can read Chinese myself, it took me a

101

Reading Hong Kong, Reading Ourselves

Supermarket in Tai Shui Hang, Ma On Shan

while to even notice the predominance of monolingual Chinese signs in the area. One day, in Wellcome (a local supermarket chain in Hong Kong) in Kam Tai Mall, I was checking the labels to see whether a root vegetable was indeed zucchini and realized all the labels were in Chinese only and I did not know the Chinese name for zucchini. Suddenly it dawned on me there are few westerners choosing to settle down in Ma On Shan or New Territories in general. Given its low population density, vast green space, and spectacular natural scenery all at a much lower price, one would think that this area has quite a lot of appeal. Perhaps it is the largely Cantonese-speaking environment that deters them. Or is the monolingual Chinese linguistic landscape a result of many expatriates' preferences for a more cosmopolitan lifestyle?

Tsim Sha Tsui (TST), Kowloon

Tsim Sha Tsui is the tip of the Kowloon Peninsula, where one can behold the famous skyline of Hong Kong rising above the other side of the Victoria Harbor. Literally meaning "sharp sandy point," this tri-syllabic Cantonese place name is not so easy for non-Chinese speakers to pronounce and thus is often shortened to "TST." Once I mentioned "TST" in class, and it took my students, mostly local Hong Kongers, a while to understand which place I was referring to. Thanks to the harbor view, many sightseeing spots, cultural facilities, and shopping malls, Tsim Sha Tsui is probably one of the places in Hong Kong where visitors outnumber locals. Yet, at the same, it remains one of the main commercial, cultural, as well as residential areas in Hong Kong. As a result, its linguistic landscape is a much more complicated hybrid than that in Ma On Shan. While I doubt words, even when accompanied by images, suffice to capture the entire picture, I will attempt in the following paragraphs to present the bits and pieces that come toward me as I walk through the crowds along Middle Road to the yoga studio where I attend classes twice a week.

The moment I get off the train in Tsim Sha Tsui East, even before out from underground, I hear the sounds of many different languages reach my ears. Unlike other stations where most passengers walk in the direction of their respective destinations without paying much attention to the signs, inside the Tsim Sha Tsui station, there are visitors stopping to read the signs or the maps on the wall. As with all official signs in Hong Kong, these are printed in Traditional Chinese characters and English. Groups of tourists often gather in front of the map, read the information in the language that they can understand, and then discuss where to go among themselves in their native tongues, including Putonghua and a variety of Chinese dialects, English, Hindi, French, Russian, and many other languages.

When I emerge from the underground station, the postcard image of Hong Kong street scenes meets my eyes. Ahead of me, I see large shop signs extending into the space above the sidewalk. They are placed so close to each other that, from afar, it looks as if they were laminated upon each other. At night, these signs will flash in bright neon colors; during the day, their colors look a bit faded. Many of them bear giant traditional Chinese characters with English names of the businesses in smaller fonts either above or below the Chinese words. More intriguingly, these overhead shop signs do not always correspond to the shops directly below them. For example, this sign reads "Sunflower Travels Xinhua Travel Agency," but the agency that it refers to is out of sight (it is probably on the upper floor of the building). Right below it are a hybrid store of traditional Chinese apothecary and Western-style pharmacy and Larry Jewellery. The signs of these street-level shops are placed flat on the wall above the storefronts and are either in Chinese or English, depending on the individual stores. The Chinese apothecary's sign is in golden Chinese writing against a bright red background. Larry's Jewellery only has an English name in silver-white lettering on a black background.

I wait to cross the road right in front of Chung King Mansion, an famous/infamous maze-like green-colored building that has been the locale of Wong Kar Wai's acclaimed film *Chung King Express*. Many Indian and African (said to have mainly come from Nigeria and Cameroon) young men are hanging out on the sidewalk, stopping pedestrians, mainly western tourists, to ask them whether they would like to buy pirated watches and handbags in English. Most of their

5. The Other Side of the Postcard: Navigating Linguistic Landscapes in Hong Kong

Tsim Sha Tsui (TST)

invitations are turned down or entirely ignored. On the other side of the road, there are more boutiques and jewelery stores. The upscale boutiques only have English shop signs, for example, the Chanel store on the ground floor of the Peninsula Hotel. But that will not stop mainland tourists from going inside, as the brand and the goods displayed in the shop windows speak another language, one that transcends linguistic boundaries.

Inside the office tower where the yoga studio is located, there is a different linguistic world. The elevator skips Floor 13 only, but not the floors that end in four as in other local buildings. Four is an inauspicious number because of its similar sound to the word "death" in Cantonese. In fact, the yoga studio is located on the 14th and 12th floors. When I called earlier to register for a class, their bilingual staff answered the phone in English, "Thanks for calling Pure Yoga. How may I help you?" I can then proceed to choose English or Cantonese to complete the rest of the phone call. English is the default, as it is the common denominator of local customers most of whom are bilingual and non-locals speaking English and/or other languages. The yoga classes are also conducted either in English by English-speaking teachers or in both English and Cantonese by local teachers with some Sanskrit chanting.

After the yoga class, I drop by one of my favorite bookstores in Hong Kong, Swindon's, on Lock Road. It sells mainly English-language books, covering a wide range of topics from academics to architecture, but it also has a small section of Chinese-language books on one bookshelf. In the front area of the bookstore, there is a table dedicated to books (for the coffee table or a scholar's bookshelf) about Hong Kong, which often attracts tourists and visitors who happen to walk by to go inside. Next to Swindon's is a small old eatery offering local food such as fish balls in rice noodle soup. Similar to the linguistic landscape in Ma On Shan as I described earlier, the more durable signage, such as the laminated menus placed underneath the glass tops of the tables, is in both Chinese and English, whereas the more fleeting kind of signage, such as the bill or chef's recommendation, is in Chinese only.

Although in a prime location with heavy foot traffic, the eatery's business seems to be dwindling. The waiters are leaning against the door and chatting with the cook. From time to time, a few mainland tourists will wander inside and place their orders in Putonghua. Once, overhearing that a group of tourists from Shanghai and an older Cantonese cook were not able to communicate because of the mutually unintelligible tongues, I stepped in to interpret for them. However, most of the time, I am the only customer. Just across the street, a new shopping mall called iSquare (i for International) offers more varieties of cuisines, including a wine section of the British supermarket chain Marks & Spencer, right across the street from the Chiuchow eatery.

Laminated bilingual menu in Chiu Fat Eatery

Causeway Bay, Hong Kong Island

About once a month, I take the subway across the harbor to Causeway Bay to go to the hairdresser's, get together with friends, or attend cultural events. As the first island which was annexed to the British, Hong Kong Island has a quite different vibe from Kowloon or the New Territories. Many places have separate English names, e.g., Causeway Bay for Tung Lo Wan. On the other hand, many other places have Chinese names that are phonetic equivalents of original English names, e.g., Wai Do Lei Ngaa for Victoria as in Victoria Park, or translations of the latter, e.g., Si Doi Gwong Ceong for Times Square. People on the street also seem to be a more balanced mix

Chiu Fat Eatery's sign reflected in Marks & Spencer's window

of tourists and locals, including local Chinese and expatriates who work and live in Hong Kong. Its linguistic landscape on the surface resembles that of TST, but if one looks more closely, it presents a subtly different hybrid.

The hair salon that I go to is located right across Russell Street (Cantonese: 'Lo Sou' [phonetic transcription of Russell] 'Gaai' [street]) from Times Square, the popular shopping mall famous for the giant plasma TV screens above the entrance. It is a part of a Japanese hair salon chain, with its headquarters in Tokyo and several branches in Causeway Bay. Their service menu is trilingual, in Chinese, Japanese, and English, as are most of their staff.

5. The Other Side of the Postcard: Navigating Linguistic Landscapes in Hong Kong

The receptionists answer the phone in English but are capable of completing the conversations in any of the three languages. My hairdresser, a middle-aged Japanese lady, speaks limited Cantonese and English, which, however, does not prevent us from communicating effectively, although sometimes she will ask one of the Cantonese-speaking assistants to interpret more complicated messages for us. While the example of the Japanese hair salon is only a tiny pixel of the entire linguistic landscape of Causeway Bay, it illustrates that any generalized description of Hong Kong's linguistic landscape as bilingual is destined to be partial.

Trilingual hair product ad

109

Conclusion: More Postcard Images?

During my first stay from 2000 and 2003, Hong Kong's linguistic landscape was a two-dimensional postcard image. I expected it to be bilingual, and when reality did not fit this expectation, it was excluded from my areas of activities. Consequently, I only saw what I expected to see. In the six years in between, not only has Hong Kong changed a lot, but my own views about Cantonese, Putonghua, and English in the city were also reshaped by my academic studies in sociolinguistics. When I came back here to work, the postcard image was shattered and reassembled into a multidimensional complex with many layers and spheres within it. In this chapter, I have tried to describe this complex through my own experiences of the various spaces in Hong Kong, moving from Ma On Shan in the New Territories, to Tsim Sha Tsui in Kowloon, and to Causeway Bay on Hong Kong Island. Although it might seem that I have covered all three major areas in the Special Administrative Region, I did not intend to reproduce the linguistic landscape in each area in yet another postcard image. As the reader might have noticed, due to my different degrees of familiarity with each area, my descriptions of their landscapes also vary. While I am able to paint the linguistic landscape of my neighborhood in relatively confident strokes, the linguistic complexity of Tsim Sha Tsui or Causeway Bay makes any attempt to characterize them completely seem futile.

A few weeks ago, a mainland Chinese student who is now studying at CityU shared with me an experience that had baffled him. When he was in an elevator in a shopping mall in Mong Kok one day, he politely asked passengers standing closer to the door to press the number of the floor that he was going to, in English. His friends who were in the elevator with him teased him for using English with local Hong Kongers, but he did not think it was a strange choice, as his Cantonese was not very good but everyone in Hong Kong speaks both English and Cantonese. He was puzzled why the same choice of language would seem normal in one part of the city yet unusual in another. If there is any practical value of this personal essay, I hope it could help students like him or myself ten years ago embrace the complexity and welcome the unexpected in the linguistic landscapes of Hong Kong.

Chapter 6
Discovering Hong Kong through Movement

Elizabeth HUEBNER

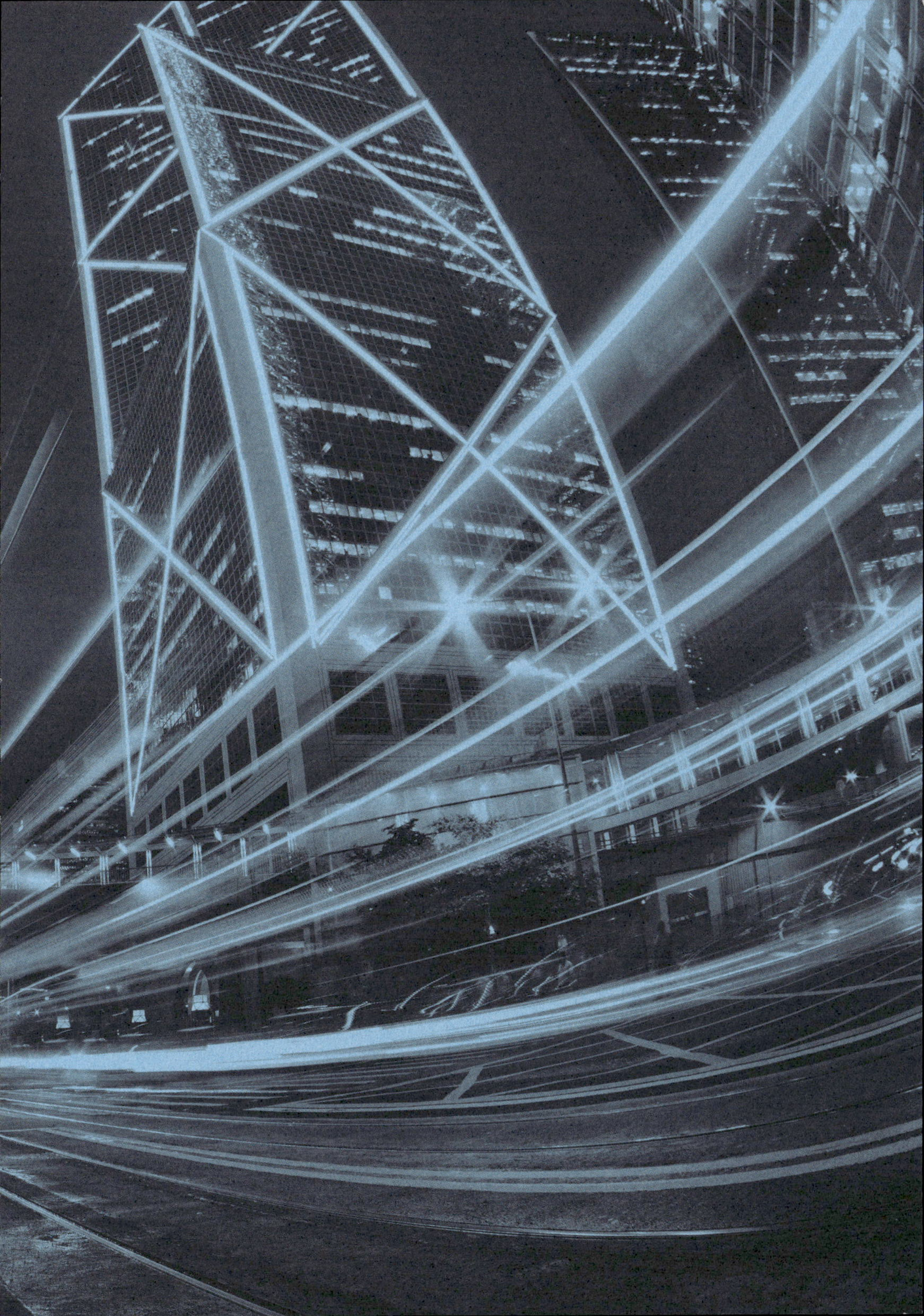

As an Alexander Technique teacher, I help people to learn to live right here, right now, in the only body they will ever have. In my practice in Connecticut, I work with many students whose "body sense" is in need of re-education; they have lost the natural poise they had as young children, and perhaps have lost self-confidence, strength, and flexibility as a result. I am aware that body sense is culturally conditioned to a great extent, so when I moved to Hong Kong, I wondered if I would see different patterns of body sense in the people I met. Some of the questions I had before I left were: How do people relate to their bodies? How embodied will people be? How much personal space do people require? How will sexism manifest in an Asian culture? How will I, an older white Western woman, be treated? In this essay I will address my questions as I relate my activities in Hong Kong.

I decided not to set up work or make other commitments before I arrived in Hong Kong. I knew that I would have a place to live and family around me for support—I was moving with my husband Hedley and my sons Duncan and Jacob but I had no idea what to expect or what opportunities would be available to me. I am organized, and like to plan ahead, so I was out of my comfort zone with this lack of planning. But my willingness to be open to what presented itself paid off. I am pleased I waited.

Street Life in Hong Kong

I did not think I would like Hong Kong. It was not a place I had aspired to live in, or even visit. I knew that Hong Kong was one of the most densely populated cities in the world. I have never liked crowds, and I just could not wrap my mind around such large

6. Discovering Hong Kong through Movement

numbers of people sharing such a small land mass. I expected to be constantly pushed and jostled in the streets. One of my first pleasant surprises was that this did not happen at all. People's personal space in Hong Kong is indeed much smaller than ours in the United States, but most residents have a clear sense of their body space. This is deftly demonstrated in what some people call the "Hong Kong weave." On the crowded walkways and crosswalks of the city, people are both tolerant and aware of people moving at different speeds around them. The rule of thumb is that one allows a faster walker to slip by oneself by rotating the body to let them pass. It is a kind of "do-si-do," as in square dancing where both parties rotate sideways as they pass each other. This happens constantly and spontaneously as you weave through the crowd. Often people come within a hairsbreadth of each other without a bit of physical contact. This requires a certain alertness to bodies in space. I was grateful daily for people's skill and willingness to maneuver around and with me in crowded spaces. It made getting around Hong Kong pleasant. Often, when stepping out into my Kowloon neighborhood, I would be entering a mass of what appeared to be wall-to-wall humanity—and suddenly I would be enjoying the dance of the "Hong Kong weave."

Street life in Hong Kong is vibrant and exciting. Life happens in the streets, where the sights and smells are intriguing and sometimes disgusting. Before arriving in Hong Kong, I had imagined that living in a densely populated city would mean that it would be dangerous for me, as a woman, to walk the streets alone. I feared having my wallet stolen, being physically hurt while being robbed, or sexually harassed. I spoke to a friend of a friend who had lived with her family on Hong Kong Island some five years earlier. She said that it was a very safe place and I would have no worries about taking taxis or walking about by myself. I found this unimaginable. The other densely populated city where I have spent time walking is New York City, and people are always warning me to not walk through Central Park alone or to avoid certain neighborhoods. I asked her why or how Hong Kong could be so safe. She said she had no idea, but assured me that it was safe. She was right! Once I got over the sheer disorientation of being in a place where I couldn't read or speak the language, I noticed that it was safe to venture wherever I wanted to go on my own. This was true for everyone in our family and most Westerners I spoke to.

Nonetheless, I often felt exposed doing things in public that I would normally do inside, such as practicing Alexander Technique or dance. I also felt embarrassed witnessing other people performing activities I had always considered to be private, such as grooming their feet, in public spaces. Apartments in Hong Kong are tiny, so people tend to gather outdoors to gossip, practice plays or dance routines, and play board games or cards. Many people venture out to do their morning exercise alone and in groups. Public parks have exercise equipment spread throughout so that people can use them to stretch or strengthen their muscles. On Saturdays groups gather in the larger spaces in the parks to dance or do *Tai Chi* with bamboo sticks, large fabric fans, and swords. Sometimes these groups have as many as fifty people in them.

The spoken sounds and cadences of the Chinese language were pleasant but unintelligible to me. I actively listened to people talking around me as I waited for the ferry or while I was in any public space. I hoped that if I kept listening intently, at some point the Cantonese language, which is the one spoken in southern China and Hong Kong, would just make sense to me and that I would begin to understand it. That never happened. Since we had planned to spend time in the People's Republic of China, I decided to take a class in Mandarin. But I found it very difficult to wrap my mind and my mouth around Mandarin. I realized early on that I had to make a choice: in the ten months that I would be in Hong Kong, I could focus single-mindedly on learning Chinese or I could go out into the streets, neighborhoods, and outlying areas and experience Hong Kong. I chose to experience Hong Kong and to use every creative means I could devise to communicate with people. I observed. I imitated.

I started out imitating what I observed the Chinese doing. This created some unexpected situations, as I didn't have much context or experience with this culture. I made embarrassing mistakes every day. I knew they were mistakes by the body language of the people around me, but I often wasn't sure what I had done wrong. I sweated through situations that I didn't understand; often, I had no way of figuring out why things were happening as they were. This was hard to accept. I was doing my best to connect into the culture all around me, but the language barrier was profound. I didn't want to just watch what was happening around me—I wanted to be part of the action. I wanted to connect with the people in my neighborhood. Since I didn't have a common language as a bridge, I dove into the culture in a more body-oriented way and decided to study *Tai Chi*. During my undergraduate studies in Modern Dance, I had learned the *Tai Chi* short form. I had had a kind of love/hate relationship with it: my body felt good doing it, but it was hard to remember, and it was so slow it drove me crazy. Yet it made an impression that stuck with me.

I noticed people practicing *Tai Chi* in various public places in

Hong Kong, but I wasn't sure where to go to learn it. When we moved into our apartment in the Whampoa Garden complex, our landlord generously walked our family around the new neighborhood. He advised that I go out in the neighborhood and look for a group of women exercising. He was confident that I could find any number of these groups early in the morning. He told me that when I found a group that looked good, I should stand and watch and wait to be invited to join in. So I found a group, stood and watched for a while, and sure enough, I was gestured to join in. I had made my first connection with the local community. I didn't know it at the time, but this moment was the beginning of my feeling at home in Hong Kong.

The Exercise Group

The exercise group consisted of about twenty-five Cantonese-speaking women, who met outside a modern sixty-story apartment building just a five-minute walk from my apartment. The class met six days a week, from 7:30 to 8:30 a.m. The leader would demonstrate what we should be doing, and we would follow her. This was good, because I couldn't follow the verbal instructions in Cantonese. In spite of the fact that I hate getting up early, I got up early every day to attend this class.

I loved the first twenty minutes best. We did dances to Chinese music in unison. My hands and arms were challenged to do new things in new ways. The music was completely new to me, and I enjoyed the feeling of it. I felt transported by the movement into the culture. After I had attended at the edge of the group for a few weeks, the women began to make room for me so that I could see the leader better. Smiling at me, they would gently prod me to the front and center of the group. I was embarrassed about being so visible, because I was always making mistakes and didn't know any of the dances, but I never felt judged or put down by the women in this group. They were friendly, kind, and supportive. They would also acknowledge when I began to get the dances right. They let me know that I was doing well even though they could not talk to me. I think of how often in the United States women compare themselves to the women around them: Who is thinner, prettier, smarter, sexier? I didn't feel any of this. These women were exercising for their health and enjoying the social contact with other women.

After the Chinese dance segment, we did calisthenics. We would stretch our legs and rotate the spine and move the hands and shoulders. My shoulders would burn at first. I wasn't used to doing so many upper-body movements. With time, my shoulders loosened up and felt wonderful. These exercises were accompanied by verbal instructions played on a tape player. After hearing them many times, I began to recognize the numbers; I learned to count from one to ten in both Mandarin and Cantonese.

The final twenty-minute segment was what had motivated me to go out and find the group: *Tai Chi*. The Chinese call it "playing" *Tai Chi*. This slow, ancient movement form, which is practiced all over China, is beautiful to watch and quite difficult to do. It takes excellent balance and flexible joints to be good at *Tai Chi*. I consider myself to be pretty flexible, but I could not squat down and fold my legs anywhere as deeply as these women could—and many of them were considerably older than I am. It takes many repetitions to learn the sequence and execute it with ease and fluidity. The form moves so that you face each of the four directions, North, East, South,

Reading Hong Kong, Reading Ourselves

Women playing Tai Chi

West. Since we were meeting next to the harbor, as I "played" *Tai Chi*, I would turn my gaze slowly to the water, where I would often see ships passing through the harbor; then to the sky and the large birds lofting above me; then to the trees, shrubs, and flowers in the garden around the apartment building; and finally to the the building itself and the people passing by our group. The very slow pacing of *Tai Chi* gave me time to notice these things. I felt very calm and centered after finishing the slow and flowing sequence of moves. I was grounded and ready to go off into my day.

Moving together is a unique kind of communication. There is a side of our personality that comes out as we move that is different and more personal than that which we project in conversation. Our bodies express things we sometimes don't know how to say. Communicating through shared action, we reveal much about ourselves that we might hesitate to reveal in other ways. As our group moved together, we had a unified purpose. Simply being in the same rhythm with other people created a sense of connection.

This group became my "girl gang." Most were older than I am. They liked each other and supported each other, and happily for me, they adopted me. I developed a closeness with a number of these women without shared language. It was frustrating that I could not speak freely with them; I wanted to ask them all kinds of questions about their lives, China, Hong Kong, and the daily practice we were doing together. I know my teacher, Mrs. Mok Kan Nui, also felt frustrated at not being able to speak directly to me. But we had a mutual interest in making a connection with each other.

The women showed great dedication to exercise; they met in the extreme heat of the summer, the brisk cold of winter, in rain and in wind. In the summer we met in the shade of the high-rise tower; in rainy weather we met under an eave; and when it was windy, in the shelter of some shrubs. The only time the class was canceled was during the Chinese New Year two-week festival, when Mrs. Mok Kan Nui went home to China to be with her family.

Navigating in the City

Soon a rhythm developed in my new life. I would get up early and go to exercise with the Whampoa women's exercise group. Afterward I would come back to my apartment, eat breakfast, and write for an hour or more in a journal which I used as source material for my Hong Kong blog. The afternoons consisted of going out into different neighborhoods and exploring the city. In the evenings the whole family would get together for dinner and compare notes on what we had learned and discovered that day. Many evenings we would spend hours preparing for the next day. We could get information in English online and map out a bus/walking route for the next day's activities.

We walked the city the whole time we lived in Hong Kong, often two to four miles a day. Although I have managed to find my way around many different corners of the world, I do not have a good sense of direction. When I moved to rural Connecticut, people gave directions like "Just go straight down this road until you see the big red barn, take a right, then go until you see the pasture with horses, and take a left." This worked fine for me, because the directions were based on physical landmarks, and I understand those. But the cityscape in Hong Kong is complex, like a three-dimensional chess board. There are the usual sidewalks beside the motorized traffic, but there are also extensive raised walkways. These are wonderful because they take you above the noise, smell, and pollution of the cars, trucks, buses, and taxis. Sometimes, however, it is tricky to figure out how to get up to them or down off them when you need to. There are also pedestrian tunnels, invisible under the road. Sometimes we would discover that the walking route we had planned would not work because we could not cross the street where we wanted to. We would stand at the corner and try to observe where other people were crossing the road. Usually somewhere in the middle of the block we would see people going downward and disappearing. They were going down a stairway to the subterranean walkway, a network of tunnels under the road. The subterranean tunnels keep pedestrians safe from the vehicles above, and in the hot, humid summer weather, they are always cool. But once I had lost sight of the landmarks above me, I was instantly disoriented. Tunnel intersections were often unmarked or marked according to the names of the streets above.

So I bought a detailed map of Hong Kong showing the names of the streets and neighborhoods. This gave me the confidence to venture outside of my immediate neighborhood alone and feel that I would be able to find my way home. (I also bought a map of China, so I could put the places people talked about in context.) The Hong Kong map lived in my purse and went everywhere with me. It is now worn to shreds.

Soon after I arrived, I discovered that some members of the group would be performing in celebration of the 60th anniversary of China's becoming the People's Republic of China. People from exercise groups all over Hong Kong were coming to an athletic field to do *Tai Chi* as one large group and then in smaller groups. The participants all wore red polo shirts and black pants. I wanted to see my "girl gang" in action. Before giving me directions to the field, the group huddled, talked together, and figured out how to tell me where to go in English. So I learned the time and place of the performance. Hedley and I went to watch 5,000 people "playing" *Tai Chi* early on a Sunday morning. It was one of our first taxi rides—cheap, fast, and scary. Pedestrians, get out of the way!

Walking on Hard Surfaces

One of the people on my contact list was a chiropractor, not a common profession in Hong Kong. We met and talked about offering Alexander Technique lessons to her clients. Most of her clients did not speak English, and that was going to be a major stumbling block.

She told me that many of her clients had serious foot problems. I found this interesting, so I began to pay attention to the shoes people wore and also the surfaces they lived and walked on. Most people wore thin-soled, flat, flimsy shoes, some because they were too poor to invest in quality shoes, others because even well-made fashionable shoes are thin-soled and flat, and provide little support. People walk a lot on hard and unrelenting surfaces. The walkways are cement; the soccer field and basketball courts are cement. Our apartment had a cement floor. Even many hiking trails are paved. It is rare that you can walk on grass or wood. Cement is inexpensive, and it survives the damp climate, but it causes wear and tear on the legs and feet. It was not surprising that people had foot problems.

After walking around the city for a couple of months, I developed a pain in my right shin. When the pain persisted, I tried one of the many places advertised for foot massage. No appointment necessary: you just show up, and are assigned a seat in the line of comfortable chairs. First your feet are soaked in warm water, and then your lower legs and feet are massaged for about twenty minutes. I enjoyed that part, but at the end I was given a quick shoulder rub, and before I knew what was happening, my neck was being thrown to the left and right. Since I didn't speak Chinese, I knew I could not explain my discomfort with the neck-throwing part, so I didn't go back for more of these foot massages. I chose instead to get help from a blind acupressurist. (Acupressure is a profession the government trains blind people to do.) The first session felt great. The accupressurist helped me a great deal, and before we left Hong Kong, I arranged for all my family and visiting friends to have a session or two with him.

Climate and Dress

Climate does affect one's body sense and appetite for movement. The year we lived in Hong Kong, the weather set records in every season; the winter set records for cold and the summer for heat and humidity. I was unprepared for all the ways that high heat and humidity impact your life. The August heat hit me like a wall and made me, a person who usually likes exercise, avoid any excess movement. I used my rain umbrella for shade from the blazing sun, and I adjusted my walking route to the shadiest part of the sidewalk. I slowed down my pace to prevent my shirt from becoming soaked in sweat. My mind slowed down, and it just didn't feel like working. My hands swelled up. For the first time in our lives, we used air conditioners in our apartment at night so we could sleep. We take pride in being a "green" family so this was a big step for us, but we knew if we were to survive this climate, we needed them. The air conditioners both cooled us enough to think and sleep and took moisture out of the air.

My idea of what to wear in such a hot climate did not match at all with the local cultural norm. In the United States, in such heat, people would be walking around nearly naked. But in Hong Kong, it is not thought proper for an older woman like myself to expose her upper arm crease. Tank tops or sleeveless shirts are out. Women can wear skirts and dresses that do not show too much skin, or long pants and short-sleeved shirts. Sandals are acceptable. The norm for men is long pants, lightweight short-sleeved shirts, and shoes (not sandals). (Exceptions are made for the young and trendy—for instance, Chinese girls get away with wearing tights under their short shorts. That way they can be trendy without disobeying the rules of modesty.) I solved the sleeve problem by wearing lightweight shirts over the tanks and sleeveless tops I had brought with me.

One Sunday we took a bus to Stanley, a town with lovely beaches and a market. The white sand looked pristine as we rolled by in the bus, yet there was not a single person on the beach or in the water. I thought that was odd. I wondered if there was a pollution problem or if there were sharks in the water. What I discovered is that no one goes to the beach in August because it is too hot on the beach!

Ours and all Chinese style apartments are equipped to deal with the extreme heat, but not the 50-degree (Fahrenheit) winter temperatures. Generally heating units are not built in. Word got out in the exercise group that we didn't have any heat in our apartment. The next week I was lent a space heater and some warm clothing.

Sex Roles in Hong Kong

Chinese culture is male-centered and male-dominated. You could say the same about most cultures of the world, but in China, sexism is more overt and more widely accepted than it is in the United States. I became aware of sexism as a teenager in the mid sixties when women's rights were in the forefront and women's liberation was in the public eye. I still take note when I see a woman doing a job that I have never seen a woman do before. In China, the traditional roles of men and women are strongly held in place by the ancient tradition of Confucianism. The four basic virtues considered to be the cornerstones of this philosophy focus on loyalty; respect for parents and elders; benevolence; and righteousness.

Perhaps because they are so clearly in charge, Chinese men don't need to act aggressively or violently toward women. The men in Hong Kong have a gentle embodied physicality that might seem effeminate by American standards. I liked the gentle, open, and caring demeanor of many of the men I met. They had a strength that was not defined by hard muscles and stiff movements or dominating behavior. Men were as likely as women to "play" *Tai Chi* in the morning, but they would do it alone or with other men. In China, family, marriage, and having children are highly valued by both men and women; yet the relationships of many couples seemed disconnected to me. I didn't see many couples spending time together. The men worked hard, and it was common for them to be out of town for weeks at a time. Historically, during the Mao period it was not uncommon for families to be separated, and the attitude seems to have persisted that separation is a hard but necessary part of life. When husbands are home, the wives are there to answer their needs. When the husbands are away, the wives are in charge and have a great deal of freedom to do as they please. This arrangement gives married women a lot of freedom to live their lives quite independently, at least part of the time. But these marriages looked lonely to me. And I noticed that loneliness often led to extramarital affairs, and many relationships were strained as a result.

Visit to Shenzhen

My "girl gang" worried about me when I told them I was going to make my first trip into southern China. The women warned me to watch for thieves and to wear my backpack on my front to prevent it from being razor-sliced and emptied. They had me pretty scared.

Mass Transit Railway (MTR)

I understood that we were potentially vulnerable, as we did not speak any Chinese. I think it was hard for my friends to imagine how I would get by without speaking or reading the language. I was told not to wear any valuable jewelry or carry any valuables with me. I later discovered that many people living in Hong Kong are afraid of traveling in China and will go only with an organized tour group. In spite of their warnings, my whole family took a day trip into Shenzhen. We rode the Mass Transit Railway (MTR) to the end of the line, less than an hour from our apartment. Then we walked across the border, showed our passports and visas, and we were in Shenzhen, China.

Most people visiting Shenzhen would shop at the Lo Wu shopping center just outside the train station. We skipped this part and ventured into the city. We found the crowds less predictable in Shenzhen than in Hong Kong. The Hong Kong weave was not evident here. A few times we got caught up in large crowd-pushing waves, which felt scary. Instead of waiting for the next train in the subway, people would surge toward the doors and potentially push us onto the train with them. These waves would involve hundreds of people; we could not see the beginning or the end of the mass of humanity. The waves resulted not from malice, but from too many people in too small a space, and a body sense that was less flexible than that which we experienced in Hong Kong. I felt a harder edge to the physical stance of people in China.

Shenzhen has grown from a small fishing village in the 1980s to city of nearly 9 million people. People have come from all over China to seek work in the factories. Each three-story building was a specialty "mall" full of shops selling the same thing. One had books, another pets, another DVDs, and another electronics; but the "mall" we went to specialized in tea. I had never seen so much tea or tea paraphernalia. The tea was being processed and packaged right there: merchants sat behind huge mounds of tea sorting the stems from the leaves.

We went from there to a large city park called Lianhuashan, and followed the music we heard. There were a number of instrumental groups performing, each surrounded by singers, dancers, and listeners. We joined a group that featured a number of men playing the erhu, a traditional two-stringed bowed fiddle. People in the crowd would join in and sing the song if they knew it. Sometimes one person would step up and sing solo. At one point, a man decided to "conduct" the musicians and the singer and crowd. I am not sure the musicians or the singer were paying attention to him, but he was thoroughly enjoying himself. Everyone was having a wonderful time in the park on a Sunday afternoon. Such group sing-alongs and dance-alongs are a common occurrence in every city we visited in China. This was a far cry from the picture I had built up in my mind of how unsafe China was compared to Hong Kong.

The people we encountered were overwhelmingly good and helpful. When we didn't know when to get off a city bus, someone stepped forward to help. When we didn't know how to work the token system in the Metro, someone showed us how to do it. When our rented leisure boat broke down, a father and son towed us back to the boat stand. After our first delightful visit to Shenzhen, we traveled numerous times into China as a family and were never threatened in any way. We had heard stories of how unsafe China was, but we were not followed, harassed, robbed, or threatened in any way. The hardest thing was dealing with people's shyness about relating to us, non-Chinese speakers. Sometimes we would have to wait a long time at a restaurant before someone would dare to come and take our order. Sometimes another customer would step in and help us order our food.

Cultural Kaleidoscope

Our family participated in the Cultural Kaleidoscope programs created by the Hong Kong Tourism Board, which introduces tourists to Chinese culture. Many of the activities were free. One of the programs I attended was on Cantonese opera. I was particularly interested in the opera, because I often give Alexander Technique lessons to opera singers in the United States to help them improve their posture and breath support. The program was held in the Chinese Heritage Museum in Sha Tin. The museum has collected and preserved many costumes and jewelry of famous opera performers from the 1960s, when the Cantonese Opera was in its heyday. (Just as in the United States, the traditional opera is not popular with young people, and some fear that the art form will die out.)

Each performance involves music, singing, acting, martial arts, and acrobatics. Unlike in the United States, where most of the training is with the voice, the Chinese opera singer has to train the voice to sing and the body for acrobatics and acting. There is none of the standing and singing in these operas that we have in Western-style opera. The singing is done in a unique style, unlike anything I had ever heard before. The men's roles are sung in the countertenor range (comparable to the natural female vocal range), and the female roles are sung in female falsetto. Like many things in China, operatic performances are full of symbolism. I had seen pictures of the elaborate makeup and costumes of the Hong Kong opera singers. Now I learned that the colors used in the face painting indicate the nature of the characters, telling the audience whether the character is ill or well, good or bad, male or female

I discovered that my exercise leader, Mrs. Mok Kan Nui, studies Cantonese opera, and that she was going to be performing soon. I wanted to see her perform. Here was another occasion for the group to huddle and try to figure out how to give me directions. No one could translate the name of the place the performance was being held. In the end it was decided that I would meet one of the exercise ladies who was also attending the performance at a bus stop near the local fresh food market called the "wet market."

The plan was that Hedley and I would ride with her on the bus, and she would lead us to the performance location. We found her at the bus stop, boarded the bus not knowing where we would end up, and headed north. We arrived at the community center of a northern suburb housing complex about 11:00 a.m. There were many people performing duets, mostly older women and a few men. The musicians shared the stage with the actors. The latter were very elaborately dressed, but did not have the face-painting and makeup used in a full operatic production. Mrs. Mok Kan Nui wore a black velvet dress decorated with pearls, sequins, and embroidery, with a high slit up one side. We were the only Western people there. The room was packed with people sitting on folding chairs. The duos performed, one after the other, to the constant din of conversation in the background. It was clear that the women loved performing these duets and had worked hard preparing them—and that the performances would go on all day long. We felt confident that we could retrace our steps homeward, so at 3:00 p.m. we left our guide (who stayed until the end) and boarded the # 220 bus to Whampoa.

The other special event I was invited to was a gathering of all of the groups that do the style of exercise that I practiced in Hong Kong. About 400 people gathered in a large room in a restaurant and sat at round banquet tables holding twelve people each. Our exercise group had two tables. I sat next to Betty Lee, who I discovered spoke English. We had been in the group together all along, but she had never let me know that she spoke English! She had learned it when she moved her family to Canada when Hong Kong went back to China. She acted as interpreter for me at the meal and the festivities. We ate in typical Chinese style with numerous courses brought to the table and shared by all. Then we were entertained by a number of groups who performed Chinese dances with elaborate, brightly colored costumes and fans. Betty became a major part of my English support team after that. Again, this group gave me entrance to an activity I otherwise would not have had access to.

Exploring Hong Kong Alone

When I was not having adventures with my "girl gang" or my family, I would explore Hong Kong alone. I spent a great deal of time roaming the Sham Shui Po neighborhood, and it became one of my favorite haunts. I first noticed this neighborhood when we rode through it to get our Hong Kong identification cards soon after we arrived. I could see that there were some pretty interesting markets, made a note of the street intersection, and went back to check it out. This is a neighborhood where the Chinese shop for electronic goods, beads, buttons, fabric, and clothing in outdoor street markets. Much of this working-class neighborhood has not been Westernized or modernized. I felt like I was stepping back in time fifty years. There are few areas of Hong Kong left like this. I was seeing something authentic—not a show put on for Westerners, but ordinary daily life. The clothing and shoes and objects for sale were more functional than those sold in the touristic night market. I enjoyed watching customers bargain the price down. Once an agreement had been reached, the merchant and the customer would often have a cup of tea together. Shopping is a social event, and people-watching was particularly good here.

I like to sew, and spent some of my sabbatical year sewing. I bought a used sewing machine and now had a reason to stroll through the streets looking for fabric and notions for my projects. Denise, a student worker at the Hong Kong Polytechnic University (PolyU), told me that there was a "fabric hut" in Sham Sui Po. She said that the fabrics were wonderful and inexpensive. I searched for the fabric hut three times, but could not find it. Each time she gave more specific directions, but still I could not find it. Being close but not being able to find something was a common occurrence for all of us Westerners in Hong Kong. We would be in exactly the right place and still have a hard time finding what we were looking for. The problem was that we didn't recognize what we were seeing when we saw it.

Finally Denise accompanied me to Sham Sui Po, and showed me the entrance to the fabric hut. It was across the street from a huge police station and just two blocks from a huge modern mall. On my solo trips, I had never perceived this as an entrance; but if I had, I would have been fearful to enter the place alone. To me the fabric hut looked like a homeless camp site. It extended for a whole city block and was covered with tarps, with chain link fences around the outer edges. There were no doors or windows—just openings in the tarps that functioned as entrance points. Inside were hundreds of stalls with colorful arrays of all kinds of fabric. Each stall is owned by a different person. If that person is not present, there are instructions in Chinese about how to contact them. Denise acted as my cultural and language translator. After I had bought some fabric, I started roaming the streets, where one could find every kind of button, ribbon, closure, thread, and bead imaginable. After that day, I returned often to the fabric hut on my own.

Much of Hong Kong strives for modern capitalist Western ways, but this neighborhood has been left behind, for a while at least. The numerous warnings I had been given about how dangerous this part of Hong Kong was seemed to be based on class bias, not reality. This is a poor neighborhood, not a dangerous one. I felt safe walking there; it was bustling, lively, and fun. I wandered into areas where I was often the only non-Asian person, and did the Hong Kong weave with the crowd. The only Western influence I could see was that the street signs were in both Chinese and English. Thank goodness for that, or I may never have found my way home!

Bringing the Exercise Group Home

It was because I felt grounded by my association with my daily exercise group that I was able to be so adventurous in the city of Hong Kong. When the time remaining became short, I realized that the exercise routine I had been practicing for nearly a year was one of the best I had ever experienced. I wanted to bring this back to my community in Connecticut to try it there. I wanted to get Mrs. Mok Kan Nui to help me and to give me recordings of the music she uses for the dances.

I located and hired a student translator to come with me to the exercise class and invited Mrs. Mok Kan Nui to have dim sum with me so I could ask her questions that had built up over the nine months I had known her. I asked her if I could have recordings of the music for the Chinese dances. I explained that I wanted to bring this exercise system to my home town and I would need her help. She agreed to help me, and gave me music and instructional videos. I went on to ask her more about her personal life and discovered that she had been born in mainland China and had escaped to Hong Kong, when she was 18 years old, by swimming across the Shenzhen River with her 19-year-old brother. They arrived with only the clothing on their backs. They had no friends, no place to live, and no jobs. But they found work and a new life in Hong Kong. I asked

"*Seafu*" (her nickname, which means "teacher") how she started teaching an exercise class. She told me that she had used this exercise style to help her through an ordeal with breast cancer. She has dedicated herself to teaching it ever since.

Saying Good-bye

I wanted to thank the women of the exercise group for all that they had given me. My gift was to choreograph a dance for them. I chose the song "My Girl Has Gone" by Smokey Robinson. It was a real challenge for them to learn this dance, partly because there was some hip sway in it. They worked really hard to master it. I had not anticipated how much of a cultural exchange we would have in the process of teaching and learning this dance!

My time in Hong Kong was coming to a close. The women decided to honor me by organizing a going-away banquet attended by about fifty people. Everyone pitched in to pay for the feast. They presented me with a crystal rice bowl as a going-away gift. Elaine explained the symbolism to me: this meant that they were wishing me good luck and that I would always have plenty. I gave each of them a photo button with a picture of the group on it. I was sad to be leaving these women. The last time I saw them was when I boarded the bus to the airport. Twenty women waved good-bye as the bus drove off. I cried.

Living in Hong Kong has left me with a deep appreciation for the goodness of people. I did many things in China and Hong Kong that would not have been possible without the spontaneous help and kindness of people who volunteered to step in when needed. My worldview is expanded and my life enriched by the ancient roots of the culture. I discovered new tastes, new sounds, new fabrics, and new ways of moving. But the thing that moved me most was the overall generosity of the people. I will always be more open and generous as a result of my year in Hong Kong.

I am glad that I made my decision to discover Hong Kong through movement. Moving together, whether in exercise groups, dance groups, or just in doing the Hong Kong weave, creates a sense of belonging to a group, and encourages an attitude of being with and for each other. There is something hopeful about a whole group moving in the same direction. We intuitively notice our natural ability to cooperate. Movement was the key to all my best adventures in China, and I believe there would be no other way for me to make the profound connection I made with these people.

Stage Three
The Search to Find and Understand the "Authentic" Other

Chapter 7
Reflections on Geography, Hong Kong, and Beyond

Janel CURRY

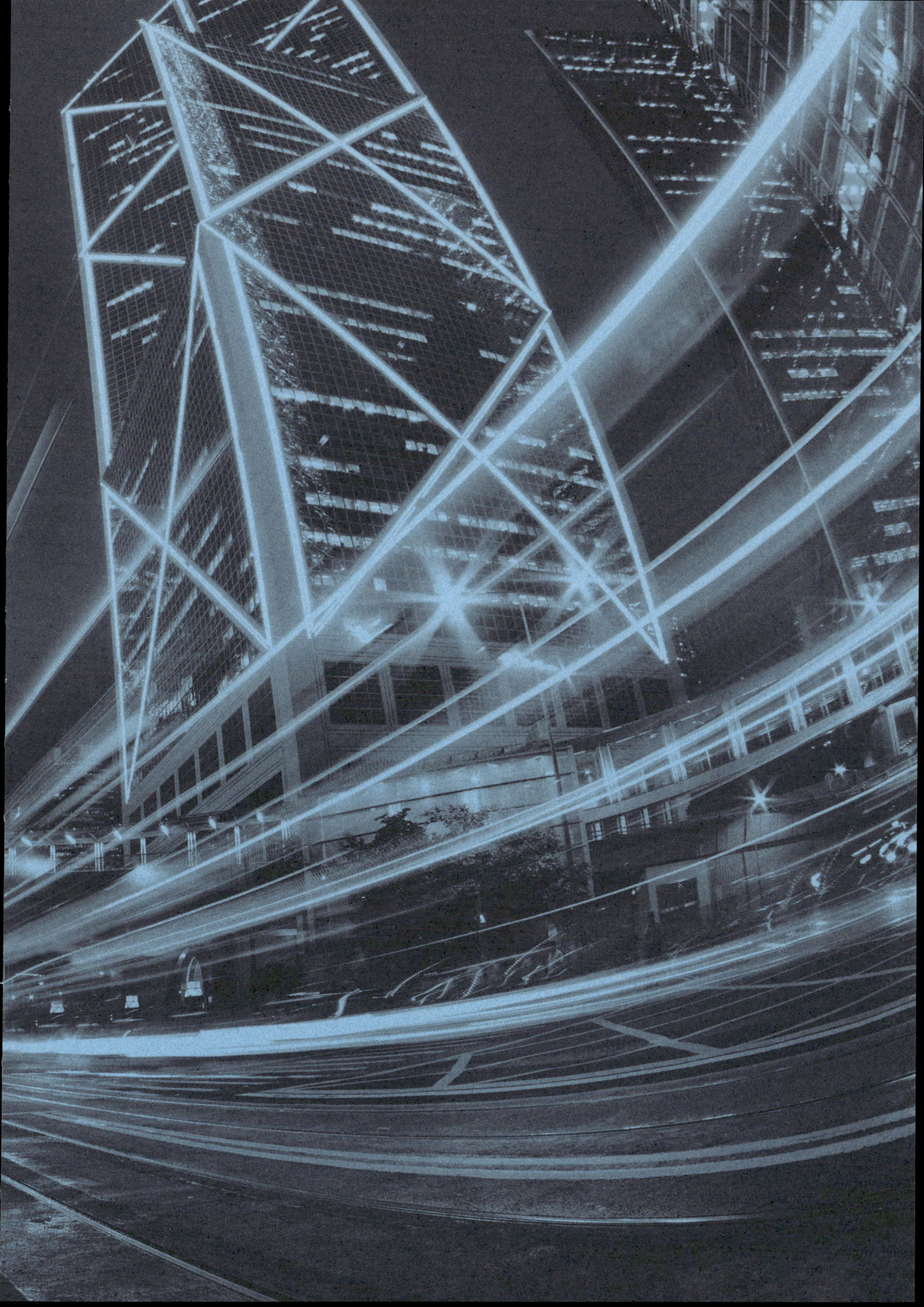

Reading Hong Kong, Reading Ourselves

Before I arrived in Hong Kong to live for five months, the city was a "site" in the most minimalist terms in my mind. I knew that Hong Kong as a site consisted of an island and mainland area along the southeast coast of China with a subtropical climate. I had some sense of its being mountainous because of the photos I had seen of Victoria Harbor and the Central District of Hong Kong Island. As a geographer, my first step is always to get a map when I know I am going someplace new in the world. So in the months prior to arriving in Hong Kong, I had pulled out my map that was beside my chair many times as I tried to imagine the surroundings that were going to be my home. This way I began to orient myself. And of course, with Google maps I could also scan the local terrain via the satellite images.

If the physical site was pretty vague in my mind, the situational setting of Hong Kong was perhaps even more so. I knew it had been part of the British colonial empire and returned to China in 1997, so in some ways, its relationship to Britain was stronger in my mental image of its situation than its relationship with China. In graduate school I had shared an office with two Chinese graduate students, one from Hong Kong and one from across the border in the People's Republic of China (PRC). We had many discussions over the anticipated return of Hong Kong to China and the impact on both of their lives. Since that time, my view of Hong Kong had remained more distant, and I was anxious to see and experience the city, its site, and its geo-political situation, close-up and personal!

Site and Situation

These two concepts, site and situation, used to describe and

7. Reflections on Geography, Hong Kong, and Beyond

understand the locational nature of places, framed my initial attempts to understand the place that was to become my home.

A city's site is the actual location of a city in terms of its physical characteristics—landforms such as mountains or bays, fresh water supplies, or soil quality for example. New York City is an example of a city where its site included a natural harbor with an unusually long sheltered coastline due to the arrangement of the physical features of the area. Many cities along the eastern part of the United States are located along the physical feature called the Fall Line, where the foothills of the Appalachians reach the coastal plain. This feature provided the opportunity for the development of early water power. The concept of "situation" is much more fluid. A city's situation is defined as the location of a place relative to its surroundings and other places—its location relative to elsewhere. Situational features might include accessibility to major transportation routes and resources. New York City grew in importance partially due to its location and accessibility relative to the Hudson River Valley and the Erie Canal, early major commercial routes that gave access to rich agricultural lands. Likewise, the poor site of New Orleans is overshadowed by its unique situation—the place where ocean ships meet river barges bringing the rich resources of the agricultural heartland of the United States to the world. Situational characteristics that affect places are extremely changeable.

Hong Kong's Site

Hong Kong's overall site and situation have long made it an entrepot for Southern China. An entrepot is a place where goods are taken off one type of transportation, sorted, stored, and then distributed out again. The historical context of the British involvement in Hong Kong is depicted in the novel, *Tai-Pan*. The novel illustrates perceptions that Hong Kong Island was a worthless "rock" evoking similar responses as those expressed in response to the US purchase of Alaska. These skeptics were soon proven wrong. Like New York City, Hong Kong Island and the Kowloon peninsula, which over time was incorporated into Hong Kong, have a long coastline enabling the development of extensive port facilities. In addition, this harbor is deep and offers a safe haven for ships while being in close proximity to the Pearl River Delta Region, a major industrial region in southern China.

In the past, cargo was taken off ships in the Victoria Harbor by longshoremen. Gradually the world has gone to packaging everything in containers. These containers are the size of semi-truck trailers or train cars. Today, Hong Kong's port is a major hub with container ships going to over 500 destinations worldwide. In 2009, Hong Kong ports handled 21 million 20-foot equivalent units (TEUs). The port is the key to Hong Kong's continued economic prosperity, and that prosperity, which in the past was tied to manufacturing within Hong Kong, is now tied to manufacturing in southern China. About 70 percent of container traffic handled in Hong Kong is related to southern China. In 2009, 205,510 ships, comprising both ocean-going vessels and river trade vessels for cargo and passenger traffic, visited the port of Hong Kong.

What else have I learned about the site of Hong Kong? Hong Kong is built on volcanic and granitic rock—85 percent of the total land area—that forms mountains and hills with steep slopes. It actually includes a group of islands, including Hong Kong Island, along with a land area on the mainland. The highest peaks are almost 1,000 meters or slightly over 3,000 feet. The arrangements of the islands and mainland provided for an extra long coastal area that allowed for the development of port terminals. This was Hong Kong's great advantage over the nearby Portuguese colonial port of Macau.

The site of Hong Kong has always been a challenge in terms of water. Seven thousand people lived in this rugged landscape when the British arrived and now there are seven million people. But the territory has few natural lakes or rivers, and no substantial groundwater—granite is not a great aquifer rock body. The many country parks in the mountains within Hong Kong provide both green space and catchment areas for the dams and reservoirs that were built under the British to help supply water for the growing population.

Hong Kong's Situation

And what is Hong Kong's situation? The situation up until 1997 involved a growing population, limited fresh water, and a hostile country next door. Many of the water projects pre-1997 were motivated by this situation. In one area the British even closed off the ocean, pumped out the sea water, and let fresh water accumulate. Today most of the water comes from the Dongjiang River in China and seawater is used for toilet flushing to limit demand for freshwater.

This change in source of water represents both a real and metaphorical change in situation for Hong Kong. Before 1997, Hong Kong was a significant outpost of a major western power—Great Britain. Hong Kong is now a Special Administrative Region of the People's Republic of China. The PRC has more than one billion people with cities like Guangzhou, Shanghai, and Beijing. The economic power of the PRC is enormous. To imagine the change in the psychology of the situation, think about the types of questions confronted regularly in Hong Kong: What would happen if all the universities in Hong Kong had to accept students from the PRC on a competitive basis with local students? How do we negotiate our way toward a more representative form of government with Beijing? What can we do to keep all the major financial institutions in Hong Kong, now that China is open for business? Many of the educational changes taking place in Hong Kong are driven by a concern that the Hong Kong SAR will become a backwater, a minor player in the Chinese context. The "situation" has been changed by the decisions of two of the world's major players and Hong Kong is left trying to sort out the results. Hong Kong's metaphorical water source, its source of life, has changed.

Space and Place

If the concepts of site and situation helped me orient myself at the larger scale, the geographic concepts of space and place helped me explore Hong Kong on the ground. Yi-Fu Tuan, in his book, *Space and Place*, talks about the concept of "space" as more abstract than "place." Abstract space, which lacks significance, becomes a place when it is filled with meaning and emotion. Space represents openness and freedom—the unknown—whereas place represents security and home—knowing. The process of encountering a region like Hong Kong involves the movement from an abstract sense of the city to greater contextual knowledge and "knowing."

Part of the experience of Hong Kong as "space" involved encounters with its population density. Hong Kong is one of the most densely populated areas in the world, with an overall density of some 6,340 people per square kilometer. This figure of 6,340 includes all the country parks so it doesn't reflect my daily lived experience of population density. For example, Kwun Tong, the most densely populated part of the city, has a density of 53,000 per square kilometer. During rush hour, I experienced the subways (officially called MTR, Mass Transit Railway in Hong Kong) as an undifferentiated mass of humanity. Even in the slower time of the day cell phones remained a necessity for finding someone, even if the person was only a short distance away on the same subway platform.

Place and Place Names in Chinatown, Washington, D.C.

Within this high density and mass of humanity—Hong Kong experienced as space—I quickly began to seek out a sense of place, a knowledge and comfort with the texture of the city. I also sought out understanding through conversations with people like linguist Jackie Lou. Her experience as a native of Shanghai, who has done research in the United States but now lives in Hong Kong, led to our having several rich conversations on sense of place in Hong Kong in comparison to various other Chinese contexts, including Chinatown, Washington, D.C. She described a fascinating problem related to sense of place and language in her Chinatown research. Within Chinatown, city planning requires that signage include Chinese language components in Chinese characters. Lou saw how the negotiations of a sense of place, expressed in signage, had generational and cultural aspects to it. When a business proposed a grammatically incorrect Chinese sign, the younger Chinese residents did not recognize that it was not correct. The older residents, who could read the Chinese characters, did not speak up but grumbled among themselves. Also, the cross-cultural translation of the meaning or messaging of the signage was not simple. Should the Chinese sign describe what was sold in the establishment rather than the actual "name" of the business ("household goods," for example)? Should the Chinese characters serve more as a decorative design element rather than provide information to consumers? Or should the Chinese characters, each of which represents a syllable in the Chinese language, be a clever transliteration so that the same sound was achieved, with some related meaning? In the latter case, Subway sandwich shops uses the Chinese characters that, when read, sound like "Saibaiwei" (賽百味) which means "better than a hundred delicacies," in Chinese.

In an area that is becoming gentrified, this is an interesting case study—what is the meaning of the Chinese text—is it to create some "image" or does it reflect the true nature of the neighborhood? What is the real significance and meaning of this to the actual local residents? Or does it eventually come down to creating what outsiders want to see—some quaint vision of what they think is there?

Hong Kong and Sense of Place

The tension between true attachment to place or attachment to an idealized "image" was played out in Hong Kong while I was there. It made big news when a block of residential apartment buildings was saved from destruction. Wing Lee Street buildings represented construction prior to 1955 in the *tong lau* style with tall ceilings, large windows, and air vents between buildings to provide lighting and air flow in the staircase. Housing pressures and rising land prices were going to lead to the replacement of most of the buildings on Wing Lee Street with a government estate—high rise housing at subsidized rates. The people who lived on the block were split over the decision, with some wanting new estate apartments and others wanting the maintenance of the present buildings. So what caused this unusual decision by the Town Planning Board to preserve the old construction? The street was recently used as a film set for the film, *Echoes of the Rainbow*, which won an award at the Berlin Film Festival. So, is the street and the past being preserved, or is a movie set being preserved? The newspaper headlines read, "Epic has a happy ending—for some." But is the "epic" the story of Hong Kong, or the story that takes place in the film? Perhaps it illustrates the general struggle with identity in Hong Kong which is often hidden under the façade of mass commercialism, where each subway stop marks the presence of yet one more shopping mall.

Neighborhoods and Sense of Place

In discussions over how Hong Kong residents experience a sense of place, Jackie Lou told me that there was no comparable word to "neighborhood" in Chinese. When you ask Americans where they are from in a city, they name a neighborhood. When you ask the same question in Hong Kong or Shanghai, from her experience, they give you the name of a building, an intersection, or perhaps a street. Their sense of place is different. Perhaps this is because the texture of the place is much finer due to the density of the population, or perhaps it reflects the prominence of familial bonds over all else. But also, in Hong Kong, many traditional neighborhoods are gone. The government began to create public housing "estates" about 50 years ago and most of the population lives in subsidized housing. This housing strategy was developed out of the tragedies of the 1960s when fires or landslides in heavy rainstorms destroyed many squatter settlements built on the hillsides. Such a tragedy was depicted in the movie of the era, *The World of Suzie Wong*, with actress Nancy Kwan. She was the first Asian actress to actually portray an Asian lead in a Hollywood movie.

Sham Shui Po and Shek Kip Mei are two adjoining neighborhoods in northwestern Kowloon, shaped by the development of public housing, that became "places" for me. These neighborhoods were not part of Hong Kong until around 1890. They are north of Boundary Street, the northern boundary of British territory until the territory was leased from China. It remained rural until the 1950s. In 1953 a large fire burned down six villages in the area, making 60,000 people homeless. As a result the government started to build public housing in this area and others in Hong Kong. Some of the original style of public housing—just after the fire of the 1950s—were 120 square feet and had three families per apartment (sometimes 18 people).

My daughter and I discovered Sham Shui Po in our search for cloth and other items for sewing. Finding where to go to buy specific items forces the development of a sense of place. In the 1970s Sham Shui Po was an area with extensive manufacturing—the garment district of Hong Kong. Much of this manufacturing has left Hong Kong for China, but the character of the neighborhood remains with button shops, lace shops, and other garment-related stores. Besides

7. Reflections on Geography, Hong Kong, and Beyond

Multiple generations of public housing in Shek Kip Mei

items related to sewing, each street has specialty street markets, from electronics to toys. It was a Eureka moment when I found the kitchen street!

Changing Spaces

For every day I grew in my sense of place, I also continued to experience Hong Kong as space. This disorientation was in part due to the fact that Hong Kong is continually changing. Even shorelines disappear as land is constructed out of the ocean. Western Kowloon is the newest of such areas. You can't easily get there from anywhere

Reading Hong Kong, Reading Ourselves

because this area of the city is part of a recent reclamation project. The West Kowloon Reclamation is the largest reclamation ever undertaken in the urban area—increasing the size of the Kowloon peninsula by one-third and extending the waterfront into the harbor by as much as one kilometer with a goal of eventually housing over 100,000 people. The land is being developed for public and private housing, commercial development and open space. But how do you create a sense of place out of seabed? At the center of this area is the Kowloon subway station. By Hong Kong standards, this subway station is empty. It has wide hallways, looks like an airport terminal, but has few people. Only ten thousand people come through the station each day because of its odd location. In fact you can check in for your flight there and then get a shuttle to the airport. When we visited this part of the city we were headed for the southern edge of the district where an arts event was planned. Walking south from the Kowloon station, we crossed an open piece of land that had not yet been developed. On one side cranes were set up, appearing like a scene from the movie "*Wall E*" according to my daughter. Behind us was a surreal view that made us feel like we had just walked into a futuristic science fiction film. Out of the scrubland this shining, modern, futuristic development arose. From the flat, vacant, unpopulated area where we stood. The disorientation of feeling placeless was intensified by the fact that the entire area has been recently reclaimed from the ocean.

Boundary Exploration

Spaces and places are separated by physical and/or cultural boundaries. Thus geographers also come to understand the world through the analysis of boundaries. These boundaries can range from political to cultural, but also include the exploration of the cultural boundaries that define the relationship between private and public space and between humans and nature. The boundary between public and private spaces differs amongst cultures and places. Within the density of Hong Kong, society has allowed a different sense of private and public space than in the United States. For example, socializing takes place in restaurants rather than in homes. And public parks are extensions of private space where individuals carry out their daily exercise routines, bring their birds in their cages, and lineup on park benches to read newspapers.

Public and Private Space

One day I identified a plot of land near my apartment that looked like open space so I went to explore. My walk ended up as an exploration of public and private space. The plot was a hill on the edge of an athletic field that I had seen many times. As I walked up this small hill, I left the neighborhood behind with its dense apartment buildings and people. When I got to the very top of the hill, I found a family playing games and many other private spaces that were allowed to exist within this public space. People constructed these spaces with materials around them and they used chairs, tables, and umbrellas. These items were left there and not bothered by anyone. In the United States we would not allow such private use of public space. We set very strict boundaries and rules around each sphere.

One of the differences between China and Hong Kong is the sense of personal space, or the boundary among individuals. In Hong

Private space with the public space of an urban park

Kong, as a friend told me, people are unaware of what is going on around them—it is as if they deal with the crowds by living within the shell of their small personal space. Americans, my friend told me, are more aware of what is going on around them. If Americans are aware of what is going on around them, then the citizens in the People's Republic of China have very little sense of personal space—they are not only aware, but get involved! We experienced several incidents which illustrated this. When on a food tour of Shanghai, we visited a park where a retired doctor did calligraphy with water on the pavement. He decided to read my friend's palm and within seconds (and I mean seconds), a huge crowd gathered around and pushed in to hear and see what was going on. This was quite typical but is in huge contrast to Hong Kong where nobody would notice, or the United States where it might be considered impolite.

Human/Nature Boundary

Besides exploring the boundaries amongst humans, private and public space, I also explored the lived boundary between humans and nature while in Hong Kong. Often you hear about Chinese culture and the ethic of harmony with nature. But that harmony is one that is very much controlled. Geographer Yi-Fu Tuan writes about the Chinese breeding carp with larger and larger eyes until they could not swim. In other writings Tuan points out the common distance between "ideal" and reality in most cultures.

Perhaps China and the United States are on opposite ends of the spectrum when it comes to their understanding of themselves and nature. Roderick Nash, in his classic work *Wilderness and the American Mind*, writes of the centrality of wilderness in American exceptionalism. From Thoreau to Muir to the 1964 legislation that established official "wilderness areas," Americans have seen the preservation of these wild places as intertwined with the preservation of the environments out of which American values and culture arose. It was this experience that made us different and "better" than older and more established European cultures.

Population densities in much of Asia create a different boundary between humans and nature. Setting aside tracts of land, untouched by humans, seems beyond the realm of possibility logistically, and many of the religious traditions of Asia do not separate nature from human society. Concepts of harmony in building and the placement of structures and site development do reflect the religious belief in *feng shui*, a Daoist belief that the "harmonious positioning of objects leads to equilibrium with the rhythms of nature and the movements of ancestral spirits."

Reading Hong Kong, Reading Ourselves

Hong Kong natives frequently refer to their utilitarian culture. This culture is evidenced in the control of nature for human use and protection. The mountainsides are paved over to protect against landslides. Most parks are covered with paving stones. I had to change my expectations when I went in search of green space in Hong Kong. On the map I would see a park, walk to it, only to find something different than I expected. First, on the map the parks look like open space. In reality it may be the side of a mountain that was paved over. The map would also show the presence of soccer fields, so I would expect a flat expanse to walk across. Wrong again. I would have to walk up flights of stairs to reach the field, placed on top of a hill that had been removed.

I was in Hong Kong for almost five months before I was finally able to begin to see the remnants of natural systems within the built-up area. A community effort to restore one natural feature is in the Kai Tak area of Kowloon. Kai Tak was the name of the old airport that closed around 1997. This part of the city remained low rise because of the flight path and now development pressures are increasing. A Chinese University of Hong Kong Professor of Architecture, Wallace Chang, has been working with locals on trying to shape the form of development. Part of that effort has been focused on bringing attention to a waterway that has now been named the Kai Tak River as a focus for community-engaged planning. Ironically, the Kai Tak River's water must be pumped into the waterway from over the mountain in the New Territories from the water treatment plant. The water cannot go into the bay on the north side of the mountains because the lack of strong current would lead to a build-up of pollution. But this water actually improves the water quality on the south side of the mountains!

7. Reflections on Geography, Hong Kong, and Beyond

The Kai Tak River in Kowloon City is named after the old airport

Flows

Finally, on my last outing, I explored some of the New Territories and outer islands on the east side of the Kowloon peninsula. For the first time I felt the density of development and intensity of Hong Kong life melt away. The quiet allowed me to reflect on the movement and flows in nature and among the people of Hong Kong.

This side of the peninsula is relatively undeveloped and has a strong ocean current. These factors have made it attractive for fish farming. On this east side of Hong Kong, a strong current comes down past Taiwan and washes out the toxins. The purity of the

Reading Hong Kong, Reading Ourselves

The main path in Wu Kai Tang village

water on this side is in great contrast to the pollution released into the waters on the west side of the Kowloon peninsula because of all the industrial development in the Pearl River Delta. The only way to know for sure where your fish come from is to go to a restaurant right by the waterfront, so well-known restaurants are located along the east side where you choose your fish from big tanks filled as fishermen unload from their boats.

On this outing we first hiked through a typical New Territories village. The residents of the New Territories migrated to the New Territories from Southern China a few centuries ago and were mostly farmers. A signature layout pattern for most of the New Territories villages developed over time. Most were built against slopes with a *feng shui* wood at the back. Wu Kau Tang village was partially abandoned in the 70s or 80s. In the 60s and 70s young people left to go to Britain to start restaurants, and search out other economic opportunities abroad. They sent money home which led to the improvement of many of the houses, but once the older generation died, many deteriorated. Now some people are coming back when they retire—they still own the houses and the weather is better than in the United Kingdom. The path through this village ran along the stretch of two-story houses, all tightly packed and attached to each other. Houses that looked newly renovated and inhabited were interspersed with those that were open to the elements with pictures still on the walls and household items still sitting on the stove, reminders of the families that were scattered across the globe as they searched for new opportunities.

The end of the day brought me to Kat O (Crooked Island). The view from the village reminded me once again of the "situational" character of Hong Kong. Local fish farms filled the foreground, while the newly developed container ports of China loomed large in the distance. The boundary between China and Hong Kong continues to be evident in culture, economics, and politics, in spite of Hong Kong's return to China in 1997. And Hong Kong continues to be a node through which the cultures of East and West flow, creating a unique landscape, culture, and experience for the visitor or short-term resident. For me personally, Hong Kong is no longer an abstract image on a map or satellite photo. When I look at my maps I imagine a great variety of real places. I also remember the graciousness of the many people who made me feel welcome. And I see a place that feels like home.

References

Clavell, James. *Tai-Pan*. New York: Atheneum, 1966.

"Epic has a happy ending—for some," *South China Morning Post*, March 17, 2010, Section C, 1.

Lou, Jackie J. (2010). "Chinese on the side: The marginalization of Chinese in the linguistic and social landscapes of Washington, D.C. Chinatown." In *Linguistic Landscape in the City*, edited by Elana Shohamy, Eli Ben-Rafael, and Monica Barni, pp. 96–114. Buffalo, New York: Multilingual Matters (forthcoming).

Lou, Jackie J. "Revitalizing Chinatown into a heterotopia: A geosemiotic analysis of shop signs in Washington, D.C.'s Chinatown." *Space and Culture* 10 (2007): 170–194.

Nash, Roderick. *Wilderness and the American Mind*. 4th edition. New Haven, CT: Yale University Press, 2001.

Tuan, Yi-Fu. *Dominance & Affection: The Making of Pets*. New Haven: Yale University Press, 1984.

Tuan, Yi-Fu. *Space and Place: The Perspective of Experience*. Minneapolis: University of Minnesota Press, 1977.

Chapter 8
The Colonial Past in Hong Kong's Present

David A. CAMPION

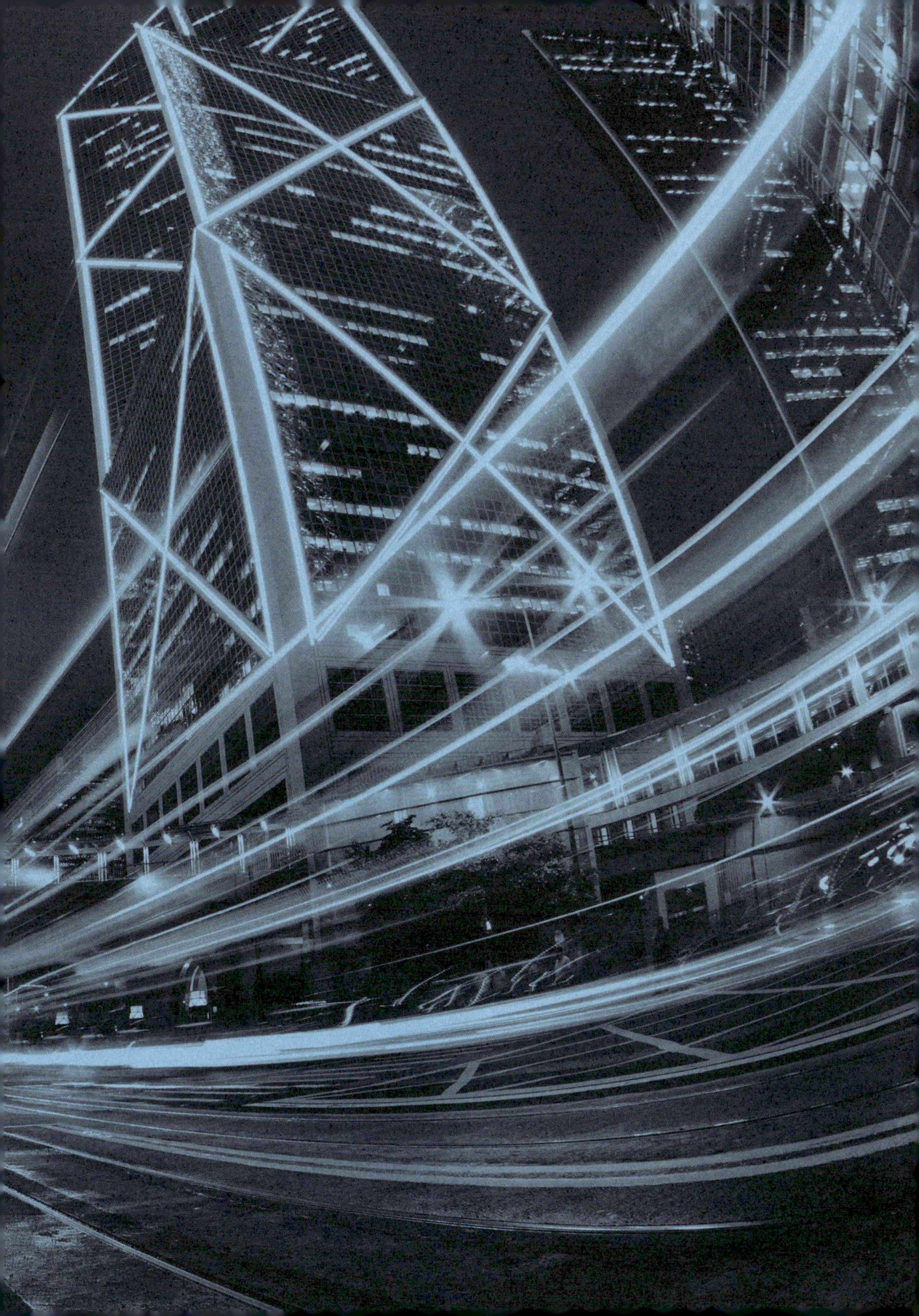

At midnight on July 1st, 1997, the territory of Hong Kong was handed over by the United Kingdom to the People's Republic of China. After 155 years of British colonial rule, Hong Kong was formally under the sovereignty of China—or "reunified with the motherland" as the Mainland Chinese would say. The handover was a lavish affair that combined wistful nostalgia for an empire on which the sun had long since set with the triumphalism and self-confidence of a world power in its ascent. The event was presided over by the Prince of Wales and Chris Patten, the last governor of the territory, and was attended by Jiang Zemin, the President of China, and Tony Blair, the new British prime minister. Amid a monsoon downpour a British military band played "Last Post," complete with bagpipe solo, as the Union Jack and Hong Kong colonial flag were slowly lowered. Moments later, a Chinese regimental band struck an especially spirited version of their anthem as the flag of the People's Republic of China and the new flag of the Hong Kong Special Administrative Region were hoisted.

The rain could not dampen the spectacular fireworks display over Victoria Harbor that began shortly after midnight, yet it was hard to describe this occasion entirely as a celebration. Indeed, the handover and the long countdown that preceded it were met with mixed feelings by many of Hong Kong's Chinese residents. While few of them embraced the elegies and nostalgia of the misty-eyed British community (some of whom had spent their entire lives in Hong Kong), they also viewed the territory's incorporation into communist China with no small measure of anxiety. It was a mere eight years after the Tiananmen Square uprising had been brutally crushed and in the midst of Beijing's increasingly aggressive policy toward Taiwan, its "renegade" province. While the former Chinese leader

8. The Colonial Past in Hong Kong's Present

Deng Xiaoping had promised under the Joint Declaration that Hong Kong's autonomy and its special role as an economic powerhouse and gateway to the West would be respected, nobody knew for certain what would happen when the British departed. Once the handover ceremony was done, the British delegation boarded the royal yacht *Britannia* and sailed away. At the same time, lorries and buses filled with soldiers of the People's Liberation Army crossed into the territory from the now unguarded border post at Shenzhen. When the sun rose the next morning, Hong Kong appeared no different than the day before, but it was the dawn of a new era.

This chapter examines the colonial foundation of Hong Kong and how its distinctiveness as both a Chinese and European society shaped it into the place that it is today. It is part history, part tour guide, and partly a personal reflection from the perspective of a foreign resident with academic training as an historian of the British Empire but with no prior experience living in East Asia.

Much has been written about Hong Kong's colonial past, and indeed much of that past is immediately evident to the newly-arrived visitor: the drive from the airport to the city center on the left side of the road, the many streets and public spaces that bear the names of English monarchs and the territory's Scottish and Irish governors, the double-decker buses, and, of course, the nearly universal use of English in the public sphere. Other remnants are more difficult to spot but like prizes in a scavenger hunt, do not remain hidden for long from the discerning eye. Among these is the occasional cast iron mailbox, with the royal initials E.R.II or G.R.VI, whose English red of the Royal Mail has been painted over with the lime green of the new Hong Kong postal service or the random building that still bears the name of British royalty. Among the latter is the Duke of

Reading Hong Kong, Reading Ourselves

Windsor Social Service Building, a drab and forgettable office tower on Hennessey Road named for the disgraced former King of England who abdicated the crown to marry the American socialite Wallis Simpson. One could easily pass it by without noticing it at all, as thousands of pedestrians surely do each day.

Many of the most important and enduring aspects of the colonial legacy, however are the ones not readily discernible to the new visitor, even one with a keen eye. Yet these invisible remnants affect the daily lives of Hong Kong people and their identity as a society in the most profound ways. To get a sense of Hong Kong's historical uniqueness, one must understand not only how it developed alongside the rest of China, but also how anomalous its situation as a colony was

The Duke of Windsor Social Service Building, Hennessey Road, Wan Chai, Hong Kong Island

compared to the rest of the British Empire. Hong Kong's colonial legacy, as much as any other aspect of its current existence, owes much to the outcome of events and policies that were forged in peace and war and which were neither imposed upon it from some fixed blueprint of imperialism nor replicated elsewhere.

An Accidental Prize

Great Britain acquired Hong Kong in 1842, in the fifth year of the reign of Queen Victoria and at a time when that nation had become the undisputed military and industrial power of the world. Britain's textile mills hummed with activity, as did the coalmines that fueled the country's steam-powered industry. Mass production allowed British exports to undersell their foreign competition in an open market while the importation of grain and other foodstuffs brought down food prices within the densely populated British Isles. The repeal of tariffs and the rise of free trade policies, along with greater political enfranchisement of the middle classes in Britain, were major victories for the merchants and manufacturers of Britain and a landmark in their political ascendancy. Along with free trade, the maintenance of vast naval and merchant fleets that could ensure open markets and freedom of the seas all contributed to the expansion of Britain's empire and to its growing economic power around the world. It was in these circumstances that imperial Britain engaged with China and ultimately took possession of the territory that would become Hong Kong.

In the 1830s, Europeans traded actively in Chinese ports. The most important of these was Canton (present-day Guangzhou) inside the Pearl River Delta. Along the waterfront of this bustling seaport, trading houses from many nationalities sat side-by-side and did brisk business with Chinese merchants. For decades European traders had grown rich exporting Chinese tea and luxury goods to affluent consumers in Europe and North America, but now Britain wished to reverse the flow and tap into the vast potential of China as a consumer market for British goods—particularly opium from India. Harsh measures by the imperial government of the Qing Dynasty to curtail the opium trade and punish the vendors prompted Britain, in an overt act of aggression, to deploy its navy to force China to open free trade. This one-sided conflict, known as the First Opium War, resulted in a decisive victory for the British. It proved, in no uncertain terms, Britain's military and technological advantage and resulted in a humiliating surrender by the Chinese. The concessions extracted from the vanquished in the Treaty of Nanking included an indemnity, access to certain treaty ports in which Europeans enjoyed special trading privileges and immunity from Chinese laws, and the ceding to Britain as its own territory of an island at the eastern side of the entrance to the Pearl River Delta.

The events of the First Opium war are well known to the Chinese and to historians of the British Empire, but what is most important for our purposes is to understand that Hong Kong was acquired as an accidental prize in a war fought not for conquest but for money. That Britain would deploy its military and naval power to advance what were mainly the interests of private enterprise demonstrate the rising influence of the commercial classes in Britain and throughout the empire. It also reveals that the gospel of free trade, which was propagated at least as zealously as that of Jesus Christ, had become an article of the faith in Victorian Britain. It became the justification for an aggressive foreign policy, one that overrode the sovereignty of other countries and forced open their markets at the point of a cannon.

8. The Colonial Past in Hong Kong's Present

Before Britain's victory in the First Opium War, the name "Hong Kong" (Fragrant Harbor) was how locals referred to the deepwater inlet between what today are known as Hong Kong Island and the Kowloon Peninsula. Until that point, the place had been a sparsely populated string of fishing villages along the coast and a few farming communities further inland. In those days, it was a geographically isolated and unimportant area compared to nearby Canton and the tiny island of Macau on the western end of the mouth of the Pearl River Delta, which by then had been occupied by the Portuguese for almost three centuries. The undeveloped island on the eastern end of the delta was relatively insignificant and ceding it to the British seemed a good way for the Chinese government to keep the troublesome, opium-pushing *gweilo* ("foreigners," also "devils") at a safe distance. From then onward the British began to use the name Hong Kong to describe the entire island that was now theirs. Two decades later they took control over Kowloon and in 1898 they gained a 99-year lease from China over the New Territories, thereby substantially increasing the size of their colony to 407 sq. miles. Today, over seven million people live in Hong Kong, making it one of the most densely populated places in the world. It would have been unimaginable to the occupants a mere century and a half ago that along muddy banks of the Fragrant Harbor would be planted the seeds of one of the world's greatest cities and a hub of the international economy.

Law and Order in an Anglo-Chinese Society

From the outset, Hong Kong as a crown colony was conceived from Britain's stubborn insistence on its right to commerce and the principles of free trade. This distinguished it from other colonies in the vast and growing British Empire of the nineteenth century. Hong Kong has no natural resources to exploit, apart from its strategic location. There were no sugar plantations as in the Caribbean, no gold and diamond mines as in South Africa, and no vast tracts of farmland as in Canada or East Africa. It was not a place where convicts could be transported as in Australia, nor did it have a vast population that could provide soldiers, policemen and contract laborers for service elsewhere in the empire as India did. Other British port colonies like Aden and the Straits Settlement (later Singapore) were similar to Hong Kong in that they were active trading centers. But in reality these were mostly stopping points along the sea routes from Europe to Asia and places from which to project military power. By contrast, Hong Kong was a terminus at the doorstep to imperial China, a place viewed by westerners as one of the largest and most untapped markets in the world. Hong Kong existed to stimulate and sustain trade between the West and China, and its administration remained focused on this goal.

At first, Hong Kong's value lay in its potential rather than in what already existed. There was little or no infrastructure and the colony's trade networks, port facilities and financial institutions would need to be built from scratch. This was in contrast to the "treaty ports" in which the British and other Europeans enjoyed special privileges. In the short term, the latter seemed more valuable since these were already fully developed cities with centuries of trading experience and well-established indigenous merchant communities. The international settlements in ports like Shanghai, Tsingtao (Qingdao), Tientsin (Tianjin), and Ningpo (Ningbo), and, of course, Canton (Guangzhou) for many years eclipsed Hong Kong in their importance to commerce with the West. In the meantime, the Fragrant Harbor struggled to build itself from the ground up. Indeed Hong Kong's earliest years were difficult ones. At first, the British struggled to understand and accommodate the culture of their new subjects and consequently the relations between Chinese and European residents remained tense and standoffish when not openly hostile. Piracy and typhoons threatened the safety of the people and constantly jeopardized the economic survival of Hong Kong. Periodic epidemics, including the deadly bubonic plague, swept through the colony and carried away tens of thousands of terrified residents. Throughout its unsteady beginnings, there was no guarantee that Hong Kong would survive, let alone prosper.

Yet in the long term, the great advantage of Hong Kong for the British was that they could administer the colony entirely on their own without interference from China or other foreign commercial rivals. At the root of Hong Kong's success were a competent and professional civil service and legal system. As the years passed, the British in Hong Kong administered (rather than ruled) a chaotic and prosperous mix of British, Chinese, and Indian entrepreneurs. The British, at first, more often Scotsmen than Englishmen, governed with the usual mix of social insularity, military heavy-handedness, and attitudes of racial and cultural superiority. Yet they also eradicated piracy in the region, initiated an ambitious series of public works projects, and established a legal regime based on English common law in which contracts were enforceable. All of this was good for business and Hong Kong became a regional commercial center to rival the great treaty ports. Hong Kong thrived and its freedom (economic, if not political) attracted thousands of Chinese immigrants as well as the Sikhs, Gurkhas, and Irishmen who guarded the territory and the Parsis and Iraqi Jews who helped found its financial system. In these years, trading companies like Jardine & Matheson, of bitter memory to China in the Opium Wars—thrived and expanded. So did the Hongkong and Shanghai Banking Corporation that was founded in 1865 by Scottish businessmen to service the growing trade and is today the international financial titan HSBC.

The Hong Kong legal system is perhaps the greatest colonial legacy and the secret of the territory's success. The imposition of laws that upheld contractual and property rights upon a largely law-abiding and entrepreneurial population allowed business and trade to move confidently forward in the knowledge that the government would protect the honest merchant and make right any violations of the law. This spirit is very much alive today in the Hong Kong Special Administrative Region. The Hong Kong judicial system has a well-deserved reputation for integrity and professionalism, and more significantly, cases in those courts cannot be appealed to the authorities in Beijing. This "hands-off" approach by China gives foreign businesses the confidence to establish themselves legally in Hong Kong even if they wish to invest in the Mainland and build factories there. Should a dispute arise, these foreigners know that their case will be placed on the docket in Hong Kong and not be subjected to the PRC legal system whose reputation for corruption and communist party influence would otherwise deter them from taking such a risk.

The visitor to Hong Kong may never notice the lasting impact of its colonial legal system; though this underscores nearly every aspect of daily life, it remains largely invisible. If one strolls through Central along the north shore of Hong Kong Island and passes by the distinctive Legislative Council building, directly across from the HSBC and Bank of China buildings on Des Voeux Road, one should

8. *The Colonial Past in Hong Kong's Present*

look upward. At the top of the building, which served as the supreme court of Hong Kong in colonial days, the viewer will see a statue of the Greek goddess Themis. She stands blindfolded in her flowing robes, grasping a sword in her left hand and the scales of justice in her right. There is no more meaningful symbol of Hong Kong's success both past and present than this.

The Legislative Council Building (formerly the Supreme Court), completed 1910, Central, Hong Kong Island

A Gateway between East and West

The city is a cultural crossroads, a gateway between East and West, a bridge between the exotic and static Orient on one side and occidental progress and expansion on the other. These essentializing clichés were for centuries applied by Europeans to İstanbul, yet since the mid-nineteenth century the ancient city on the Bosporus has shared this distinction with Hong Kong. Such stereotypical descriptions, however, do an immense disservice to the visitor in the territory and to its

Reading Hong Kong, Reading Ourselves

residents since they invariably gloss over the deeper complexities and richness of Hong Kong society. Nevertheless, these characterizations often feature prominently in the imagination of many westerners and so they must be reckoned with.

At the outset, one must not overstate the western influence in Hong Kong. From 1898 onward, the British controlled Hong Kong Island, Kowloon, and the New Territories that included Lantau Island and hundreds of smaller outlying islands. Yet the colonial establishment in the territory was confined largely to Hong Kong Island and the southern end of the Kowloon Peninsula. In the outer regions, one would have hardly ever seen a European face, except perhaps for the soldiers guarding the border with the Mainland or the occasional civilian out for a hike in the mountains. Although under the political control of the British Empire and beholden to its laws, most of the territory was composed of traditional Cantonese-speaking communities that experienced minimal cultural intrusion from their British rulers. Where the English language may have resonated in the halls of government, the court chambers, the colonial social clubs, the racetrack at Happy Valley, and the lecture halls of Hong Kong University it did not extend much further. In most of the markets and dockyards, along the streets and alleyways, and in the rural fishing villages and farms, Cantonese remained the lingua franca of Hong Kong. Chinese culture and language predominated, with the occasional sprinkling of English, Hindi, Punjabi, and Arabic. Chinese festivals set the rhythm of the calendar and most buildings and streets, even in the European sections, were laid out with due regard to *feng shui.*

To their credit, the British had the good sense not to try to fix something that wasn't broken. The mystery of Hong Kong's enduring prosperity continues to be debated, but as far back as the nineteenth century the British adopted a colonial policy of economic non-interference—perhaps a more successful version of the "benign neglect" shown toward the American colonies in the eighteenth century. The Chinese in Hong Kong may have chafed at their racial exclusion from high office but, as mentioned earlier, they did enjoy the protection of a relatively honest and impartial legal system. By the late twentieth century, the racial prohibitions were gone and Chinese civil servants served at the highest levels of the Hong Kong government. On average, its residents enjoyed a higher standard of living and fewer economic regulations than people in Britain, so by then Hong Kong could no longer be considered a colony in any real sense. More importantly, throughout its history Hong Kong's British keepers had mercifully shielded the territory from the worst horrors of modern China's tumultuous and tragic history: among these the Taiping Rebellion, the warlordism of the 1920s and 30s, the civil war between the Kuomintang and the communists, the famines of the Great Leap Forward, and the insanity of the Cultural Revolution. The exception, of course, was Japanese occupation during the Second World War. Toward the end of the twentieth century the situation in China was improving—somewhat. Yet while the Beijing leadership under the "Four Modernizations" seemed to be shedding its atavistic hatred for capitalism, it showed no sign of tempering its centralizing and authoritarian style of government anytime soon. As the certainty and stability of British non-interference, such as it was, approached its final hour, nobody knew what would replace it.

War, Occupation, and Regeneration

British colonial rule in Hong Kong was interrupted during the

Second World War when the Japanese army invaded the territory and held it for three and a half years. The Battle of Hong Kong in December 1941 and the occupation that followed were the darkest days in Hong Kong's history and they changed the nature of colonial rule irreversibly. Today, however, amid the prosperity, energy, and self-confidence of Hong Kong, it is difficult to find any remnant of the dreadful experience of this war. The Hong Kong Museum of History and the Museum of Coastal Defence both do an admirable job educating their visitors about what happened there in World War II, but the public memorializing of that experience is virtually non-existent compared to what has been done in places like London, Dresden, and Hiroshima. There may be several reasons for this. The first is that the loss of Hong Kong was a bitter humiliation for the British Empire that was only exceeded in the East by the fall of Singapore a few months later. The second is that during the occupation, the territory's most energetic resistance came from Chinese communists. The third and most significant reason may have to do with the fact that British colonization in Hong Kong, as elsewhere in Asia, rested on the rarely questioned presumption of the cultural and racial superiority of westerners over Asians. This view was completely demolished during the war and it could never again return in the minds either of the colonizers or the colonized.

The fall of Hong Kong began when Japan attacked the territory on December 8, 1941 (this was actually the same time as the attack on Pearl Harbor since Hawaii and China are on opposites sides of the international dateline). Japanese land forces smashed their way across the border into the New Territories and within days had moved south and taken Kowloon. Battalions of the Royal Scots and Middlesex regiments manned their concrete fortifications and gun emplacements in the mountain ridge around Shing Mun separating Kowloon from the New Territories. This maze of concrete tunnels and bunkers, nicknamed "Gin Drinker's Lane," had been built earlier to stop any invaders from the north. The ruins of this redoubt are still there and nowadays the more intrepid hikers on the McLehose Trail can crawl through them. Some of the passageways bear such names as "Regent Street," "Shaftesbury Avenue" and "Charing Cross Road." Perhaps these were meant to cheer up homesick soldiers or confuse Japanese attackers. In any event, the defenses proved no match for the enemy and were overrun in a matter of days.

The remains of "Gin Drinker's Lane" off the McLehose Trail in Shing Mun, New Territories

The attack was not unexpected. British army units on Hong Kong Island had earlier been reinforced by Indian battalions from Punjab and Rajasthan and by Canadians from Winnipeg, Québec and the Maritime Provinces. These men were untested in combat and hastily dispatched in a rearguard action as thousands of civilians were evacuated to Singapore and Australia in the final months of 1941. After the attack began they managed to hold out for two weeks, but the constant air assaults, the prospect of high civilian casualties, and the knowledge that they were outnumbered three to one and would not be relieved anytime soon forced them finally to surrender. The capitulation took place on Christmas Day 1941, just a few months shy of the one-hundredth anniversary of British rule over Hong Kong. Britain's great trading center and flagship colony in East Asia was now lost to the enemy. To add further insult, the governor of the colony, Sir Mark Young, was forced to sign the surrender document in the lobby of the posh Peninsula Hotel in Tsim Sha Tsui—a symbol for the British and Chinese of Hong Kong alike of the former's prestige, power, and racial exclusivity.

The three and a half years that followed were the harshest in the history of Hong Kong. British soldiers and civilians were rounded up and put into prison camps in which many perished from disease and malnutrition. Chinese residents of the territory lived in fear of the mercurial cruelty of their new colonial masters. Japanese soldiers arbitrarily killed civilians in the street for no apparent reason other than to ensure that the population lived in a state of constant terror. Women and girls of all ages were randomly raped for the same purpose as well as to allow Japanese commanders a way to indulge the baser instincts of their battle-hardened troops and to keep their morale up. Those civilians who escaped such direct brutality were forced to submit to food rationing that often reduced them to near-starvation. They were also made to exchange their Hong Kong dollars for Japanese occupation currency whose unstable value caused sudden hyperinflation crises. The forced currency exchanges helped pay for the occupation but resulted in the widespread loss of personal savings for rich and poor alike. Fuel and medicine shortages meant that flu outbreaks and winter dampness carried away even more of the weakest and hungriest people, mostly children and the elderly. Japanese-run schools and newspapers attempted to indoctrinate residents with a sense of loyalty and respect for the new rulers of East Asia, meanwhile thousands of unemployed Hong Kong civilians were deported to distant parts of China to work as forced laborers throughout the Japanese-occupied areas.

Resistance throughout the occupation was minimal but small bands of partisans did manage to hide out in the wooded hills of the New Territories and Lantau Island where they waged sporadic attacks on Japanese military and government facilities. Most of these fighters were communists who operated independently of any support from the British, Americans, or nationalist Chinese. Japanese reprisals for partisan activities were directed against the civilian population but the attacks did not stop, nor did they have any significant effect on Japanese control over Hong Kong. The combined effect of the massacres, starvation, illness, and deportation over three and a half years resulted in a loss of more than half the population. Even the growing prospect of a Japanese defeat as the war progressed did not guarantee a return to the status quo ante for Hong Kong. The nationalist Chinese leader Chiang Kai-shek made no secret of his desire to see Hong Kong returned to China immediately after the war and President Roosevelt seemed willing to concede this to America's ally. When the Japanese surrendered in August 1945 the British fleet in the Pacific made a beeline to Hong Kong at full speed in order to prevent the Americans from arriving there first. British soldiers liberated their fellow countrymen and women, as well as what was left of the Chinese population. The Japanese occupation governor of the territory, General Takashi Sakai, was brought before the Allied war tribunal and executed in 1946. In the end, the British restored their rule over Hong Kong, but their image would never be the same.

Understanding the experience of the Second World War in Hong Kong does help to put a lot of things in perspective. The resilience of human beings is indeed extraordinary. In Hong Kong the postwar recovery was remarkably swift. The apparatus of British administration was reestablished within a few weeks of the Japanese surrender and economic prosperity returned so quickly that within three months all rationing and price controls were ended. Much of the prewar colonial racial segregation ended as well. The spectacle of British humiliation at the hands of an Asian power ensured that any assumptions of western racial superiority were gone forever. Whites-only beaches in Hong Kong were abolished and Chinese people were allowed to buy property anywhere in the territory, even in the highly coveted and formerly restricted enclave of Victoria Peak.

Today there is virtually no evidence in Hong Kong of the Second World War. Maybe time does indeed heal all wounds—including physical as well as psychological ones. And maybe this can happen more quickly in a place like Hong Kong, with its relatively short history and its orientation toward the future rather than the past. It is a truism of Hong Kong that the old is constantly being torn down to make room for the new, and thus it may be easy to forget what happened during the war. A noteworthy exception to this is the Hong Kong Museum of Coastal Defence set inside the remains of the fort at Lei Yue Mun built in 1887 by the British at Shau Kei Wan.

8. The Colonial Past in Hong Kong's Present

Seven-inch gun of the Central Battery at the Lei Yue Mun Fort (presently the Museum of Coastal Defence) Shau Kei Wan, Hong Kong Island

For decades this massive redoubt on Hong Kong Island guarded the eastern entrance to Victoria Harbor and today its pillboxes, bunkers, and heavy artillery are preserved for visitors to wander around. Its exhibits preserve well the details of this dark episode in the colonial history of Hong Kong for those with the determination to search them out.

Walking among the Living and the Dead

The visitor to Hong Kong may notice a large stone structure in the garden along Chater Street in Central, just across from the

Reading Hong Kong, Reading Ourselves

Legislative Council facing north. From the distance it seems neither distinctly Chinese nor European, but at close view it appears to be a sarcophagus set atop a tall stone pedestal. In fact, it is the Hong Kong Cenotaph, a memorial dedicated in 1923 to residents who died in the First World War. It is an almost exact replica of the Cenotaph at Whitehall in London designed by the great imperial architect Edwin Lutyens and unveiled three years earlier. The memorial now commemorates the dead of both world wars, the majority of the latter group having died in Hong Kong itself. The inscription in Cantonese and English reads simply "The Glorious Dead"—an august but anonymous epitaph.

The Cenotaph (dedicated 1923), memorial to the dead of the two world wars, Central, Hong Kong Island

If one wishes to make a more personal acquaintance with some of these dead, one must go to the MTR station at Central and take the Island Line to the last stop at Chai Wan. The station there lets out, not surprisingly, directly into a shopping mall. One exits from the mall and heads a few blocks south to the Lin Shing Road and begins the slow climb up the hill. After half a mile, a hairpin turn to the right leads to Cape Collinson

8. The Colonial Past in Hong Kong's Present

Sai Wan War Cemetery, Chai Wan, Hong Kong Island

Road and up past one of the largest cemeteries in the territory. The graves are packed into steep concrete terraces that hug the contours of the hill. From a distance the whole structure gives the appearance of an open mine, but one into which the most precious treasures are deposited rather than extracted. Near the top of the road, in a tranquil and isolated park, is the Sai Wan War Cemetery.

It is here that one enters the most haunting and humbling remnant of Hong Kong's colonial encounter—and its most human. Sai Wan contains the remains of hundreds of soldiers who died in the defense of Hong Kong in 1941 and in the terrible occupation that followed. The white headstones stand alongside each other in rows along a gentle downward slope. Each tells its own story but all of them together are a roll call of the British Empire and its intimate and deeply rooted place in the grand narrative of Hong Kong. The first graves are of British men and women: infantrymen, sailors, nurses and engineers. A few rows further down are the Indians, mostly Punjabi Sikhs and Muslims. Another section contains headstones that bear the royal seal of the Netherlands and mark the resting places of the Dutch servicemen interned in Hong Kong after the fall of the Dutch East Indies (present-day Indonesia). Finally one walks among the Canadians, their headstones marked with the iconic maple leaf of their home on the other side of the Pacific. Above them all stands a large white cross, a somewhat presumptuous and unrepresentative symbol since Sai Wan's residents are indeed a much more ecumenical assembly. The individual headstones bear Christian crosses, Stars of David, and calligraphy verses in Arabic from the Koran and in Hindi for those whose cremated remains are buried there. Underneath the names of each of the dead are inscriptions chosen by the bereaved family. "Far away from England, but heaven is his home, ever in our thoughts—Wife and family." "Peacefully sleeping, free from pain, in God's own time we shall meet again." "Sadly missed by wife and family, brothers and sisters, Thy will be done." Most moving of all are those stones marking the graves of the unknown, the dead that could not be positively identified. They bear such simple epitaphs as "a soldier of the Indian Army is honoured here" or "a sailor of the 1939–1945 War." At the bottom of each is written, "Known unto God." Returning to the entrance one finds a large marble slab listing the names of 72 soldiers of the Hong Kong forces buried in China and dozens more for whom no remains were ever recovered. Before leaving Sai Wan one can glance back at the marble cenotaph in front of the grave markers on which is inscribed Kipling's epitaph, "Their Name Liveth Forever More."

Sai Wan is a sad and beautiful place, and a lonely one. Set into the side of a hill overlooking the high-rise towers of Chai Wan, it gets few visitors. Except for groundskeepers' trucks and the occasional beige minibus that plies its route up and down the hill, there is little traffic on the access road. Beyond the peaceful buzzing of insects and the fragrant smell of flowers and freshly cut grass is the distant but ever-present sound of traffic and construction. It is a peaceful retreat but also a site that wears heavily the human cost of Hong Kong's colonial history and the burdens of empire. It may remind the visitor of "The Soldier," Rupert Brooke's famous poem from the First World War: "If I should die, think only this of me: that there's some corner of a foreign field that is for ever England." Sai Wan is such a field but for the larger empire: one that links an isolated corner of Hong Kong intimately in sorrow and sacrifice to the working-class neighborhoods of Glasgow and London, the villages of Punjab, the plains of Manitoba, and the fishing communities of New Brunswick.

Borrowed Time in a Borrowed Place

Britain acquired its 99-year lease for the New Territories in 1898 at the height of its empire, the greatest the world had ever known. Only a year earlier, Queen Victoria had celebrated her Diamond Jubilee commemorating sixty years on the throne. Britain's economic and military power may have been in relative decline but it was still unmatched by any of its rivals. Hong Kong was then merely one of dozens of British colonies across the globe in an empire that directly or indirectly encompassed a fifth of the dry surface of the earth and a quarter of its people. Less than a century later, Britain had declined dramatically in power and had lost its empire. Within two decades after the Second World War, the "wind of change," as Prime Minister Harold Macmillan put it, had proved too much for the old European empires as the demand among colonized peoples across the world for independence could no longer be forestalled.

Hong Kong was the last important British possession to leave the former empire, yet even at the beginning its residents must have known that they could never be independent. From the signing of the lease for the New Territories onward, Britain held most of Hong Kong as the tenant of a patient landlord rather than as an imperial conqueror in the truest sense. For those who called it home, their existence as separate from the rest of China proceeded on borrowed time. When the lease ran out in 1997 the territory merely traded a distant ruler for a not-so-distant one. Yet today Hong Kong enjoys remarkable autonomy from China, much as it did from Britain. It has its own currency, a remarkably free press and freedom of assembly, a separate police force and civil service, and, above all, an independent judiciary. Its economic freedoms are as broad as they were in the past, and its political freedoms are likewise as proscribed. Clearly neither of the two powers to hold Hong Kong, whether in the past or present, has shown much appetite for interference in a society that functions so well and has proved so enigmatic yet so useful to whoever possesses it.

8. *The Colonial Past in Hong Kong's Present*

Further Reading

Booth, Martin. Gweilo: *Memories of a Hong Kong Childhood*. London: Bantam Books, 2005.

Buckley, Roger. *Hong Kong: The Road to 1997*. Cambridge: Cambridge University Press, 1997.

Carroll, John. *A Concise History of Hong Kong*. Lanham, MD: Rowman & Littlefield, 2007.

Keay, John. *Empire's End: A History of the Far East from High Colonialism to Hong Kong*. New York: Scribner, 1997.

Lau, C. K. *Hong Kong's Colonial Legacy: A Hong Kong Chinese's View of the British Heritage*. Hong Kong: The Chinese University Press, 1997.

Lee, Leo Ou-fan. *City Between Worlds: My Hong Kong*. Cambridge MA: Belknap Press, 2010

Morris, Jan. *Hong Kong*. New York, Vintage, 2011.

Snow, Philip. *The Fall of Hong Kong: Britain, China and the Japanese Occupation*. New Haven: Yale University Press, 2004.

Whaley-Cohen, Joanna., ed. *Picturing Hong Kong: Photography, 1855–1910.* New York: George Braziller, 1997.

Chapter 9
Hamlet in Hong Kong

Joseph CHANEY

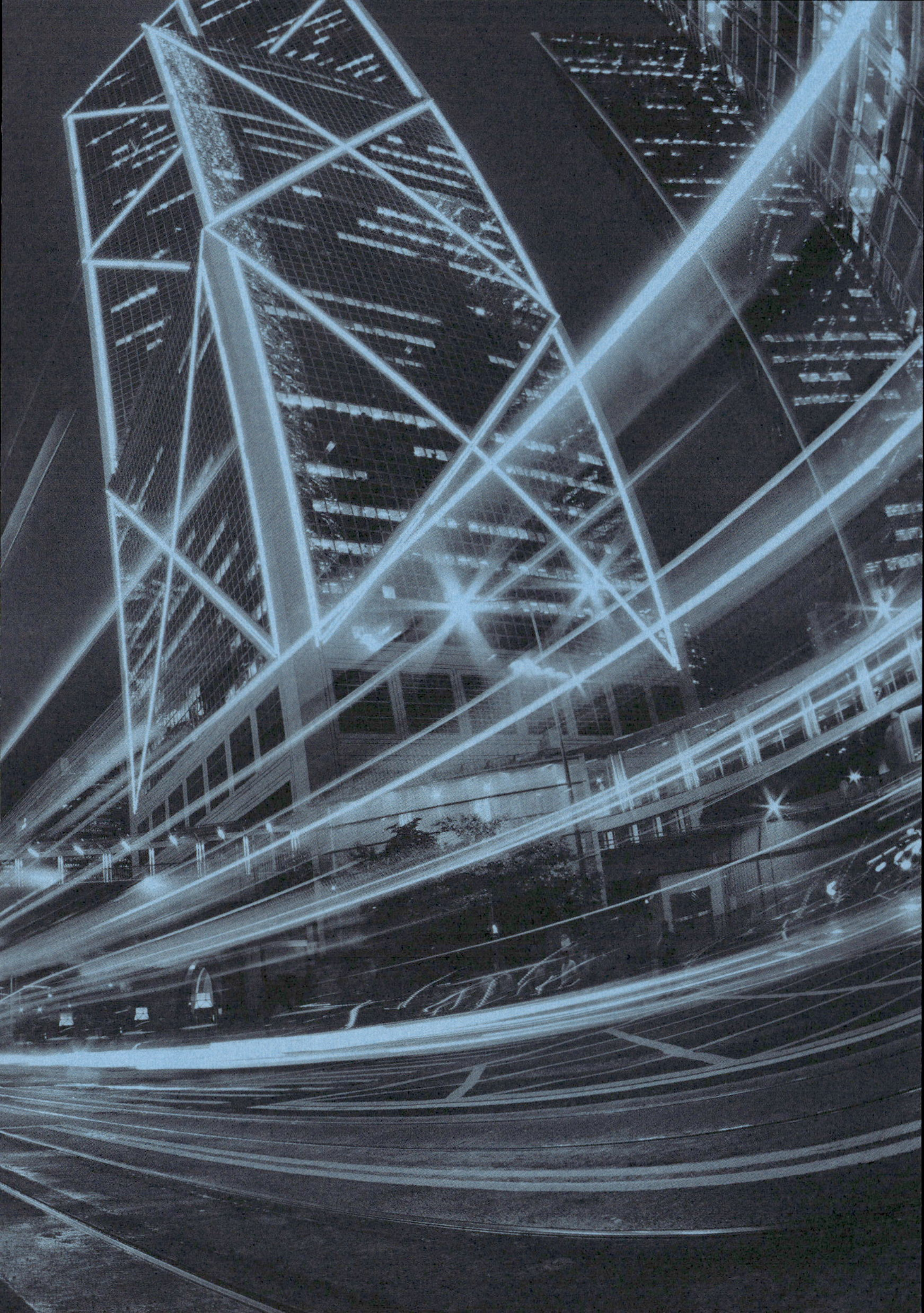

送畀我嘅好朋友茱莉 / *Dedicated to my good friend Julie*

The Island

The specter of Hamlet haunts Hong Kong, lingering on the ramparts of Shaw College Student Hostel 2, disappearing hurriedly down an alley in Mong Kok, or hiking alone under the pines of Tai Po Kau on a Sunday afternoon, lost in thought. Like Shakespeare's young Hamlet, the Hamlet of Hong Kong doesn't quite know what he's about, but he knows that the time is out of joint, that there is something rotten in the state of Hong Kong, and that his family is no longer the refuge it once was.

Ophelia is here too, also on her own, exiting the MTR station at Central, climbing into the smog-filtered midday sunshine and being lost, even losing herself, amid the traffic of Queen's Road. She is certainly no more suicidal than Hamlet, and she is equally Hamlet-like in her playfulness of mind, a quality that leads her toward despair almost as often as it raises her spirits to an astonishing height. Like the Hamlet of Hong Kong, she has two names, one Chinese (even Cantonese, if one may say so) and the other English. Mandarin is always in the air, as well, running its constant linguistic interference. In fact, Ophelia is always speaking three languages at once. On most important questions, she is of at least two minds.

She is of two minds about Hamlet, of whom she is now thinking. The day before, a Saturday, they met for dim sum. What she remembers is that they argued. She never argues with other friends, only with Hamlet, who insists on being called Hau and on calling her Miss Shum, even though they were introduced as Hamlet and

Ophelia. All of her school friends call her Ophelia, and most of her friends at church know her as Ophie. Among family, she is On-lai. Why call her Miss Shum?

She and Hamlet almost always converse in Cantonese. She remembers that he teased her about her clothing—the American and European brands. Her vanity. Through the glass front of the restaurant, they had a perfectly framed view of a billboard-sized ad showing a blonde, angular Westerner in a skirt and heels who seemed to be either dancing or tumbling down a city sidewalk.

"That's you, isn't it?" he asked.

"Yes, I want to be an American!" she said. But what she was really thinking, what she later wished she had said, was, "You are one hundred times more American than I!"

Hamlet was never angry, never exactly hurtful. He smiled. He criticized in a, somehow, loving way.

"I disappoint you, Hau."

"I'm completely happy with you, Miss Shum. Completely happy. You are in fact like dim sum."

"How?"

"Your menu is inexhaustible. I'll never be done thinking about you."

"But when you think about me, you think it would be good if I were different than I am. You think I'm unserious."

"We're all hopelessly unserious, aren't we? And as long as we have dim sum, why should we be serious?"

Hong Kong S.A.R.

Hong Kong is an international crossroads, but also, oddly, an isolated community. An immense, teeming village. A haven of high rise apartments, glossy shopping malls, and corporate towers. As Hong Kong people acquainted with the rest of Asia know, merely to live here is the result of an improbably lucky stroke of fortune. Possessors of Hong Kong ID cards and MTR Octopus cards, they are fortunate sons and daughters of the dragon.

Hamlet and Ophelia are students—Hamlet at the Chinese University of Hong Kong (CUHK), and Ophelia at the University of Hong Kong (HKU), each having scored high enough on the Certificate of Education examination to qualify for university—three years of freedom. University life is an extension of childhood, but without the heavy oversight of parents. It is an easy slide if you know how to pass exams, and everybody does. Flunking out of college would mark a person as implausibly creative. It is not known to happen.

Nan Lian Garden

Strolling in the midday heat, Ophelia passes by the gift shop in Nan Lian Garden and spies Hamlet descending from the entrance bridge to Chi Lin Nunnery. It seems they had the same notion of arriving early, but chose different parts of the complex to wander through. The Tang architecture of the Buddhist nunnery is too formal, too severe for Ophelia's taste. On the garden side, the trees and flowering shrubs grow more profusely, and the ponds make for a variety of

The facade of Nan Lian Garden

refreshing prospects. The garden is one of those hidden delights that one visits rarely but is always happy to know about.

On her walk, which began with a short passage through shops at the exit of Diamond Hill MTR Station, she has actually struggled to stay focused on her surroundings. The previous evening she made the mistake of telling her mother of her lunch date with Hamlet. Her walk has included involuntary flashbacks to their conversation. At one point, although she thought she had been careful to represent the whole business as casually as possible, her mother leaned in and looked at her hard and said, "Hau could never marry you."

Ophelia was stunned.

"Mama, there hasn't been any talk of marriage! Why are you saying this?"

"I know you. I know how you think, On-lai," she said, reaching out with her finger and tapping her daughter lightly on the temple. "But I want you to know that his father will certainly want him to have a rich bride. We aren't rich. Are you covered in gold?"

These were her words. And in such a small apartment, how can she avoid her mother?

"You are an ordinary, unremarkable girl. He can't possibly love you. Study! Study! That is your way to happiness. Don't count on Hau to rescue you!"

* * * * * * * * * * * *

Ophelia sees that Hamlet is smiling broadly as he approaches. "I've just been walking around in the Tang Dynasty," he says, by way of greeting.

"I've been gardening. When did you get here?"

"Maybe half an hour ago. I visited the Sakyamuni Buddha. The Tang is when all of that started, you know. Civilized Chinese religion. We weren't fully Chinese until the Tang."

"Oh?" She is relieved to hear him speak lightly. The brightness of his face throws her mother into the shadows.

Hamlet steps back to look at her. She is dressed all in red. "You look like Princess Pingyang."

"Did she wear red Converses?"

"She might have. Like you, she kicked ass." He says this in English, with an American accent, and it makes Ophelia laugh.

"All that history is bad for you, you know? It's a weight on your back."

"A weight, yes. And the heavy lesson of history is, 'You must wait'."

They are walking now toward the restaurant, which stands beside a water wheel at the eastern end of the garden. Ophelia walks with her head bowed, smiling. An older woman seeing them pass would say she was in love.

* * * * * * * * * * * * *

At the restaurant they are able—without waiting—to get a small table by the picture window. Water flowing over the roof from the water wheel cascades down this broad surface of glass. The garden is still visible through the changing stream, but distorted beautifully.

Their order arrives in many small bowls. A variety of spiced vegetables and textured tofu. Rice. Tea.

"The waterfall is to remind you," says Hamlet.

"Of what?"

"Simply to remember. That's the purpose of falling water."

"I can't tell when you're being serious, Hau. I'd rather think of you as a philosopher than as a comedian."

"I became both at the same time, you know. That's always the way it goes. I'll tell you how. This was before my time at Princeton. My second semester at CUHK, I took a general education course on 'the great ideas'. A simple course, taught in Cantonese, just short readings and discussion; but it was just about the only course that ever changed me."

Ophelia leaned forward on her elbow. "Changed you? I want to hear about this!"

"You want to know how to change me. It's too late. Dr. Chiu got to me first. One day we were discussing *The Social Contract* by Rousseau."

"What's that?"

"Political theory—but it doesn't matter. I mean, the book itself is not the point. The teacher asked whether we understood the term 'Romanticism'. We didn't, so she explained this movement of thought and art that swept Europe in the early 19th century. Then she asked, 'So, what do you think about Romanticism?' My classmate raised his hand and answered, and all of us were in awe, because he answered so clearly and perfectly, recalling the teacher's every word, and talking about Romanticism as if he had known it his whole life. Even the teacher said, 'That was amazing, Terence!' Then she smiled and asked, 'But do you know what you did? You repeated (really quite perfectly!) everything I just said. You said it better than I did! But I am sorry to tell you that everything you said was wrong'. Well, we were all shocked. But she was still smiling. 'Don't blush', she said to Terence. 'Everything you said was correct, if only according to me! But this seminar is not about correctness. Why does it matter what I think? If you leave this university only with my ideas in your head, what good are you? The world doesn't need another Dr. Chiu. I'm already here! Who are you? What do you believe? What is your opinion?'"

Here Hamlet pauses and peers into his tea cup. "She changed my life."

"I don't understand. Until that moment—what? Did you think you were Dr. Chiu?"

"Actually, mimicking the teacher would have been better than what I was doing. That's our so-called Confucian tradition. But me—maybe I wanted to please my teacher, but usually I saw no point in any of it. I have a strong memory, so school was easy. I'd like to think I could have done what Terence did! But there's no point."

"You mean you now realized school is pointless?"

"I realized it was wrong to let anyone do my thinking for me."

"I'm surprised by your claim."

"Why?"

"You've always been a contrarian. This wasn't anything new! For example, when have you not disagreed with me? It's your habit."

"This will be the first time I've ever disagreed with you. Maybe I was once a rebel, but now I'm not. A rebel reacts. He says 'no' to the old established ways. But I set aside all authority, and I ignore the rebel, too."

"So, then, what do you believe in?" Something has driven Ophelia toward this question, a need to understand whether they, in any sense, walk on the same ground.

The bill has arrived, and Hamlet pays it. "Let's take the air," he says in English, reflecting upon his feeling that certain conversations shouldn't be pursued while sitting by a water window in a Buddhist restaurant.

* * * * * * * * * * * * *

Once out in the open air of the garden, Hamlet begins, "I know, of course, that you consider yourself a Christian."

"Why put it that way? I am a Christian. You, too, I think. Your parents are Christians."

"Maybe you know more about that than I do. My parents, I think, are Chinese. I am Chinese. To call them Christians is to say that they're lost."

"Saved. They're saved by the resurrection. That's the only way to forgiveness and eternal life. What? What do you believe?"

Hamlet doesn't answer.

It angers Ophelia that Hamlet would force her into this hurtful debate through pure obstinacy. He clearly has no argument. He just wants me to defend myself, she thinks. But why? She is fearful of making a wrong step, but she realizes that what she means by "wrong step" is not what she ought to mean. "So, you don't believe in anything? The story of Christ is something to believe in. It shows us who God is and why we need Him, and how we can reestablish a relationship with Him and restore meaning to our lives."

"It's only a story."

"A true story."

"No story is true. And China has no god."

"The world has a God."

"The world."

"The God of Creation."

Clouds have drifted overhead, and a breeze is blowing. They arrive at the pond and stand leaning against the railing of the pavilion, facing the water together. It seems to Hamlet that all the details of the scene, the fountain, the buildings, the rocks and trees, are the furniture of his argument which he reviews as he speaks. "I see no evidence. Even if I could believe that the world was created in six days, I see no evidence that anyone actually lives with this God, in the spirit of this God's love. Christianity is a Western myth. It was imposed on us by the Europeans and Americans. We are the heathens, the ones who need their wisdom, their truth. If you come to me and tell me to change my life, to follow you, or else I will go to hell, I'm not going to enjoy your company. Of course, if you have all the wealth and all the power, and you tell me that the only way to get work, the only way to provide for my family, is to go to your church and believe in your god, then, okay, I may agree to go to your church. I'm hungry. My family is begging me to feed them. Okay, I believe! I believe!"

This speech seems to Ophelia personally insulting, dismissive of her experience of faith. You are talking politics, not faith, she wants to say; but what she says is, "How will you find forgiveness?"

"I don't mean this in a bad way, but my parents can't be forgiven. Not that way. I don't seek forgiveness of that kind. I don't want it. It may be infinitely difficult to be entirely good, but there is no easy way, no magic answer. We live with our evils. Our culture has its own resources, Miss Shum. We don't need to turn to the West in order to understand ourselves, to know what is right to do, and to practice forgiveness."

Miss Shum, again! Ophelia doesn't know how to respond. How can he be so wrong? How can he abandon his faith? Why must he speak so cruelly? She wants to continue the fight, but another impulse is working to defeat her resolve. She doesn't want to lose him. And she wonders whether this feeling, this softness towards Hamlet, is a sin. Should you love someone you believe is going to hell?

By evening she will regret two contradictory things: not having defended her faith more vigorously, and not having dropped the matter as soon as possible and asked Hamlet for his forgiveness. Because it will seem then, as she lies in bed, not able to sleep, that all of Hamlet's philosophical seriousness, like his cheerfulness, barely conceals a sadness that only she may have the power and the reason to discover.

* * * * * * * * * * * * *

Hamlet, for his part, on his MTR ride back to Sha Tin, wonders whether he made any sense at all of his actual thoughts. I'm a fool, he says to himself. What good does it do to argue with her? To provoke her? Even if everything I say is true—if everything I say is true, there is no point in arguing as if I were trying to win a case, as if some magistrate were listening and deciding! Am I arguing with her, or am I arguing with the Westerner in my head?

His ride across campus in the university bus to Shaw College isn't an especially happy one. Not only must he sit with his thoughts, but also he must witness two of his least favorite scenes at the Chinese University of Hong Kong: here and there, new graduates being photographed under the trees, each of them clutching a large stuffed bear or bunny and smiling under a mortar board; and a large troupe of undergraduates from the Business Faculty, dressed uniformly in black suits and ties or black skirts, loading onto the bus like so many store-bought dolls. Children! Babies! he hisses under his breath.

9. Hamlet in Hong Kong

June 4th memorial event held at Victoria Park every year

Victoria Park

It is June 4, a day of commemoration, and Hamlet paces the floor of his father's apartment high in a tower at Causeway Bay. He has raised all the blinds in order to take in the sweeping view of Victoria Harbor and Kowloon. Soon the crowds will gather for the vigil in honor of the victims of the Tiananmen massacre—the annual pro-democracy protest aimed at Beijing. He has invited his American friend Horatio to join him for the evening, to see Hong Kong at its most impressive.

His father is away on his first business trip since Hamlet's mother demanded a divorce. His mother is home with her mother in

Guangzhou. Hamlet finds it hard to speak to her now—strangely, because he knows—everyone knows—his father is at fault; he is the unfaithful one. But when he had dinner with his father, the evening before his departure to Shanghai, he was moved by him, by his fragility, his awkwardness. His shame. Surely that's what he saw in his father's face. His father was guilty already, but when his mother left, it was to shame him. It seemed to Hamlet that the shame itself had partially redeemed him. Hamlet found that he could talk to him without anger, this man who has for so long represented much of what Hamlet finds disturbing about his country—the thoughtless enjoyment of prosperity, the acceptance of control by Beijing, the casual honoring of all forms of colonialism.

They talked about Hamlet's friend Horatio, the young man from Princeton who would be his guest at the private vigil. Hamlet had spent a semester at Princeton as an exchange student, and this year his friend from America was at CUHK on exchange. The two were inseparable. But now the semester was over, and Horatio was planning to leave on a tour of Southeast Asia. June 4 would be a sort of going-away party for him. Hamlet's father could see—because for once he was paying attention—what he had only vaguely sensed for the past year, that Hamlet's short stay in New Jersey had changed him. He could sense a new desire for, he wasn't sure what. There was an intensity about his son. No longer was it a matter of what had seemed before to be nothing more than peevishness.

"I assume you want to go back to America."

"Yes," said Hamlet, "sometime, but not now. Not anytime soon. Hong Kong is my city. I want to make it my home."

"Then you are happy here, at home?" his father asked cautiously, because this would be news. His son seemed to hate the business world of Hong Kong, even though he had tried to show him over the years, in many ways, what a comfortable and rewarding life he could have if only he would decide to join the corporation.

"Not happy, determined. I'm determined to stay and make the best of it."

"Well, I'm very happy to hear that!" His father couldn't suppress his laughter, and Hamlet found himself laughing with him. Suddenly it seemed hilarious to both of them that he had no intention of running away forever to some foreign land.

* * * * * * * * * * * * *

Horatio arrives as the sun is setting over the harbor. "The penthouse! Your father has quite a view!" he says.

"Yes!" As much as he wants to diminish the power of beauty wherever he finds it, Hamlet has to admit that the view is captivating.

Soon people will begin to congregate in the park below. He has set out food and drinks, and the two of them are feeling spirited and voracious.

"It's illegal, though, this set-up," Hamlet says, waving his hand down the length of the room. "This is a middle-class neighborhood, but my father bought all four apartments on this floor and hired a firm to knock down the walls and redesign it this way. One big apartment, a wall of windows. He may have paid off the downstairs neighbors to keep them from talking."

"Hmm. Well, let's enjoy it. With a view like this, I can see why you don't want to mingle with the crowd down there. Here, we're above it all—the drama, the statue of the Goddess of Democracy."

"We could go down there and join them …."

"No, no. I like this!" He sits down on one of the stools by the windows.

"I've held a candle many times. I would be happy to do it again, to give you the experience. Let's go. It would be good for you." Suddenly it strikes him how selfish he has been in formulating this plan.

"No, really. I'm not budging, so give up."

"It would be good for you, and you might learn something. You know our motto."

"Our motto?"

"The motto of Shaw College, 修德講學, 'cultivate virtue, acquire knowledge'."

"Maybe I've heard it. In America, school mottos are often several single words in Latin: Light, Knowledge, Virtue, Truth. Veritas, you know. Princeton's is actually a phrase: 'Under God's power, she flourishes'. But it isn't like Shaw's; it doesn't tell you to do anything. Where's it from?"

"It's Confucius, more or less. Do you want to know the whole saying? It goes something like this: 'The Master said, It's because I don't always cultivate virtue, because I don't always question more deeply what I've learned, because I don't, when I hear what is the right thing to do, I don't always do it, and because when I have done something wrong I can't always correct myself—these failures make me worry constantly'."

"What? He says he can't do these things, and they call him the Master? So the point is to worry. Okay, I can see that."

"Our mission, as students at Shaw College, is to do what the Master himself couldn't do, and to do it without worrying! Are you prepared?"

"No, but I'm no longer a student of Shaw College. I do find it interesting that Confucius was a worrier. I'm also a worrier."

"That's a point the scholars try to exhaust with their commentary. Worry, they say, is different from concern. The Master is never concerned, never nervous or disturbed. But he worries, he worries constantly—"

"I would reverse that. 'Concern' is lighter than 'worry'. Worry is all about nervousness."

"This worry isn't light, but there is no nervousness in it. The Master isn't worrying just because he's the worrying type. He's paying attention."

"He stays focused on his shortcomings?"

"Yes, he stays focused. He doesn't stop thinking about them. It would be wrong not to worry about his shortcomings."

"Because a master has to be perfect."

"I wouldn't say that. No, not at all. But listen to what he says. He says, 'I should question more deeply what I've learned'. So, it isn't simply, 'acquire knowledge'."

"Our motto is stupid."

"There's no real thinking behind it. It shows the easy way, which is really not a way at all. To the administrators, who don't read Confucius anyway, the Master is an authority, any old authority. Like them, he's just someone who knows things. A schoolmaster. Naturally, he speaks in mottos. 'Make a difference'. 'Never give up'. 'Say yes to happiness'. 'Cultivate virtue'. But Confucius is not a cheerleader. In fact, he never stops asking questions. By the way, you are forever a student of Shaw College."

"Are we expected to be virtuous, at Shaw College? I hope not."

"Yes, we are! But virtue isn't following rules. I don't actually know what Shaw College has in mind. Virtue also implies courage. Maybe, partly, the courage to be good. The courage to lead others toward what is good."

"And what's good? You'd think I would know."

"What's good, Ratio, is to do as the Master does, to think about how we fail to be virtuous, and to worry about it." Hamlet points down. "There. Watch."

The horizon has darkened. People are still flowing in through the gates and walkways of Victoria Park, but many have already gathered on the grounds. On the courts and playing fields, they sit close together, cross-legged, a mosaic of bright colors under the electric field lights, but Hamlet knows that many have already lit their candles, passing the fire from wick to wick, from hand to hand, cupping it in the white paper candle holders. He proceeds to turn off the lights throughout the apartment before rejoining Horatio at the window.

"Almost," whispers Hamlet, "almost. Now, now."

He and Horatio look down for a moment in silence. Then the field lights go black, leaving behind a carpet of soft light, a spreading expanse of shimmering ground. Before long, the entire park is brimming with light. It seems to radiate from this point or that, to flow in streams and waves—a trick of the eye. Hamlet knows that they're all seated now. He describes the proceedings to Horatio. From memory, he can hear the words over the amplifier, the measured speeches, the naming of the student protesters, the invocation of their dreams and of their blood. He can see the listeners wiping tears from their cheeks. Some will appear to be praying. This is the part he has chosen to miss. The incense of bodies pressed together in the humid evening. The oneness, the melting of the candles of their bodies, the melting and the joining of flesh as a cathedral of darkness lifts its arches above them. In his tower, Hamlet stands atop a buttress of that imaginary structure. He can't really escape, because from his ethereal perch he sees what was always true about this memorial event: the park below, that immense square, is Tiananmen. In small flames, the spirits of the massacred impose themselves on the space, claiming it as their own. And not only that. The district of light amid the darkness below, that community of light in a dark land, is Hong Kong itself. Tiananmen is Hong Kong. Hong Kong is Tiananmen. Each person there, each inhabitant of Hong Kong, glows with a faint light.

And one of those lights, he knows, so small and purposeful, is Miss Shum. He sees her stoic, sad face. Her expression tonight may be unusual, but it's the same face he sees everywhere. Why is it that he thinks about her constantly? Not thinks, but worries. All day long, and half the night, he is aware of her presence and influence. And it is wrong of him. This seems beyond doubt now. It is not virtuous. It is not the way.

He turns to his friend. "Something is wrong with us, we Hong Kong people, Ratio."

"I think it's beautiful."

"It is. But for us, there is a day for everything, you know. This is the day to be political. Tomorrow we'll be done with it. People marvel that in Hong Kong we express ourselves so freely. But there are limits, and we know them after all these years. We've learned what it means to obey the authorities, to obey always just enough —to turn the other cheek. We don't know what it means to take responsibility for Hong Kong. That's the thought we can't entertain. Or we only entertain it and never embrace it. That's the thought I've been trying to hold in my mind."

"Hong Kong is a great place, Hamlet."

"It isn't great."

Chapter 10

Are You in the Safe Zone? Cultural Sensitization and Religion for a Teaching Traveler

Ivette VARGAS-O'BRYAN

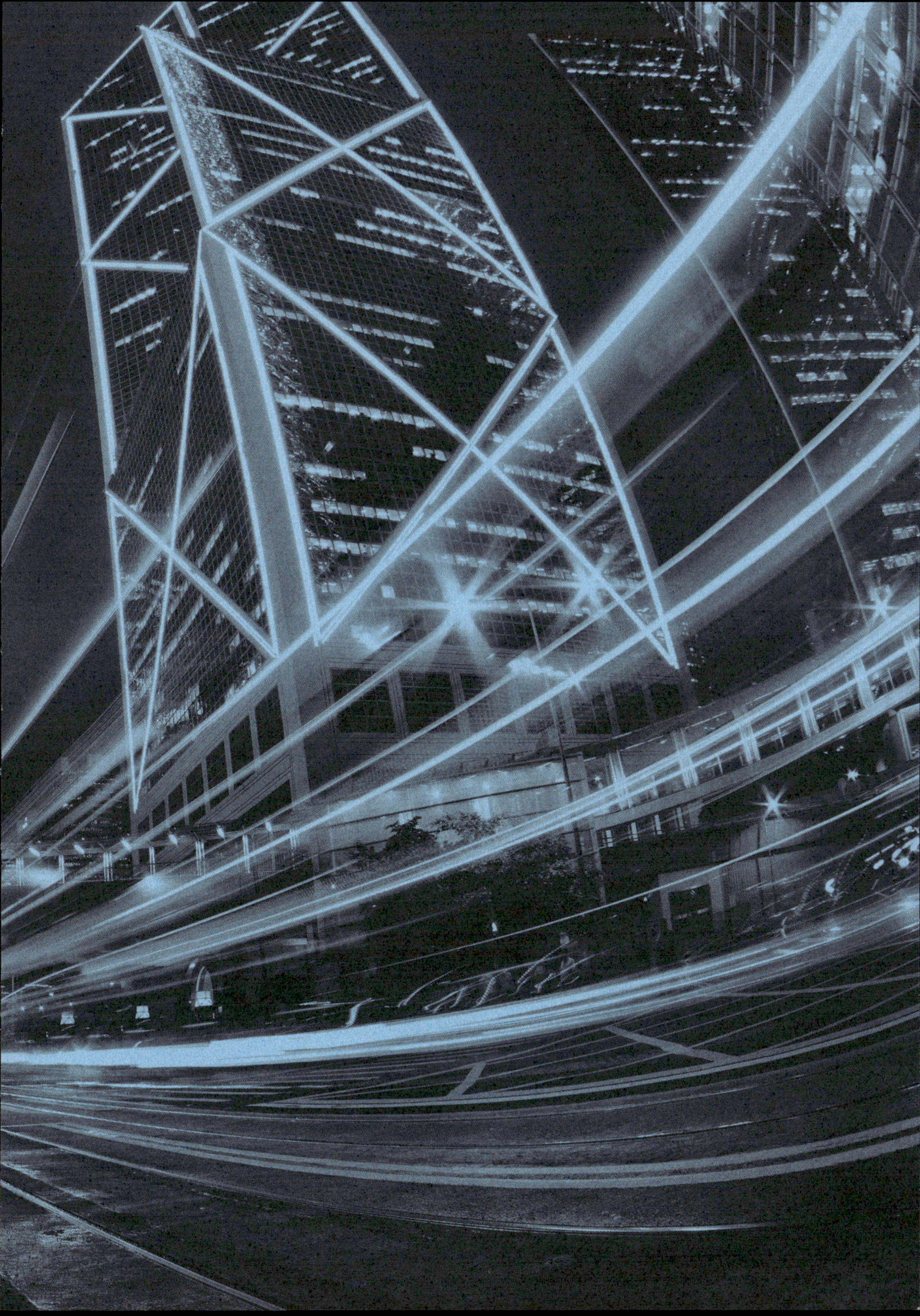

A landscape is a series of named locales, a set of relational places linked by paths, movements, and narratives. It is a cultural code for living ...[1]

Christopher Tilley, *A Phenomenology of Landscape.*

Traveling with Cultural Sensitization and Religion

Whether you are teaching English abroad for the first time, conducting an internship or immersing yourself in a culture through traveling or combining activities, you cannot take for granted how relevant cultural sensitivity is for communication and establishing relationships especially in terms of how a culture deals with the issue of religion. It does not matter how in tune you are with the latest data, how many religious groups you have belonged to, or how sensitive you think you are, encounters with religion and religious views in a different cultural context, especially if they are closely linked with the country's political policies, do challenge your sense of belonging. You become self-reflective about your own cultural values as you learn about others'. After traveling to over 15 countries, I've gotten a feel for these things. Even so, as an American professor in a Chinese context, my appreciation for religious values were challenged and turned topsy-turvy, making me walk a tight rope balancing what was appropriate for different audiences. Religion marks a liminal

---

1. Christopher Tilley, *A Phenomenology of Landscape* (Oxford, UK: Berg Publishers, 1994), 34.

space in China where the distinction between what is appropriate behavior, teachable, or legal is blurred, and where locals often appear as what anthropologist Victor Turner, in his *Dramas, Fields, and Metaphors*, called the "marginals" without "cultural assurance of a final stable resolution of their ambiguity."[2] The "marginal" search for meaning required that I search for better means of communication, and attempt to be sensitive to the fast changing views that the Chinese were experiencing each day. There was no book that could fully prepare me for my experiences and snapshot encounters that reflected the modern Chinese people's own search for meaning. This essay is about my teaching about religion and how it became the instrument for my increased cultural sensitization in China.

Trained in Buddhist Studies and healing traditions and having lived in Asia, I was particularly interested in the search for meaning and cultural identity in the People's Republic of China context. Based on my experiences teaching as a Fulbright scholar in Hong Kong, subsequent teaching in the PRC, and several years of fieldwork research in China, religion provided a lens through which to understand the underlying paradoxical cultural transformations encountered in Hong Kong and China, regions of blurred borders and imaginative spaces. I will briefly explore my encounters with religion and teaching in the classroom at City University of Hong Kong and at a college in Zhuhai.

---

2. Victor Turner, *Dramas, Fields, and Metaphors: Symbolic Action in Human Society* (Cornell University Press, 1974), 233

Encounters of Conversion and Misunderstanding

Sometime in the middle of the spring semester in a university in China I received an email thanking me for teaching the "Applied Ethics" course. Before I read further I quietly chuckled to myself thinking that teaching that course was perhaps the most challenging teaching assignment in my career since it was outside my field and interest. I also thought about how fulfilling the task became as I saw my students, largely non-native English-speakers, transformed by their encounter with religious and philosophical literature. Having reflected, I continued reading the email. The student stated that he was so inspired by my lectures on Augustine that he had converted to Christianity! I immediately drew a deep breath and thought about the numerous times I had told my students in China over the past two years that religion can be studied academically as a subject of study—a strange, new perspective for them. China is a place where religion is a sensitive subject and has political implications. Knowing full well that this email and my response were likely to be closely monitored by the academic institution and others outside of it, I wrote a careful reply, something to the effect that although I was thrilled about him being inspired, conversion was not the intention of the course. This was the academic study of religion. It was not so much the conversion experience that disturbed me, but my encounter with students' desperate search for meaning at this and other institutions.

Emails such as the one described previously were typical as Chinese students encountered and learned about their own cultural traditions in novel ways in my other courses on Asian religions.

They had to analyze and not just memorize. The surprising result led me to think about religion as a critical lens through which to examine cultural transformation underway in China. These experiences made me think more intentionally about the purpose of education. These students were in contrast to those I have had with American undergraduates in Texas, who either approach non-American cultures with idealism and fascination, while viewing their own with either disdain or unquestioned fervor. In China, I was keenly aware of the unidirectional flow of ideas across the waters from Hong Kong (a former British colony) or the United States. There is growing anxiety over Western influences in China. Worried government officials are implementing measures to address what they see as the deterioration of Chinese culture due to Western influence. Such concern is expressed by top officials like President Hu Jintao who said, "We must clearly see that the international hostile forces are stepping up strategic attempts to westernize China, and ideological and cultural fields are a focus for long-term infiltration."[3] Aside from influences by Facebook, Twitter and Lady Gaga videos, China is focused on economic development although officials express ambivalence in terms of identity within a religious space. Such questions as, "What is Chinese culture today?" "What should China hold onto from the past?" loom large in people's minds.

The controversy surrounding religion in China is partially related to how religion is defined and contextualized. Religious studies

---

3. "China sees culture as a crucial battleground," *CNN Staff*, January 5, 2012.

scholars such as Russell McCutcheon and J. Z. Smith[4] argue that how we classify the term "religion" has a tremendous effect on how we use it. Furthermore, the context of its use also transforms its meaning despite careful examinations of history. The emphasis on understanding classification has been used by Anthropologist Mary Douglas in *Purity and Pollution* to look at the distinction between "soil" and "dirt."[5] We need to keep in mind the classifier, the system of classification, and that which is being classified. As such today, classification in every academic study is seen by some to be an inherently and inescapably political, albeit, social activity. This is the case with the term *religion*.

Some scholars note that Chinese religious policy today can be described as the freedom to believe and practice alongside with government oversight of organizations and political actions. Historically, the governmental hostility toward religion in China, evident both before and after the 1949 revolution, was in part a reaction to the negative colonial and missionary experience. Today, according to the Chinese Constitution, religion is enforced by legal legislation as a mechanism through which to promote social harmony,[6] controlled through legal sanctions related to specific churches. But the diversity of religious expression goes beyond the

---

4. Russell McCutcheon, *Manufacturing Religion: The Discourse on Sui Generis Religion and the Politics of Nostalgia* (London: Oxford University Press, 2003); Jonathan Z. Smith, *Imagining Religion: From Babylon to Jonestown (Chicago Studies in the History of Judaism)* (Chicago: University of Chicago, 1988).

5. Mary Douglas, *Purity and Danger: An Analysis of Concepts of Pollution and Taboo.* (New York: Routledge, 2002), 36. In our culture, dirt is essentially a question of "matter out of place" of that which we find inappropriate in a given context. It is concomitant with the creation of order.

6. White Papers, www.china-embassy.org/eng/zt/zjxy/t36492.htm.

structures enforced by law. This is evident in religious expressions that are found everywhere from temples to traditional Chinese medicine clinics. Not only is there syncreticism, but also creativity that shows no bounds.[7] Within these expressions, there is a hybridic manifestation of cultural identity laden with religious symbols and representations. As I walked in local communities like Tangjia, Zhuhai; or the backstreets of Shanghai, Beijing or even Macau, I encountered the fervor of religious expression.

Religion continues as a source of fascination in Chinese life that cannot be contained or structured by the government. People are ambivalent toward religion, yet have a desire and need to preserve its expression, bringing out a critical attitude toward the Chinese economic boom.

Teaching "Not Teaching" about Religion and Local Encounters in a Strange New Universe

My positions at two universities were on the surface quite different. One of the positions was as a Fulbright lecturer at City University of Hong Kong teaching a general education course in sociology entitled, "Religion and Society in Asia." The other position was as an Asian

---

7. David Palmer, Glenn Shive and Philip Wickeri, eds. *Chinese Religious Life* (New York: Oxford University Press, 2011); Mark Green, "The Alchemical Lore of Wong Tai Sin and the Contemporary Pursuit of Transformational Wellbeing," in *History and Culture: Chinese Cross Currents* 5, No. 4 (October 2008), 90–101; Adam Yuet Chau, *Religion in Contemporary China: Revitalization and Innovation* (New York: Routledge, 2011); Andrew B. Kipnis, "The Flourishing of Religion in Post-Mao China and the Anthropological Category of Religion," in *The Australian Journal of Anthropology* 12, No. 1 (2001), 32–46. .

philosophy professor at United International College in Zhuhai, part of Beijing Normal University and Hong Kong Baptist University. Both of these positions enabled me to encounter local communities of religious practice, and revealed current Chinese attraction to religion. Likewise they provided me with contexts where I could observe people's search for meaning including desires for a greater cultural identity grounded in Chinese traditions. I soon learned though that addressing religion in South China was also about not addressing it. The discourse of silence as well as verbal affirmations were held in an often uneasy but necessary balance.

There are several issues that an academic trained in the study of religion had to face. One regarded the presence of religion as a discipline in the academy. The other was about an acceptable pedagogical approach to teaching religion. While there are difficult issues in North America, I was even more sensitive to the difficulty of religion as a concept in the communist Chinese context. I felt that I had to identify myself in a neutral manner. Therefore, my representation of my professional identity was shaped by such considerations. I was represented as a scholar of Asian Studies, or a historian versed in medical anthropology.

In the Department of Asian and International Studies in Hong Kong I was surrounded by an international faculty with a primarily Chinese student body so negotiating identity was less complicated than in mainland China. In this latter context, it was important that I was represented as a philosopher because of the deep respect many scholars held for philosophers like Laozi and Zhuangzi, and because of the stigma regarding religion, especially coming from a Westerner. Even saying I was a historian of religion would have been quite problematic, drawing attention to me as a teacher and possible "preacher."

10. Are You in the Safe Zone? Cultural Sensitization and Religion for a Teaching Traveler

In addition to negotiating my own sense of identity in these contexts, I also had to negotiate the nature and expectations of the student body. In the case of Hong Kong, the students in my course on religion and society in Asia were mostly from Hong Kong with a few mainland Chinese students. These few mainland students often stood out like sore thumbs since they were quite demure in comparison to the Hong Kong students and were often quietly disparaged by Hong Kong students who took pride on being "freer" in terms of publically expressing their views and more modern in their perspectives.

While teaching and giving such lectures I was often reminded that religion in each culture has its unique history and therefore that history defines it and its place in society. At this point in history, religion in the Western context has been given a legitimate voice, one taken seriously in top academic institutions. The history of teaching about religion in the academic context in the West is a complex story however. This story includes the eventual division between the study of religion and the study of theology. Such organizations as the American Study of Religion (AAR) arose as a nonprofit member organization serving to give voice to scholars involved in the academic study of religion. Religion has held a central (and still does) place in American history and has directly marked its cultural identity. Through the study of religion in the American context we also know that religion is as much a part of public life as it is part of the private sphere. Religion inevitably affects and is affected by politics. It is not a matter here whether people are affiliated with churches or creating new religions, but rather about the underlying rhetoric about religion in public discourse that is quite evident.

Although organizations like the AAR do not exist in China and discussions about the academic study of religion is at its infancy, there is evidence in China of a developing interest in religious studies. Programs have developed in religious studies, Tibetan Studies, and even Sanskrit in the mainland. However, Hong Kong scholars revealed to me misunderstandings about how to approach the study of religion.

Teaching the Academic Study of Religion with the Stigma on Religion

In the context of Hong Kong, there were several factors that shaped students' responses, and my subsequent representation, of religion. A unique legacy of religion remains because of the multiple impacts of the history of British colonialism, a past and current missionary presence, and the influence of the Chinese mainland since the return of Hong Kong in 1997. My campus was surrounded by this complexity. The neighborhoods surrounding it showed colonial and post-colonial influences, and included several Catholic organizations and academic institutions like Caritas and the Marion Sisters, many Protestant churches, local Daoist and Buddhist temples, and a Mormon Church.

In spite of the presence of religion, I found it a challenge to teach a course on religion and society. The major focus at this university as well as others in Hong Kong was on technology and business. The motivation of the students was less about learning and more about obtaining the diploma so they could go on with their lives and make money. What did religion have to do with *their lives*? Fortunately, they quickly found out it did, and they had to view their world with new lenses even if it came from a Western woman.

The course in Hong Kong itself was structured as a combination lecture and tutorial session; the tutorials provided students a chance to express themselves and engage with the materials. The stereotype that Asian students were passive in the classroom was easily dispelled. I found that, in comparison to my students in Texas, religion was not readily discussed in an academic context nor in any other classes other than religious studies courses. For my Hong Kong students, religion was the corner Buddhist or Daoist temple where they would socialize on special holidays or where they would see their mothers (frequently grandmothers) go to request special favors. If they were Christian, they remembered the basic lessons from their time at a private Christian school or from evangelical sessions at church they frequented during special holidays. Any course on the subject was thought of as "bible-study" focused on conversion. Many had only rudimentary knowledge of these many traditions even though Buddhism, Daoism and Christianity were central to their history.

Other students expressed the standard Marxist-Maoist perspective on religion ("religion as poison"). It was also significant that I never encountered a Hong Kong student who critiqued Christianity from a Marxist perspective. This was in great contrast to my students across the Pearl estuary at Zhuhai in mainland China. My Hong Kong students could not clearly distinguish between Buddhism and Daoism. Buddhism was not really understood because of its perceived "mysterious" or "difficult" philosophy and association with monks. It was often lumped together with Daoism, and Daoism was something almost everyone practiced at some level. On the whole, there was a lack of sophistication on the part of students in relation to the study of religion and a lack of understanding of the nuanced nature of religion in society.

My approach with the Hong Kong students was to emphasize the importance and the real world value of studying religion. Through the study of religion in Sri Lanka, India, Myanmar, Tibet, China, and Japan, students quickly realized that without having a more open perspective on religion and a solid historical background, they would easily miss the significance of current events, especially when it came to connections between religion and politics, economics, or the arts. They began to see the place of religion in terms of their own identity as well and the latter really mattered to them.

Like mainland Chinese students, Hong Kong students were particularly interested in learning about their own history and traditions. There was almost a sense of urgency in learning more. They knew little of their own culture and traditions even though they lived right next door to temples and churches. I did not expect this urgency in Hong Kong, a world city with an international flavor, sheltered from the ravages of the Cultural Revolution. But the absence of memory of their traditions or legacies was starkly evident. For these students, life was making money, it is a materialistic world. But in my classroom they had to be the Sri Lankans, the Tibetans, the Indians, and the Burmese, thinking about issues of religion tied to identity, choice, and violence. Although I could have easily just focused on the commercialization of religion, I saw that these students needed more. They needed a base on which to build and from which they could build their critical thinking skills. I remember one particular class period when students sat on the edge of their seats and exclaimed that they did not know about the violence between the Sinhalese and the Tamils or the Indian partition, even though South Asia was their neighbor! I quickly realized that the study of religion is a route needed to help students become better informed "world" citizens.

This need for preservation, or more so, "recovery" was sorely lacking in Hong Kong, a metropolis dominated by modern architecture. In Hong Kong, the students showed particular enjoyment in fieldtrips to the famous Wong Tai Sin Temple and to the Buddhist nunnery and garden, Chi Lin Nunnery. It was both fascinating and sad to see students at Wong Tai Sin Temple ask what the religious purposes of the joss stick (incense sticks used for devotion) and the divination sticks (for predictions) were. They expressed surprise at all three traditions (Wong Tai Sin's Daoism, Buddhism through Guanyin and Confucianism through Kongfuzi) being represented; and listened attentively to the Daoist immortal story in relation to the large marble image of the sheep in front of them.

Looking at Tradition

Across the waters traveling to Jiuzhou Ferry port I found myself in another world of education, development and modernization that led me to further examine the role of religion in the Chinese context. However in both Hong Kong and mainland China, pedagogical techniques took a turn toward engagement so that students' history of silence and lack of exposure were faced.

The process of having students work on projects about religion in the context of space was helpful. It helped me decipher what my students knew of their own history in terms of religion, and how much they were open to moving beyond their past limited exposure. Their mixed responses included bewilderment, excitement, openness, and resistance. They asked questions such as: How can these institutions be significant to our worldview that are focused on development and modernization? Aren't these remnants of "our" grandparents, superstitions or outdated medical treatments? In researching local temples and conducting fieldwork at Chinese medical institutions students found themselves discovering new things about traditions they thought they knew and noticing places they ignored. Studying and visiting these sites seemed to have given these students a renewed respect for their own traditions, another dimension of themselves they were not aware of. I saw this also in many instances during my UIC courses in Zhuhai. Students often would say that they wanted to learn about Chinese philosophy. Sometimes it reminded me of the Texan attitude I often encountered in my students at Austin College in which Texas (and the United States) is the center of their universe. They want to learn about the religions that affect their home and their history to help them with a sense of identity.

As I exposed my Chinese students in both universities to alternative histories and unknown philosophical perspectives in Chinese religious history, I remember encountering the personal memories of the students. This was more evident in Zhuhai however, it was certainly reflected in the Hong Kong classroom. Some of the mainland students and those with families from China reflected on the traumatic history of their parents. As Erik Mueggler in *The Age of Wild Ghosts: Memory, Violence, and Place in Southwest China* states, "memory plays a powerful placemarker for a culture, pointing to a constructed and evolving identity."[8] For those students, the older generation's memory of the Great Leap Forward and the Cultural Revolution with their specter of legal sanctions, silence along with

---

8. Erik Mueggler, *The Age of Wild Ghosts: Memory, Violence, and Place in Southwest China* (Berkeley: University of California, 2001).

masked verbal communication was more of a communication than direct verbal speech.

In deconstructing their assumptions about what the term religion represented to them, exposing them to the history of the term, and engaging them in case studies, students began to express their feelings about what they saw as religious (or as some would insist on saying, "spiritual"). In their readings about religion in Japan, for example, they found that like the Japanese, religious traditions are cultural traditions even though the significance of the rituals may have lost their original meanings. However, I challenged them to uncover the earlier meanings, to develop a sense of responsible preservation.

Conclusion

In the ritual of our lives, we are often confronted with dichotomies—the written words from news reports, official government documents, scriptures, and literature—and then the actions, the practices, the feelings, and the expressions of ordinary people themselves. The space between what is said and what is actually done is what I am concerned about in this essay. As the academic study of religion and anthropological studies of Asian societies have shown, the relationship between word and practice reveals a society's tension between its standards and divergences. Prior to my trip to Hong Kong and mainland China, I remember reading several articles that stated that with the increased economic boom in the mainland,[9]

---

9. Mayfair Mei-hui Yang, *Chinese Religiosities: Afflictions of Modernity and State Formation* (Berkley, CA: University of California Press, 2008).

there was also a resurgence of religion. Religion was not just seen in the official organized form but in eclectic sorts borrowing elements from Christianity, Buddhism, Daoism, and local traditions. A presentation I attended in Hong Kong also pointed out that such traditions are unofficially allowed in mainland China as long as they contribute to harmony in society. I remember also encountering many students and instructors in mainland China saying that there is a lack of spirituality, that although people are more financially successful, they also find that they lack something and so there is an urgent need to fill that void. I am not sure if I helped fill that urgent need in my students in Hong Kong or on the mainland, but I did encounter a need to find or make sense of their identities through religious traditions. As mentioned earlier, paradoxical representation of Chinese society revealed a fervent search for identity. I was also participating in that paradox as an educator. It was through understanding more deeply Daoism, Buddhism, Confucianism, and Christianity that students rediscovered themselves as Hongkongese and as Chinese through the inspiration of the antics of a Western-trained female academic. It was by learning through teaching that I also understood the meaning and relative nature of my own constructed categories.

References

Ashiwa, Yoshiko, ed. *Making Religion, Making the State: The Politics of Religion in Modern China.* Stanford, CA: Stanford University Press, 2009.

Chau, Adam Yuet. *Religion in Contemporary China: Revitalization and Innovation.* New York: Routledge, 2011.

Chunwa, Kwong. *The Public Role of Religion in Post-Colonial Hong Kong.* Bern: Peter Lang Press, 2002.

Durkheim, Émile. *The Elementary Forms of the Religious Life: A Study in Religious Sociology.* London: G. Allen & Unwin; New York, Macmillan, 1915.

Evans, Carolyn. "Chinese Law and the International Protection of Religious Freedom." *Journal of Church and State* 44, No. 4 (2002): 749–774.

Foley, D. E. *The Heartland Chronicles. Multicultural Education in a Pluralistic Society.* Philadelphia, PA: University of Pennsylvania,1998.

Gooch, Todd A. *The Numinous and Modernity: An Interpretation of Rudolf Otto's Philosophy of Religion.* Berlin and New York: Walter de Gruyter, 2000.

Greene, Mark. "The Alchemical Lore of Wong Tai Sin and the Contemporary Pursuit of Transformational Wellbeing." *History and Culture: Chinese Cross Currents* 5, No. 4 (October 2008): 90–101.

Kipnis, Andrew B. "The Flourishing of Religion in Post-Mao China and the Anthropological Category of Religion." *The Australian Journal of Anthropology* 12, No. 1 (2001): 32–46.

Ko, Tinming. *The Sacred Citizens and the Secular City.* London: Ashgate Pub Ltd. 2000.

Kwok Siu-tong and Kirti Narain. *Co-Prosperity in Cross-Culturalism: Indians in Hong Kong.* Hong Kong: The Commercial Press, 2003.

McCutcheon, Russell. *Manufacturing Religion: The Discourse on Sui Generis Religion and the Politics of Nostalgia.* London: Oxford University Press, 2003.

Mueggler, Erik. *The Age of Wild Ghosts: Memory, Violence, and Place in Southwest China*. Berkeley: University of California, 2001.

Palmer, David, Glenn Shive and Philip Wickeri, eds. *Chinese Religious Life*. New York: Oxford University Press, 2011.

Rosaldo, Renato. *Culture & Truth: The Remaking of Social Analysis: With a New Introduction.* NY: Routledge, 1993.

Smith, Jonathan Z. *Imagining Religion: From Babylon to Jonestown (Chicago Studies in the History of Judaism)*. Chicago: University of Chicago, 1988.

Tilley, Christopher. *A Phenomenology of Landscape*. Oxford, UK: Berg Publishers, 1994.

Turner, Victor. *The Ritual Process: Structure and Anti-Structure*. London: Aldine Transaction, 1995.

Yang, Mayfair Mei-hui. *Chinese Religiosities: Afflictions of Modernity and State Formation*. Berkley, CA: University of California Press, 2008.

Stage Four
Learning and Communicating in Place

Chapter 11
How Good Am I? Self Evaluation in an Examination Culture

Christopher DENEEN

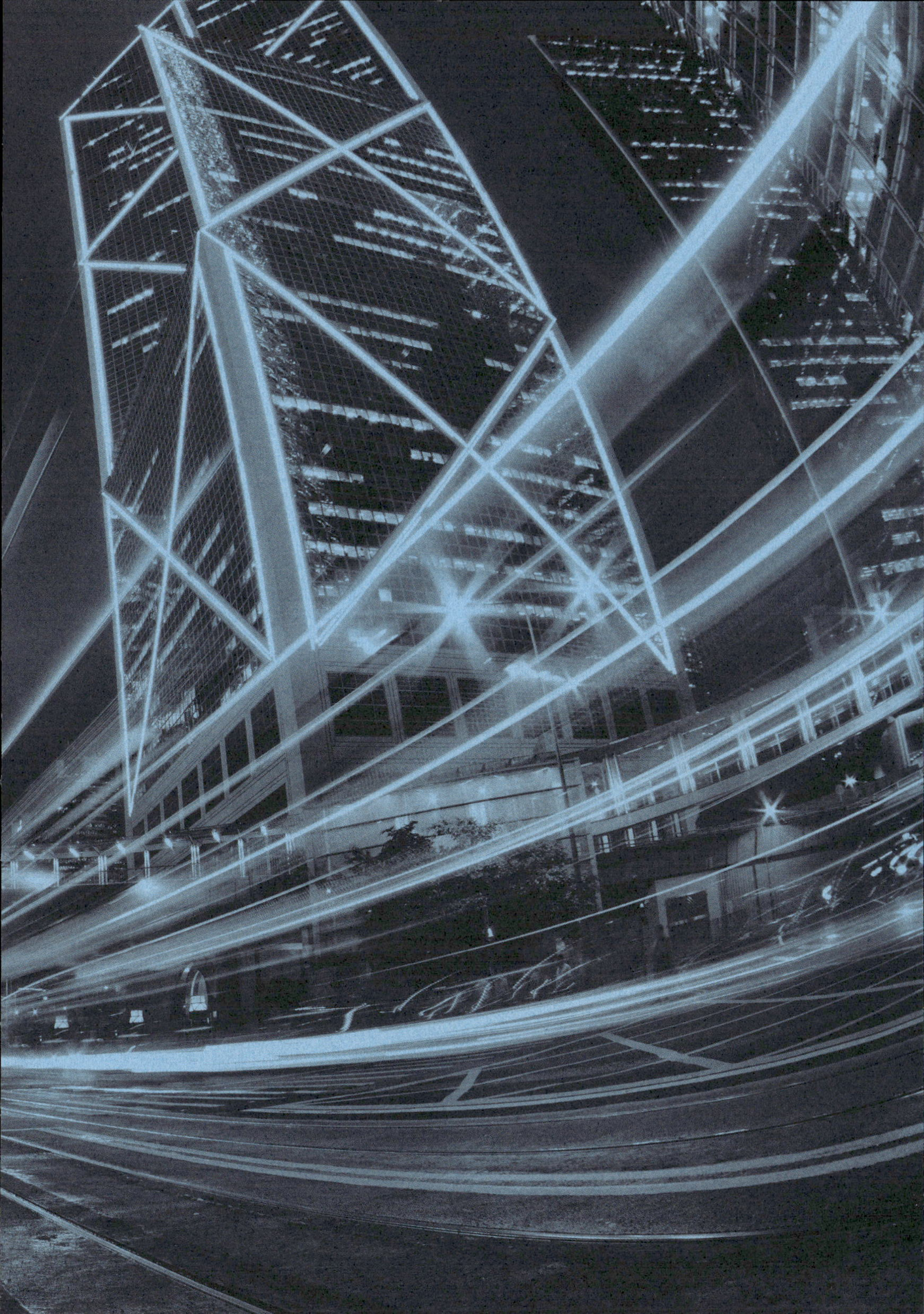

γνῶθι σεαυτόν
(know thyself)

Ancient Greek proverb

A few weeks ago, my wife Valerie and I were out at dinner with my former research assistant. Jen had left Hong Kong to pursue her doctoral studies in linguistics at Cambridge University. She was back visiting friends and family. We were catching up over dinner in Tsim Sha Tsui, a busy, vibrant district of Hong Kong and celebrating her successful first semester. I had something I was particularly proud to tell her about: I was finally studying Cantonese. If anyone would appreciate this, I thought, it would be a developing expert in linguistics. Before the entrees arrived, I tried out some rudimentary phrases. Valerie, a native speaker who had been patiently suffering through my attempts to navigate her mother tongue, rolled her eyes but said nothing.

"Oh! You're learning Cantonese! Are you going to formal lessons or a tutor?"

"No; I'm using recordings where I learn and sound out words and phrases. I'm studying about half an hour a day, five days a week." I adopted an appropriately humble tone.

"That's great ... but what are you using as your examination book?"

"Oh, I'm not using an exam book. Like I said, I'm using recordings. They're on my iPhone."

Jen looked embarrassed, "I'm sorry; since I got back to Hong Kong, I've been speaking mostly Cantonese. My English is already getting rusty. I meant, what is the text you are using to administer tests to yourself?"

She spoke the last part slowly. I couldn't tell if she doubted her grasp of English or mine.

"Yes, I understood you. I'm not using one."

She started at me, aghast.

"But, but ..." she spluttered, "How do you know how good you are?"

Valerie nodded solemnly in agreement.

I was spared committing any further heresies by the arrival of pizza and pasta. The conversation moved on, and we all had an enjoyable evening. However, Jen's question lingered with me in the days following the meal. How good am I?

Placing the Self in Self-assessment

It is a question I've asked myself many times. I ask it so often, I am often not fully conscious I am doing so. Like breathing, it has become regular and autonomic. The question surfaces when I approach a task or test, when I face some new challenge, or during a moment of existential crisis. Sometimes the question is specific, as in "how good am I at factor analysis?" Other times, it appears as a vast, holistic inquiry that pounces on me in the shower: "how good a person am I?" Self-inquiry is a part of our modern personal, educational and professional lives. The question is woven into my life and likely into yours as well.

When I step back and look at the process of asking and answering, I see self-assessment. I'm predisposed to seeing it this way, as I work in educational assessment. Much of my professional life is built around building better assessments that support and determine competencies. "How good am I?" is central to my professional interests. That means you are central to my interests as well. When people develop the skills of self-assessment, good things happen. Enhanced ability to self-regulate one's learning, more accurate understandings of the quality of one's work, and even more accurate sense of self-confidence are benefits tied to developing one's self-assessment skills (Boud & Falchikov, 2006; McDonald & Boud, 2003). Thus, "how good am I?" is fundamental to education. People who are good at asking and answering this question are fundamental to our future.

It's a tough task, though. We are not inherently very good at self-assessment. Compounding the problem is our stubborn refusal to acknowledge this limitation. We convince ourselves that we are naturally competent self-assessors. We believe our self-judgments of performance, knowledge and skills to be valid and reliable, "nobody knows me like I know me!" Research suggests otherwise. Without training, people tend to be very inaccurate at self-judgment (Brown & Harris, 2013). Those who perform well in school may have an edge in making specific judgments about their academic achievement, but even among top students there is a general tendency towards misestimating one's capacities. This is inaccuracy that if left unaddressed, extends into professional life (Dunning, Heath, & Suls, 2004). Challenging this in an educational arena means confronting limitations and providing a lot of practice.

Building people's capacity to self assess is seen as a key priority for the future, but it is one of education's most difficult tasks. Thus, educators throughout the world are pushing for the explicit development of self-assessment skills within school curricula. Hong Kong is no exception to this trend; in fact it is trying to lead it. As Hong Kong works to position itself as a world-class hub of cutting-edge learning and achievement, self-assessment has become a centerpiece of the agenda.

It is proving to be an uphill battle. Part of the problem lies with the inherent difficulties I mention above. However, there are other factors especially relevant to Hong Kong. The greatest value in self-assessment lies in going beyond a rote script (Boud & Falchikov, 2006). In other words, valuable self-assessment is best achieved through developing the learner's ability to construct questions and arrive at judgments. This is fundamentally different than an external authority telling learners how good they are and then expecting that they internalize that message. The former is self-assessment; the latter is not. Self-assessment requires educational systems to develop the learner's agency to explore, determine and articulate their achievement. It is not at all clear that Hong Kong is ready to commit to this.

Different cultures have different understandings of the role of learners in the educational process. This has, historically produced different expectations about what a learner is encouraged or even allowed to do on their own. When people from different cultures meet at an educational crossroads, there is often misunderstanding and even shock at the baggage the other is traveling with. Jen's surprise at my response and my dwelling on her question are examples of this. Having lived and worked in Hong Kong for five years, I have come to understand that these meetings have implications for Hong Kong's agenda of educational change: self-assessment and learner agency are contested spaces.

Meaningful progress requires that we know ourselves. Just as we want this for learners, we need it for societies. In Hong Kong, this requires that the people meeting at educational crossroads understand the historical and modern forces that make self-assessment and learner agency problematic. In this chapter, I hope to introduce the reader to some of these forces and explain how they powerfully influence Hong Kong, its education systems and its learners. Many of the issues Hong Kong faces resonate with educational issues of international concern. As we come to understand Hong Kong's struggles, I hope as well we may better understand similar struggles elsewhere.

A History of Knowing and Being

Hong Kong is a place where many cultural currents meet and commingle. Two traditions dominate, though. One may be seen in the architecture of the courthouse, the tradition of scones with afternoon tea and the meticulously kept lawn of the Kowloon Cricket Club. With the cession of Hong Kong under the Treaty of Nanking, the British Empire began to shape the region. This can be seen as much in the educational architecture as in the buildings. In 1865, under the direction of British Colonial Secretary Fredrick Steward, the Government Education Department of Hong Kong imposed a system of education closely aligned with the British, exam-driven model. Examinations played a crucial role in determining how students moved through the system, how far they got and the opportunities they might have upon exiting. For over 130 years, "How good am I?" was answered through memorization and recitation. Validity of one's answer lay in the results of an examination paper. Any other answers that learners might arrive at were of subordinate concern. Hong Kong had been colonized, and so had its learners. Knight and Yorke (2003) describe the colonizing of a learner's educational identity as when systemic and external priorities move into the internal space of the learner, a space that might otherwise be filled with the learner's own inquiries and determinations. Just as the physical and educational architecture of Hong Kong were adapted to the desires of the British Empire, the internal architectures of learners were molded as well.

It would be an oversimplification, though to see Hong Kong's investment in examinations as beginning with the British take-over. The colonial system capitalized on a much older tradition: the Chinese imperial examination system. Established in 605 CE and sustained on Mainland China until the early 20th century, the imperial examination system was essential to maintaining governance, military strength and cultural identity (Carless, 2011). Title and authority in society, civil service and the military were granted in large part based on examination results. Like the British system, there were sequential and stratified levels of examinations that determined the learner's path and outcomes. Examinees who scored well secured a future for themselves and their entire family. Their prospects grew even brighter if and when they passed through the progressive levels of examination.

The system was complex, having evolved over multiple dynasties. The rudimentary explanation is that an examinee's journey began with local *tongshi* examinations. Those who succeeded at the *tongshi* and wished to progress further could make the journey to the provincial capital and sit for the more demanding province-wide *xiangshi*. Obtaining a degree at this level allowed one to sit for the *huishi*, a triennial examination held in the national capital. For a rarified few, there was the *dianshi*. Also a triennial examination, the *dianshi* was held at the imperial palace. The emperor himself would often preside over its administration.

These examinations focused on areas modern students would recognize, such as mathematics. However, they also drew heavily from an agreed upon, highly specific body of classic Chinese texts. This body of literature conveyed the quintessential virtues and understanding of the Chinese people. Those who took the exams were asked to apply this knowledge in civil or military situations where it was deemed essential to correct decision-making. Creativity mattered, but it was of subordinate concern. The desired outcome was for the examinee to serve as a conduit, channeling the applicable text in the correct manner to obtain the ideal response.

The examinations were not simply about learner achievement; they were the foundation of a civil, social and military meritocracy. The exams were egalitarian; any man of the empire could sit for the examination, regardless of their status. Hypothetically, the son of an illiterate farmer from the furthest-flung province could sit in front of the emperor himself and then be ushered into the highest echelons of civil or military service ... if their essay was good enough. Of course, as with modern examination systems, those with the means to hire private tutors had a clear advantage. Passing degrees on the lower-level examinations could also be purchased by the wealthy, thus assuring the stability of a family's status, even if brilliance skipped a generation. Even still, the examinations were seen as a reliable and equitable route to success.

Modern Hong Kong with its silver skyscrapers, luxury cars and neon-clad streets seems a far cry from the days of either empire. The last imperial examination in China was given in 1904. British rule ended nearly two decades ago and the territory of Hong Kong is now the special administrative region of the People's Republic of China. Ostensibly, the education system has changed as well. As China races into industrial and economic modernity, Hong Kong's educational system claims to be turning away from its exam-centric focus. The language of reform in Hong Kong embraces agency, inquiry and development of learner capacity. "How good am I?" is an explicit part of the modern Hong Kong agenda. As I wrote earlier, these changes are not going exactly as planned. Behind the bright modern lights of Hong Kong lie shadows, the largest of which lurks in education.

A Shadow of Ourselves

As you walk through the city, looking at billboards and the sides of buses, you will see dozens of advertisements featuring smiling, glamorous young men and women. They are clad in well-tailored and trendy clothes; their hair is perfectly coiffed. One might assume these ads are for the latest boy/girl bands, were it not for academic credentials and subject specialties spelled out beneath each figure. These are the "tutor idols," academic tutors marketed as pop stars. The advertisements range from eye-catching to wonderfully bizarre. There are the "Tutor Queens" of King's Glory Education Center,

Reading Hong Kong, Reading Ourselves

A bus advertisement for tutor services

slender, tall young women who might as easily be strutting the catwalk of a fashion show as teaching math. There is Amanda Tan and her "Task Force" of tutors, their heraldic crest framed by a rampant unicorn and Pegasus. My personal favorite is Joseph Li who bills himself as "The Exam Prophet." Wreathed in fog and sporting a giant, but well-maintained afro, he looks past the viewer with a serious, otherworldly gaze. Mr. Li claims to have a preternatural grasp of the questions on future rounds of the region-wide examinations. His clairvoyance is accurate enough that it warranted formal investigation by the authorities, several years ago. As far as I know, they never found any stolen test sheets taped under his crystal ball.

11. How Good Am I? Self Evaluation in an Examination Culture

This is Hong Kong's shadow education system. The marketing tactics that have launched dozens of teen bands are used to draw students into tutor centers, where they are drilled in the new Chinese classics: English, calculus, chemistry and other disciplines. This for-profit system exerts at least as much power as the formal education system, but is not subject to the same oversight or regulations. This makes it hard to get firm numbers, but in 2010 it was estimated that 76% of primary students and up to 86% of secondary students were receiving tutoring (Bray & Lykins, 2012). In a city of seven million, the shadow education industry is estimated to be a US$255 million per year industry (*ibid*).

The schedule is brutal. Secondary school students might spend three to four hours a week in tutor centers and primary students, up to ten hours a week. There is the expectation that many more hours each week will be devoted to homework. Keep in mind, this is homework assigned by their tutors. Students still have to slog through the formidable amount of homework assigned through their formal schooling.

Shadow educators insinuate themselves into students' lives, becoming friends and confidants. Not long ago, I was at a dinner party and happened to sit next to a tutor idol. As we discussed our mutual interest in Hong Kong education, she told me about her relationships with students outside the tutor center. "I expect my students to friend me on Facebook. I don't require it, but I strongly encourage them to." She showed me her page. Her list of "friends" numbered in the hundreds. "These are all current and former students," she proudly exclaimed. "We talk and post about our dreams, our hopes, what we had for dinner last night ..." When I asked whether this might intrude too deeply into her life, she laughed, "Oh no, this is my tutor Facebook page. My real life Facebook page is totally different."

Shadow education markets itself as having broad educational benefits. The core focus, though is on obtaining high examination scores. The staggering time commitment and degree of intimacy have profound, identity-shaping consequences. From math drills to commenting on their latest Facebook post, the tutor is in the student's life, hour after hour, week after week. The focus may be narrow, but the engagement is vast. Inevitably, students' assessments of themselves are colored by this engagement. Like the imperial system, shadow education is more than just prepping for an exam; it is a structure that impacts the student at a personal level. As the tutor steps into the student's life, they also step into the space where questions and answers about the self have their genesis. Shadow education markets itself as supplementing the formal educational system. We must, however understand that it is fundamentally at odds with systemic educational reforms aimed at developing learner agency and self-assessment. Like the systems that preceded it, shadow education colonizes the learner's identity.

Given the extraordinary demands and invasiveness of shadow education, what could possibly motivate parents and students to participate? Part of the answer lies in the history of the region, and the long-standing faith in examinations and scores as a reliable and egalitarian route to success. As the formal education system becomes less exam-centric and more learner-centric, people are becoming nervous. One of my colleagues, a professor of education and the mother of a Hong Kong schoolchild, put it thusly, "The more the formal education system turns away from examinations as underlying architecture, the more parents, especially ones who came up in the older, British system are looking to tutors. They feel like the schools are failing them by trying to do all these things that don't produce an exam score."

Even still, history and culture cannot account for the massive appeal, size or revenue of shadow education. For that, we must turn to a more modern and pragmatic concern. We must also acknowledge the failure of progressive reformers to adequately negotiate this concern. I am referring to the competition for university attendance.

Squeezing through the Bottleneck

In Hong Kong, there are eight University Grants Committee (UGC)-funded institutions. The public ranks these informally but rigidly, with a clear top and bottom. Getting in at the top is like passing the *dianshi* and receiving a nod from the emperor, himself. But getting in anywhere is desirable ... and tough. Just like the imperial examination system, success is rarified. In total, the eight UGC-funded institutions accept about 18% of applicants. Given that 65% of Hong Kong's graduating secondary school students apply to university, this creates fearsome competition.

There are other options. Hong Kong has other higher education institutions but they are not held in nearly as high regard as the UGC universities. Mainland China has many universities. However, most of these institutions are still emerging in terms of quality and name recognition. The well-known and respected institutions on the mainland China are just as tough to get into as their Hong Kong counterparts. Alternately, there are foreign universities. These options can be cripplingly expensive, especially in comparison to a Hong Kong university. A resident of Hong Kong attending the top-ranked and internationally well-regarded University of Hong Kong (HKU) need only pay HK$42,100 or a little under US$5,400 tuition per year. Many students continue to live at home during their university years, thus saving on room and board. Compare that with attending the University of California at Berkeley. At the time of writing this, a Hong Kong student would pay US$35,750 in tuition and fees. That's not including room, board, books, or tickets to travel halfway around the world and back to see family. All in all, Berkeley would cost a Hong Kong family ten times as much as HKU.

For most Hong Kongers, that leaves local universities as the best or only choice. This leads to a predictable question: What will give a student the necessary competitive edge to get accepted? As the curriculum shifts from focusing on exam results to building students' capacity, parents, teachers and students are asking this question with increasing anxiety and bewilderment. "What does it mean for the admissions process that I am more accurate at assessing my competency?" "Does increasing learners' agency increase their chances of getting into a UGC institution?" I have heard these exact questions posed at educational forums. The panelists are often educational reformers, many of whom work at these UGC institutions. The answers they give focus on how students will become deeper thinkers, more desirable job candidates and better citizens. Sometimes the responses center on life- and career-long benefit to the learner or how much better a student's performance will be on complex tasks, even in their first year of university.

On the one hand, these answers describe candidates best prepared to use higher education as a road to success. The principles underlying these answers may inform curricula that support longitudinal success across careers and lives. On the other hand, these answers fail to speak directly to the socio-economic and competitive priorities of getting into a university. It's no wonder that stressed-out students and parents find these answers lacking. When people feel pressed by immediate concerns, they look for pragmatic, concrete answers. Examination-centered shadow education adroitly markets itself as providing those answers. Nobody likes it, but an exam-centered curriculum is perceived as the most immediate and practical responses to that seminal question, "How do I get on the road to success?"

This is a costly answer. Besides time, energy and resources, commitment to an exam-centered regimen robs learners of the very capacities that allow them to make the most of their educational experiences. As exam tutors step into the learners' interior space, self-regulation, self-assessment and self-inquiry are crowded out.

The long-term deficits to the learner and to society produced by this approach are exactly the reason change is so strongly advocated for. This advocacy, though must better market itself. The pressing and urgent questions of stakeholders have to be answered directly and effectively. Doing this requires progressive educators to confront the weight of history, a well-marketed, multi-million dollar industry and the hard realities of socio-economics. It's not enough that Hong Kong's learners are well prepared to travel the road to success; we have to make the clear case that building learner capacity helps get them on that road in the first place.

Getting Past the Crossroads

In Hong Kong, self-assessment and learner agency are areas of contention. They represent a departure from historical and modern practices that have powerful associations with egalitarianism and success. At the same time, these ideas represent what research tells us are the best solutions for life- and career-long navigation of the 21st century. Which path will Hong Kong take? Will exams and exam-centric curricula remain dominant, crowding the learner out of their own learning? Will learner agency and the capacity to inquire deeply and accurately into the self find purchase? The future will be determined by what principal stakeholders decide are the best answers to the most important questions. I value the research informed answers and I believe in them. I recognize, though the pressing urgency and responsibility of getting others to buy in to these answers. It's up to me and other educators to advocate for learner agency and self assessment in ways that are understood and accepted by a general public concerned about the future. I also recognize that this is not a problem endemic to Hong Kong.

The United States is in the midst of what Diane Ravitch refers to as the fetishizing of examinations (2013). Examination-based accountability has been touted as the means to improving both the system and the prospects of individual learners. The public is being told that there is a terrible crisis in how we are educating our children. True or not, there is certainly a very real crisis in paying for higher education. Just as in Hong Kong, the competition for affordable higher education is an immediate and urgent concern. For these and other related reasons, the United States has an educationally stressed population. More testing is being sold as the cure.

Lucrative industries have blossomed to meet the almighty goal of high examination scores. Like Hong Kong's shadow education system, these industries thrive on the promise of delivering practical answers to practical questions. Many educators in the United States perceive this as a threat. They cite curricula, once rich with discovery and self-inquiry as now thinned to a narrow trajectory pointing in the direction of standardized test scores. Interestingly, it is Hong Kong's tantalizingly high scores that are often cited as the goal. "If we can get scores like these, America's future will be secure!" The naiveté and provincialism of this thinking is only matched by the equally naïve belief that educators can challenge this thinking and the financial and political machinery it has given birth to without providing answers that principal stakeholders will accept.

How Good Am I?

Jen's question is important: "How do you know how good you are?"

My first response is, I know how good I am because thanks to a good education, knowing my limitations and a lot of practice, I am fairly competent at self-assessment. At the same time, my judgment must contend with certain external realities. For example, I am not actually very good at speaking Cantonese. I know this due to the looks of bewilderment I often get when I try to speak it with Hong Kongers. As an educator, how good I am cannot be separated from the results of my work. Positive change in my students, improvement of curricula I work with and the impact of my research are important. These external realities and indicators mediate my self-judgment. This mediation is necessary if I want my self-assessment to be valid. So, accurate self-assessment may start within me, but it has to extend outwards in a negotiation with the rest of the world.

Becoming a hub of educational excellence requires enhancing learner agency and the capacity to self assess. If we want this to happen, we need to practice what we preach. It's not enough that as a community of scholars and educators, we have assessed the situation and come to evidence-based answers. Just as individuals' judgments have to contend with external imperatives, our judgments as an educational community have to better negotiate the hard realities that shape perception and practice.

Hong Kong is trying to move away from a monolithic focus on examinations. The United States is trying to resist being dragged into the same situation. These are difficult battles. The systems and people that profit by overemphasizing examinations know their market. They are good at selling answers that speak to very real concerns. These answers are unpalatable; the time commitment, stress and sheer exhaustion of test prep are invasive and disempowering. However, until the answers of greatest benefit can address the most immediate concerns, we won't see much progress. Progressive educators must make the best possible case for how enhancing agency and self-assessment gets learners on the road to success in the first place. Until that happens, "How good am I?" will remain a question asked and answered on an examination sheet.

References

Boud, David and Nancy Falchikov. "Aligning Assessment with Long-term Learning." *Assessment & Evaluation in Higher Education* 31.4 (2006): 399–413.

Bray, Mark and Chad Lykins. *Shadow Education: Private Supplementary Tutoring and Its Implications for Policy Makers in Asia*. Mandaluyong City, Philippines: Asian Development Bank, 2012.

Brown, Gavin T. L. and Lois R. Harris. "Student Self-assessment." *The SAGE Handbook of Research on Classroom Assessment*. Ed. by James H. McMillan. Thousand Oaks, CA: Sage, 2013. 367–393.

Carless, David. *From Testing to Productive Student Learning: Implementing Formative Assessment in Confucian–Heritage Settings*. New York: Routledge, 2011.

Dunning, David, Chip Heath, and Jerry M. Suls. "Flawed Self-assessment: Implications for Health, Education, and the Workplace." *Psychological Science in the Public Interest* 5.3 (2004): 69–106.

Knight, Peter and Mantz Yorke. *Assessment, Learning and Employability*. Maidenhead, UK: McGraw-Hill International, 2003.

McDonald, Betty and David Boud. "The Impact of Self-assessment on Achievement: The Effects of Self-assessment Training on Performance in External Examinations." *Assessment in Education: Principles, Policy & Practice* 10.2 (2003): 209–220.

Ravitch, Diane. *"Reign of Error: The Hoax of the Privatization Movement and the Danger to America's Public Schools."* New York: Alfred A. Knopf, 2013.

Chapter 12
Reflections on Learning and Teaching in Hong Kong

Susan GANO-PHILLIPS

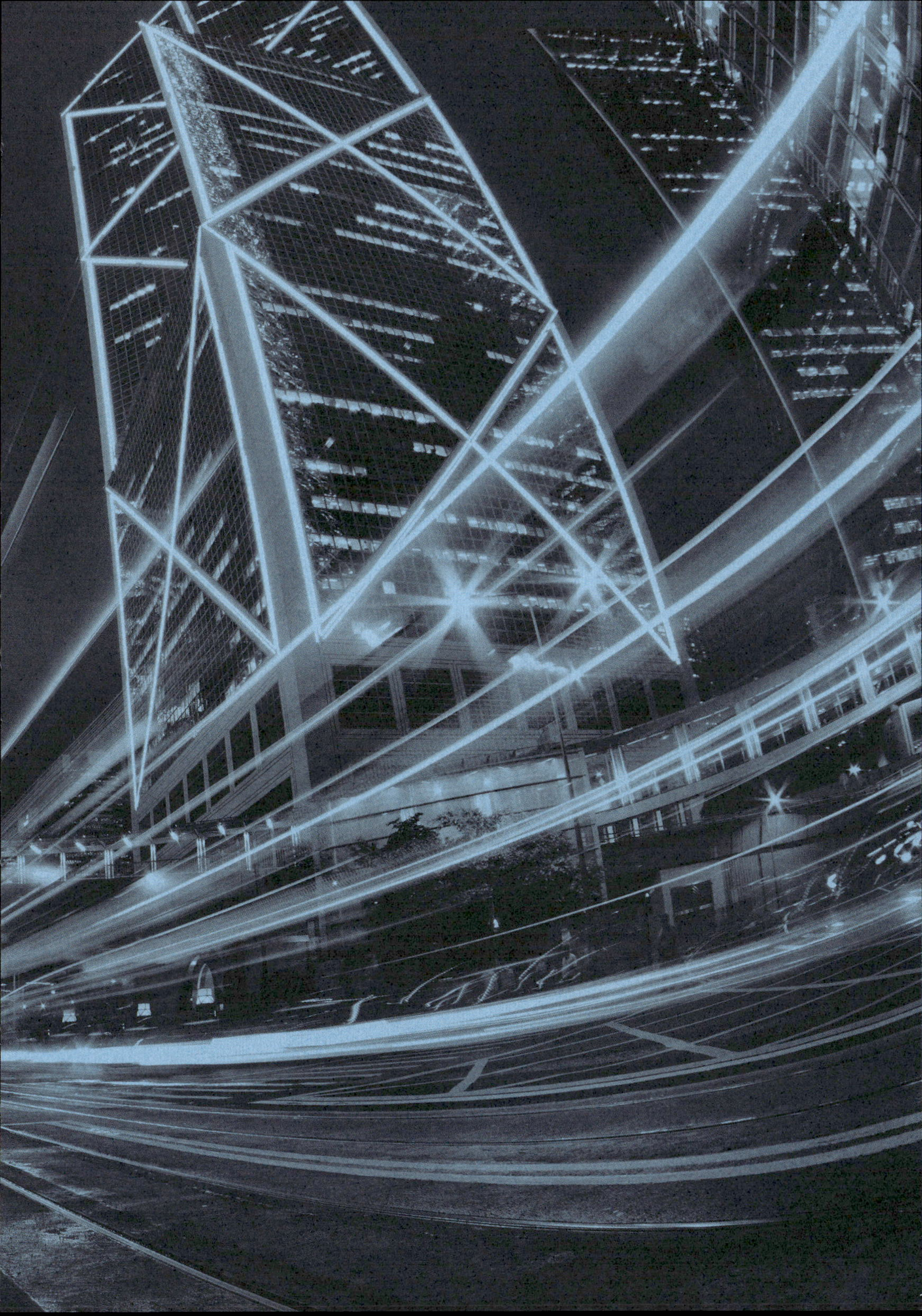

It was an extremely hot early September morning. I had wound my way through the cavernous university building, so large that it is broken into five color coded "zones" to aid in finding one's way around, and I waited in a crowded hallway for the previous class to be dismissed before I entered the classroom. It was a very typical university classroom, by all accounts, containing 54 movable side-arm desks arranged in six wide rows, with a center aisle leading to the front, and a white board and computer/projector set up in one of the front corners at a podium. I was beginning a new class, something I had done tens of times before, with all the normal excitement and anticipation that typically occurs, but this time was different. I was teaching in Hong Kong. I had been invited to team–teach a graduate level course to master's degree students, and in planning for my inclusion in this course, the existing course instructors invited my ideas for new content and teaching approaches.

After introducing ourselves and distributing the syllabus to students, who had dutifully filed into the class and filled nearly all 54 seats in the classroom, it was my turn to present. I had decided that I wanted to introduce an active style of learning to the classroom as the course was designed to prepare graduate students for their teaching roles with undergraduate students in the upcoming semesters, and I wanted to model for these students various ways of engaging others in interaction in the classroom. I was told that students would be unfamiliar with active learning strategies in the classroom (having rarely been asked to respond to professor's questions, work in groups, or actively complete a task and report the outcomes of that task to the larger group). Fearlessly, perhaps naïvely, I launched into my first classroom activity, one which I believed was a fairly low-stakes effort. I asked classmates to work in pairs to answer a simple opinion question, as there had been no prior readings assigned for this first class period ("What do you think motivates student learning?"). Students seemed bewildered and uncomfortable by this request to pair off and discuss an opinion question. The students' response seemed as almost as if I had asked them to turn and engage in long, passionate kiss with a stranger, rather than turn and speak to a fellow student. They stiffened in their chairs and seemed unwilling or unable to turn their heads to either side to engage their classmates. Eventually, after what seemed like minutes, but was more like, about thirty seconds, a few fearless students began to turn toward a neighbor and spoke in soft, whispered tones. Within three minutes, everyone seemed to be paired off and engaged in a quiet conversation of some type. I was thinking, "All right! I've turned the corner—getting these students to engage with one another is not going to be that hard… I wonder why my Hong Kong colleagues predicted I'd have so much trouble with classroom engagement."

Little did I know, my biggest challenge was staring me in the face. As I would typically do in my US classes, after allowing sufficient time for paired discussions, I turned to the class and asked for their reports concerning their discussion, saying something like, "OK everyone. Now that you've had a few minutes to talk about this question of what motivates student learning with a partner, I'd like to hear what answers you came up with." In my experience, this sort of comment invites participation from the class and leads to a nice sharing of ideas from many individuals. After offering that comment, I turned to the class and waited. "They are processing their ideas, sorting through the ideas they had shared with one another," I said to myself. So I waited …. Surely, they had come up with some responses relevant to my question and were just about to share, so I waited. Ok, now I began to panic—I was used to wait time—the time needed for processing and thinking prior to responding to a complex question—but this was getting ridiculous. Ten seconds, twenty seconds, now sixty seconds had passed. "Please, someone answer" I began to think—"I am going to completely embarrass myself in front of my Hong Kong colleagues if my efforts at active learning flop right here and now." So I did what any teacher would do, I restated the question, assuming that I hadn't been clear in asking my question. I thought to myself, students must be hesitant to respond because of the uncertainty I have created in the way I asked the question—after all, I am teaching in English, which is a 2nd or 3rd language to all of these students. "Please, share with me and the class any interesting responses you have had or heard regarding what motivates student learning." And I waited—students shifted nervously in their chairs, almost none making eye contact, and if I turned my gaze in their direction, they most certainly diverted their gaze to their notebooks or the floor. Ten seconds, twenty seconds more. I thought to myself, "Ok, what am I going to do if no one speaks up?" Finally, a faint sound from a student on the aisle in the second row, "My classmate suggested that grading is a significant motivation for students to learn." I repeated back what I had heard the student say—offering, an "Exactly! That's a great idea regarding what motivates student learning," and expanded a bit on the topic of grading as an external or extrinsic motivator for learning. Then a hand was raised in the back row, and the student offered, "My classmate suggested that having some interest in the topic may motivate student learning." And we were off and running ....

Those 80 or 120 seconds of silence—what felt like a lifetime, and brought me perilously through a wide range of emotions—

they provided quite a lesson to me in how different the classroom environment in Hong Kong really is from that in the United States. Had I known the culture in Hong Kong better at that time, that silence would have been perfectly expected—in fact, to have expected something different was very naïve and ethnocentric on my part. Over that year in Hong Kong, I learned a great deal about the educational system, the culture, and the life experiences of typical university students that helped me to appreciate the many reasons why active engagement in the Hong Kong classroom was so challenging. I'd like to tell you about those reasons and explain how developing a more thorough understanding of the factors which were influencing students' behavior helped me to adjust my teaching and helped students' to find new ways to engage in the classroom.

The most immediate reason for the reluctance of students to engage in the classroom can be traced to the history of education within Hong Kong. Students' prior experiences of education are a major influence on their current and future classroom behavior and Hong Kong and mainland Chinese students are accustomed to certain practices that are influenced by instructor philosophies, class sizes, typical teaching techniques, and patterns of assessing learning that do not necessarily promote active classroom engagement, as I had envisioned it.

Philosophically, higher education and thinking about the teaching and learning process has been revolutionized in some places in the world over the past two decades, originating with Barr and Tagg's 1995 article, "From Teaching to Learning—A New Paradigm for Undergraduate Education." As an American educator whose training and early career work occurred since the mid-1990s, I had come to believe that everyone viewed education from this new perspective. The critical change involves a shift from focusing on faculty members' roles as teachers, to an unequivocal focus on students' actual learning—and how faculty members can create climates and conditions that promote student learning. High impact learning practices (Kuh, 2008), first year experiences (Upcraft, Gardner, & Barefoot, 2004), a variety of active learning approaches such as problem-based learning, just in time teaching, cooperative learning, team-based learning, and various forms of experiential learning (e.g., Millis & Cottell, 1995; Duch, Groh, & Allen, 2001) have resulted from this shift toward learner-centered education. However, I quickly learned that the ideas inherent in this approach have been embraced to greater or lesser extents in various places around the world and in differing disciplines. Programs and higher education systems that are accountable to accreditation processes have, for the most part, been quicker to adopt this learner-centered approach than have those not subject to these sorts of external pressures. Thus, in the United States, accreditation processes and increasing government scrutiny of higher education have led to wide scale adoption of this new paradigm—with a variety of curricular and co-curricular reforms helping to accomplish these goals. In Hong Kong however, these ideas have been introduced more recently (in the last five years) and are being adopted in a more piece-meal fashion, by individual faculty members, or by faculty members within a specified program, but rarely at an institutional level. Thus the philosophy of education as student-centric rather than faculty-centric has not become universal in Hong Kong universities.

Another factor influencing students' classroom engagement and behavior is class size in higher education. Like in the United States, there are a wide range of class sizes in Hong Kong universities, with a typical pattern of very large introductory courses, with somewhat smaller, more specialized upper division courses within the various majors. However, Hong Kong classes, on the whole, are considerably larger than in the United States. This trend holds throughout the entire K-16 system. Introductory-level university courses typically involve 200 to 300 or more students, and upper division and graduate courses typically have approximately 50 students per course. While active learning is possible in such classes, these class sizes do not naturally lend themselves to active student participation.

The implications of these somewhat larger class sizes combined with a traditional faculty-centered philosophy of teaching can be seen in the pedagogies or teaching approaches typically employed by faculty, a third factor influencing student engagement in the classroom. Traditional lecture-based courses, where the faculty member is the "sage on the stage" are extremely common in Hong Kong. This is not to say that some faculty are not utilizing innovative active learning strategies within the classroom, but rather, to say that the lecture continues to strongly predominate students' classroom experiences. Even the lecture style itself seems to vary across cultures. Unlike in larger US courses, Hong Kong students are much less likely to interact with the instructor during such courses, as many instructors neither welcome nor tolerate questions. Faculty-student relations are viewed as less warm and more authoritarian than in US classrooms and praise of student behaviors or responses is rare (Hofstede & Hofstede, 2005). Hong Kong students rarely ask questions or speak out in class, and almost never disagree with professors. It might be tempting to interpret students' relative lack of participation in class as a lack of motivation, but in fact, it may reflect historical and deeply-seated cultural differences between the United States and Hong Kong rather than motivational issues.

Much has been written about the differences in student behaviors across Asian and Western classrooms as well. Watkins and Biggs (1996) coined the phrase, the "paradox of the Chinese learner" to help us to understand how apparently similar behaviors in students from different cultures may, in fact, reflect quite different learning processes. This paradox notes that students in Confucian-heritage cultures (including China, Hong Kong, Taiwan, Singapore, Korea, and Japan) are taught in classroom conditions that are not typically related to good learning outcomes according to Western standards, including: large classes, expository methods, harsh classroom climates, and strict norm-referenced assessments. However, despite these learning conditions, Confucian-heritage students typically outperform Western students in some curricular areas (science and math) and have deeper, meaning oriented approaches to learning. Subsequent research has revealed that while Chinese students are perceived as passive rote learners in the classroom, in much the same way that many US students are, Chinese students show high levels of understanding and an ability to see deeper meanings from their classroom and independent learning experiences. It appears that Chinese students focus on understanding while listening to lectures or reading independently whereas Western students focus more on memorizing. When the point of learning is to advance understanding, as it is for Hong Kong students, quiet individual classroom engagement with course materials or instructor lectures can lead to deeper understandings (Dahlin & Watkins, 2000).

A fourth factor influencing students' classroom engagement and behavior relates to students' interactions with one another. On the whole, there is also much less student-to-student interaction in Hong Kong university classrooms than is typical in the United States.

Largely, Hong Kong students attend classes to hear lectures presented by their esteemed faculty and interact very little with the instructor or with one another (Watkins & Biggs, 2001). Hong Kong students may be uncomfortable in unstructured situations or group settings where their roles and responsibilities are ill-defined, in disagreeing with classmates publicly, or in volunteering to lead an initiative or project because such situations call for an individual to assume a leadership role, a position which is not looked upon favorably in the Chinese culture because it requires an act of individualism and self-promotion rather than collective action. The importance attributed to social harmony within the Hong Kong culture influences students' classroom behaviors by suggesting to students that raising their hands or engaging in any behavior which draws attention away from the group and toward a single individual or oneself is to be avoided. Thus, such behaviors fly in the face of the socio-cultural context of Confucian-heritage cultures.

A fifth noteworthy factor that influences Hong Kong students' classroom participation relates to the typical processes used to assess student learning. Traditionally Hong Kong courses have placed a heavy emphasis on standardized, norm-referenced, cumulative examinations as the measure of student performance. It is not uncommon for final essay examinations to count sixty percent or more toward the final course grade. In an effort to provide evidence of the legitimacy of student instruction, I had even heard of some cases where instructors from outside the university who were unaffiliated with specific courses were brought in to write the examination questions for the final exams. Such a strategy was perceived as a rigorous assessment of student learning, though depending on the nature of examination questions generated relative to the course contents presented, may have been completely invalid. These essay examinations were then graded on a normative basis, with a certain percentage of essays being assigned to each of the various possible grades, and without regard to any specific learning criteria that had previously been made known to the students or to the examination writer. This approach to assessment argues for strong individual mastery of the content of the course materials, wherein sharing a common understanding or knowledge base through classroom discussion would not add value to one's performance on examinations.

Experiencing K-12 Educational Culture

There are a number of other, more distal factors, which may influence students' classroom participation and behavior during university-study, beyond those mentioned above. I'd like to talk about the primary and secondary education (K-12) of Hong Kong students as a way of explaining how cultural and societal context influences university students' mindsets and behaviors. I begin with a few anecdotes that demonstrate my beginning awareness of the cultural and social context into which my family was embarking when we decided to move to Hong Kong. I was quickly confronted with a range of school options for my then 6th and 4th grade children—local public schools (taught in Cantonese), private schools (English language, Cantonese, or Mandarin instruction), international schools, religiously-affiliated schools, and others. I also realized almost immediately that I was not entering an educational system that paralleled the one with which I was familiar in the United States. I learned for example, that applications were required for my children

12. Reflections on Learning and Teaching in Hong Kong

There are a wide range of school options for primary and secondary students in Hong Kong

to be admitted to schools and that my timing (seeking a placement 6 months in advance of the need for enrollment) was already putting us at a disadvantage. Application processes varied from school to school but most involved essays, review of school records, recommendations, application fees, and in some cases, in-person assessments of performance—all for admissions for elementary and middle school students! Clearly, I was out of my element and had much to learn about the K-12 education system in Hong Kong.

One of my first lessons was just how significant the demand for high quality education is at the primary and secondary levels in Hong Kong. Many schools I contacted had long waiting lists and

I was discouraged from even applying. Mine was not a unique experience. After moving to Hong Kong, I became acquaintances with a woman who worked in kindergarten admissions at a private religiously-affiliated school each spring. At this school, much like those I had contacted, applications were carefully reviewed, and each applicant and their parent(s) were given a face to face interview and formal assessment. Despite significant annual fees for study at this elementary school (in excess of US$6,000), the school admitted only one-third of its more than 400 applicants for kindergarten! The consequence of this high demand for quality education is felt far beyond admission to elementary schools—in fact, it is the bedrock for subsequent competition and high-stakes testing among students that is felt throughout the rest of the educational system. Historically, Hong Kong students have been "tracked" at a relatively early age toward university preparation or alternative educational goals. Nationwide, standardized, high-stakes testing begins with students around 5th grade and those test results determine which students are placed on a "University track." Further, until 2009, students were tracked into relatively narrow and more specialized secondary school education focusing on either "Arts and Humanities" or "Science and Math." Since 2009, secondary students are being provided a more general program of study. This tracking and high stakes testing culminates in a national examination known as the Hong Kong Advanced Level Examination (HKALE), which, in combination with the Joint University Programmes Admissions System (JUPAS), determines students' admission to university study. Thus, while it is uncommon for United States students to give serious consideration toward college until they are well into high school, students in Hong Kong are narrowing their focus and experiencing the pressures of selection at much earlier times in their educational progression. My elementary and middle school aged children quickly felt this increasing emphasis and pressure to compete, through the high levels of co-curricular and extra-curricular engagement in which their classmates participated. Children often were scheduled for language, music, gymnastics, or fitness classes every weekday after school, lasting into the evening hours. Even during lunch and recess at school, children routinely signed up for web design, digital photography, language, fitness, or cooking classes. While not typical, one of my son's 4th grade classmates was already studying four languages—imagine being quadralingual at age ten!

Another phenomenon which differs significantly between Hong Kong and the United States and which influences students' interactions with one another is the fact that Hong Kong students

Classroom experiences in Hong Kong are different from that in the United States

typically do not attend schools within a limited geographical region near their homes, but rather, students tend to be dispersed broadly throughout the entire territory of Hong Kong, based on their test scores. Thus, students who perform very strongly in the Math/Science area or in the Humanities area are, because of their tracking system, offered positions in schools with strong reputations for those areas of the curriculum. It is not uncommon for students to use public transportation (over ninety percent of all transport is public in Hong Kong—buses, trains, etc., or private school bus) for thirty, sixty, or even ninety minutes, one way, to attend a school which their test scores have allowed admission. It is also not uncommon for families that have two or more children to have those children attending different schools throughout Hong Kong. These phenomena have implications for social contacts between children attending school together as well as for the connections of siblings and families with schools. Having been through an educational system which does not emphasize long term social relationships among peers results in students having different interests and motivations for forming friendships or relationships among peers in university classes.

A third feature of Hong Kong primary and secondary education that appears rather trivial at first glance but which may actually signal a deeper contextual difference between Hong Kong and the United States students is the fact that students in all primary and secondary schools in Hong Kong wear uniforms to school on a daily basis. Sometimes these are simple traditional smocks and/or white slacks and shirts, while in other cases a colored dress or even sweaters, polo shirts, and scarves or neck ties are part of the outfit. Uniformity is the name of the game for all children in the K-12 system—students are expected to comply with a strict dress code, even with respect to their outerwear (coats, jackets, or hats that are worn), and with their clothes for Physical Education classes. Consistency, right down to the socks or shoes one might wear, is tightly regulated by the schools. In many ways this use of uniforms as a way of signaling conformity and uniformity was unfamiliar to my family—while some schools in the United States require uniforms, most students attending public schools are free to wear almost anything within a broad dress code approved by the school board. The use of uniforms may speak to the British colonial heritage of Hong Kong as well as to the collectivism and efforts to promote social harmony which pervade Confucian-heritage cultures throughout Asia. Individualism and self-promotion, whether through clothing or behavior within a school or university classroom, are strongly discouraged in the K-12 system.

A final variable that may impact student engagement in the classroom relates to students' views of the purposes of undergraduate education. Hong Kong students' views are not unlike most of the rest of the world: Hong Kong students tend to see higher education as a ticket to a career and employment security. However, the reasons to seek a career and job security seem to differ somewhat across cultures. Americans tend to focus on education to allow *personal gain*—wealth, status, career achievement, etc. On the other hand, Hong Kong students, whose culture has focused on collectivist ideals for centuries, tend to view education as *a means to develop society as a whole,* with less regard for personal gain (Watkins & Biggs, 1996, p. 26). Historically, a university education in Hong Kong has meant a job that could provide a good wage and social stability for the graduate and his or her family, including adult parents as they aged, in a society where relatively few public support services exist for the elderly. This stands in stark contrast to the United States where a social security administration and Medicare offer a basic social net for elderly family members. So while Hong Kong graduates seek to earn a good wage, their primary motivation is not status or personal recognition. Rather, it is due to fulfillment of a family or social obligation to provide for one's aging parents. This ability to care for oneself and one's aging parents has been essential in a society where public support of the elderly has not been substantial.

However, multiple factors in the Hong Kong society are beginning to chip away at the perception of undergraduate education as simply facilitating job security. Globalization and recent economic crises have led both employers and students to question the value of a university education. Employers in Hong Kong as well as throughout Asia and much of the rest of the world are lamenting the lack of adequate preparation of students for the work force. Employers are increasingly noting the need for greater creativity, critical thinking, problem-solving skills, inter-cultural sensitivity and communication skills, and team-work in the graduates that they employ. These transferable or "soft" skills have traditionally not been the focus of the specialized 3-year undergraduate degree programs in Hong Kong. Students, while not clamoring for change, quietly lament the emphasis on mass production of graduates and rote-learning which have dominated their educational experiences. There is increasing recognition that the vast stores of knowledge being developed in university students today are quickly becoming obsolete and are an insufficient preparation for the uncertain and complex futures which graduates face. Together, employers, parents, students, and society are coming to recognize the mismatch between the needs of society and the preparation of undergraduates (Weimer, 2002). This is, therefore, the point where more active learning strategies and student-centered approaches to education may have the most impact—in preparing students for the sorts of employment opportunities that will be available to them in the 21st century marketplace. In describing how active learning approaches can better prepare students for career success (whether for personal gain or for social and family stability), educators may find a common ground for changing the approaches currently used in classrooms throughout Hong Kong.

Looking back now, I can see how my personal and family experiences in the K-12 system highlighted several key themes about education in Hong Kong that, I later discovered, rang true in the higher education system: there is high demand for education leading to fierce competition for admissions; students are not place-bound for education, instead they go wherever the opportunities and high-stakes testing and assessment practices allow; students are accustomed to uniformity/conformity within the schools as exemplified in the K-12 system by strict standards of dress codes, and students' views about the purpose and value of education are influenced by societal and cultural expectations. Each of these factors also influences how and whether students feel comfortable engaging actively with one another or with the professor during university study.

Cultural Context and Teaching and Learning

As a psychologist, I found my work to improve teaching and learning at a university, as well as my life experiences as a whole, to be fascinating and frequently challenging my previously held assumptions and beliefs. Having had the opportunity to immerse myself in the educational system of Hong Kong for a year, I came to appreciate the importance of context—culture, place, and time —in defining teaching and learning experiences. To be certain, the stories and scripts of teaching and learning in Hong Kong are different than those in the United States at every level of the educational system. It was fascinating to watch my own children test out and discover things about their implicit expectations for learning and for school experiences through their everyday activities. I watched their bewilderment at not being able to "have a friend over" because their friends schedules were so filled with scheduled extracurricular activities that they had no time for idle "hanging out." I was intrigued by their assessment of collectivist values—particularly as it related to something as mundane as wearing school uniforms and I observed with intrigue, how their reactions and feelings about uniforms changed over time. Before our move, my pre-teen daughter was perhaps most distraught by the thought of losing her identity by being forced to wear a school uniform than by any other aspect of the move we were making to half-way around the world. By two months into the school year, her views had changed dramatically, to one expressing genuine appreciation for the uniforms that allowed an emphasis to be placed on learning rather than on clothes or social status. Finally, I took great pleasure in seeing my children learn about themselves and their cultural history through their daily interactions, which challenged many previously-held assumptions.

Through both my observations of my own children, and through my varied interactions with the higher education system in Hong Kong, I have come to realize the importance of understanding and making explicit the features of the context in which interpretations are being made. I learned that differences in teaching or learning practices are not better or worse—they are simply something that requires consideration and interpretation. I found, for example, that some aspects of American education that I thought were common to all educational experiences were actually quite American-centric ideas—warm and open faculty-student relationships, broad use of criterion-referenced testing, motivations for classroom behavior, and even basic strategies for learning were all surprisingly different than I had expected in Hong Kong. I suppose you could say I learned as much about myself and the American context as I did with the Hong Kong one through this experience of studying our differences. And the experiences have made me a more reflective teacher and learner than I could ever have been without having had the opportunity to work in a different cultural context. Rather than rushing to judgment or assuming I understand an issue within the teaching or learning process, I have learned to be a more careful observer and to ask questions. After all, attempting to solve a problem which is poorly defined or understood, or which does not make sense in a particular context, is likely a frustrating and futile effort.

In closing, it is clear that that the behavior of students in classrooms around the world is highly influenced by their prior schooling, their history and upbringing, and the specific cultural values and traditions which define their lives. My Hong Kong teaching colleagues were right, that in the absence of a clear and compelling explanation for using an alternate approach in the classroom, engagement would be difficult. In the end, my direct explanation to students as to why we were engaging in an experimental approach in the classroom combined, perhaps, with their willingness to help out a confused and bewildered foreign teacher, and my ability to create a safe and rewarding space in which to share ideas, allowed active learning to win out. As the class progressed, my Hong Kong colleagues were able to ask and obtain more and more independent thinking and action from our students. We modified our approaches in slight ways that honored aspects of students' histories within the Hong Kong context—for example, rather than asking students to report on their own ideas, we asked students to share good ideas that they had heard offered by their group members. In doing so, we respected the cultural traditions that suggest bringing attention to oneself is boastful and unproductive for the harmony of the group, but instead allowed students the ability to focus on the "good ideas" rather than people to whom the ideas were associated. Within three consecutive class sessions, my fellow instructors and I had shaped students' willingness to volunteer ideas as part of the classroom routine, by recognizing and respecting their cultural expectations. Eventually, these students began offering their own ideas, opinions, and responses to instructor-generated questions. I am hopeful they are now doing the same with the classes for which they have instructional responsibilities.

References

Barr, R. B., & Tagg, J. "From teaching to learning—A new paradigm for undergraduate education." *Change* (Nov-Dec,1995): 13–25.

Dahlin, B. & Watkins, D. A. "The role of repetition in the processes of memorizing and understanding: A comparison of the views of Western and Chinese secondary school students in Hong Kong." *British Journal of Educational Psychology*, 70 (2000): 65–84.

Duch, B. J., Groh, S. E., & Allen, D. E., eds. *The Power of Problem-Based Learning.* Sterling, VA: Stylus, 2001

Hofstede, G., & Hofstede, G. J. *Cultures and Organizations: Software of the Mind.* 2nd edition. New York: McGraw-Hill, 2005

Kuh, G. *High-Impact Educational Practices: What They Are, Who Has Access to Them, and Why They Matter.* Washington, DC: Association of American Colleges and Universities, 2008.

Millis, B. J., & Cottell, P. G. *Cooperative Learning for Higher Education Faculty.* Washington, DC: American Council on Education/Oryx Press Series on Higher Education, 1997.

Upcraft, M. L., Gardner, J. N., & Barefoot, B. O. *Challenging and Supporting the First-Year Student: A Handbook for Improving the First Year of College.* San Francisco: Jossey-Bass, 2004.

Watkins, D. A., & Biggs, J. B., eds. *Teaching the Chinese Learner: Psychological and Pedagogical Perspectives.* Hong Kong: Comparative Education Research Center, University of Hong Kong, 2001.

Watkins, D. A., & Biggs, J. B., eds. *The Chinese Learner: Cultural, Psychological, and Contextual Influences.* Hong Kong: Comparative Education Research Center, University of Hong Kong, 1996.

Chapter 13
Rhetoric and the Art of Mid-Level Administration in Hong Kong

Paul HANSTEDT

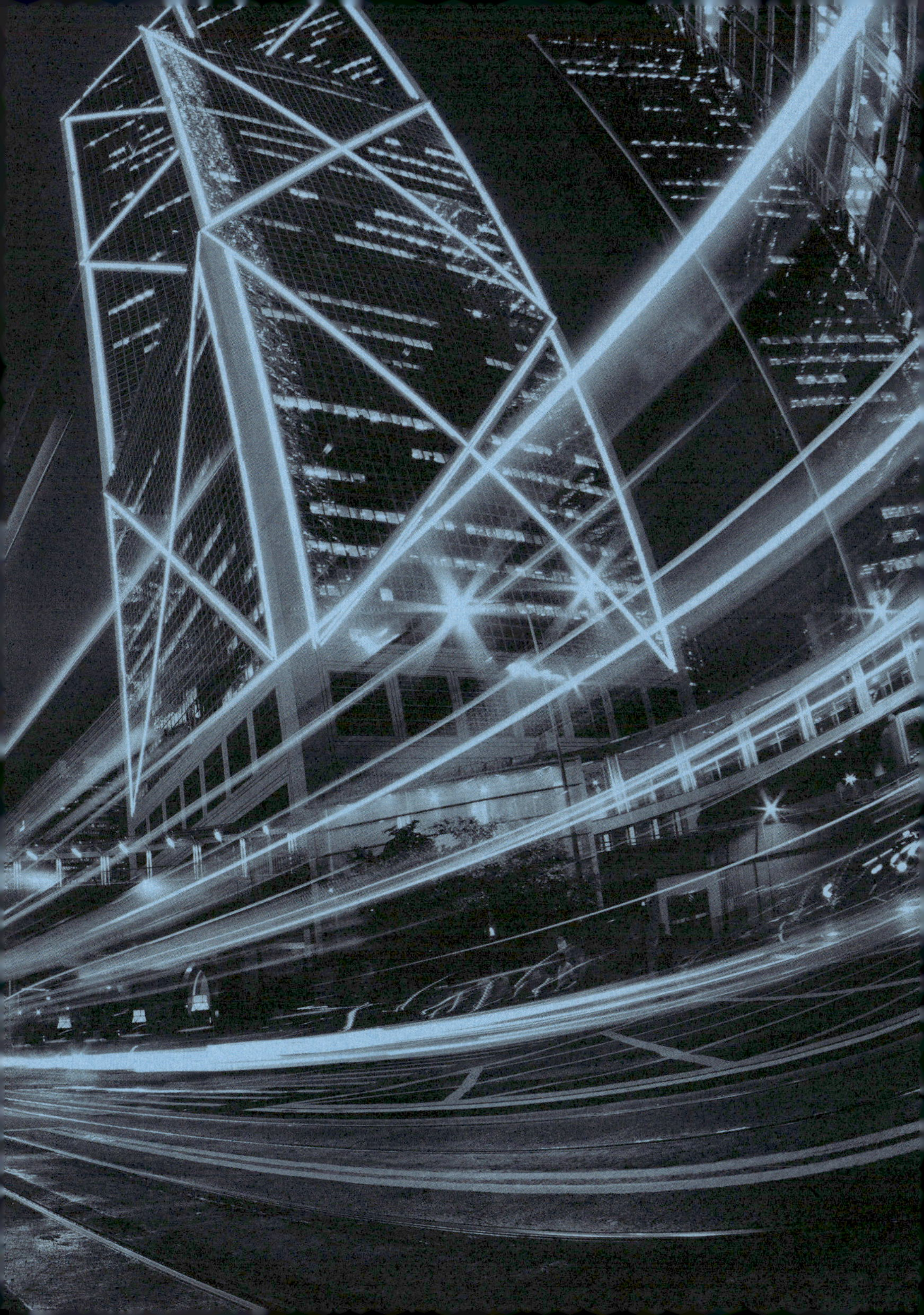

I was walking back from a departmental briefing the other day—filling in a group of faculty about the new GE (General Education) program at my host institution—when I made the mistake of asking my colleague William how he felt it went.

He paused. "It went well," he said. And then he paused again.

I frowned. Though a Hong Konger, William usually says what he thinks. These pauses—and his slightly constipated look—were unusual.

"Just 'well'?" I said. We'd done nearly a dozen of these briefings in the last few weeks; this one, as far as I was concerned, had been better than most.

"Don't take this the wrong way ...." William bit his lip. "It was very good, but at points, just points mind you, you seemed a little—" Here, he pinched his thumb and forefinger together, leaving the smallest of gaps. "Just a little—and only at times—just a tiny bit—"

"Tell me," I said, "I'm a grown up. I can take it."

"—condescending."

I hit him. Hard.

Okay, no, I didn't. The funny thing is, his words didn't hurt as much as you might expect. For one thing, I enjoyed watching William squirm—that just doesn't happen very often. For another thing, I knew beyond a shadow of a doubt that of all the emotions I carried into that meeting, condescension wasn't one of them. I like my work, yes. And I know Gen Ed very well, having worked in it and lived it for a quarter of a century. Was I enthusiastic? Yes. Maybe a little too enthusiastic? Likely. Long-winded? Most certainly. My whole life I've dreamed of being the man of few words, but as you can tell from the length of this article, that seldom happens. But deliberately condescending? Positive I knew more than anyone else in the room? Absolutely not. My host institution is filed with brilliant people, many of whom have published brilliant books. I know when I'm out of my league.

William's next words helped a bit. "When you go into the part of the presentation where you ask them questions—you know what I mean?"

"Uh-huh."

"You just go into it right away. No pause. Just put the slide up and start questioning them. I don't know, maybe you could just—" He gave a shrug. "Just pause for a minute and say, 'Now, if we might consider this for a moment.' Ask them. Invite them. Don't tell them."

He watched me out of the corner of one eye, the afternoon sun glancing off his glasses. What we were experiencing, obviously, was a moment that, if not illustrative of east and west, certainly demonstrated how Americans differ from Hong Kongers. Americans want you to cut to the chase. Don't waste their time. "Pause for a minute"? "Perhaps we can consider"? About as un-American as bombing Ben & Jerry's.

But when in Hong Kong ...

"Okay," I said to William. "Anything else?"

Aristotle says that every rhetorical situation—written or spoken—has three parts: Writer, Topic and Audience. Change one of these and everything else in the situation shifts: An e-mail by a college kid to his grandmother about a party sounds completely different than an e-mail about the same party sent to a friend. And an e-mail to the friend about a funeral will sound even more different.

A lot of people think that for students, topic is the tricky part. But that's not true. What really screws up student writers is the teacher standing at the other end, staring at them, red pen in one hand, grade book in the other.

Audience sucks. And not just for college kids: it's because of audience that we lose sleep at night. It's because of audience that we try desperately to imagine folks in their underwear. It's because of audience that lots of writers drink too much.

Anyone who's ever had to write a memo to their boss knows the terror of audience. At moments like this we don't even consider imagining friendly readers. No, at high-stress moments like these, we think about all the jerks who ever beat us up in high school, all the women who ever laughed in our faces when we tried to chat them up, every teacher we ever had who frowned when we tried to answer a question in class and, when we were finished, stared at us silently for a minute, biting their lower lip.

Making this all the more difficult is the fact that Hong Kong can be a tough audience. On the one hand, Hong Kong is known for its obsession with brand names. The newspapers say this. The students say this. My colleagues say this. Strolling through the malls here is like being in an E! fashion special: Christian Dior, Prada, Gucci, Chanel, Yves Saint Laurent, and Versace and a couple dozen brands I've never heard of and can't pronounce.

Some I've talked take this a step further and argue that Hong Kong academics are similarly obsessed with brand name scholars—

that is to say, what counts is how many books you've published and your reputation in the field. The quality of those books, the sales of those books, the relevance of those books to the work of an academic institution—all of that is secondary. This is in contrast to the States, where, after decades of increasing publication demands for tenure, some institutions and organizations—the 10,000-member Modern Language Association, for instance—are starting to question the value of the monograph.

All of that said, I can't say I've actually noticed much publication obsession in Hong Kong myself: while a lot of the people I work with here have books most seem to recognize that it's the quality of the scholarship that counts, not the length of the CV.

But still, there are some who don't see it that way. "All people care about around here," a friend of mine told me once, "is what level you got hired at. If you got hired at assistant or associate, fine. But if you got hired over them, then watch out."

Titles matter in Hong Kong. I'm a Full Professor at my home institution, having reached or surpassed every benchmark necessary for that rank. The thing is, the standards are different at my small liberal arts college—teaching means EVERYTHING, service counts for a lot, and publications are important, but not the end-game. So when I got to Hong Kong and the matter of making my business card came up, my boss asked me how I wanted to be titled.

"I don't care," I said. "Professor, I guess."

This seemed like a fairly innocuous answer: everyone in the States is called Professor, including adjuncts with Ph.D.s. But my colleague in Hong Kong looked a little uncomfortable. "This might be difficult," she said. "We would need to get approval." And then she went on to explain that here, "Professor" is a term reserved only for the best of the best, the top in their field.

The flip-side of all of this is that, as much as title, rank, and brand matter in Hong Kong, so does humility. On the face of it, this is a culture where putting oneself forward as superior is not tolerated. Eugene Eoyang, a distinguished professor in comparative literature and the former GE director for Lingnan University, talks about how asking for volunteers in the Hong Kong classroom can lead to dead silence. No student will raise his or her hand, because to speak out is to put yourself forward as superior, to make the implicit claim that your thoughts matter more than those of your classmates.

I've seen this in my briefings. When my colleagues and I first designed the GE presentation, I insisted on including slides that asked the departmental members to participate in the discussion. "This is how the brain works," I said. "If we don't have the audience act on the information we're presenting, they'll forget it the minute we leave."

Nice theory. The first time I gave the presentation and came to the slides with "activities," I was greeted with stony silence.

"I'm sure you all have some nice ideas," I said, after waiting a good 15 seconds.

No reply. Just determinedly blank looks.

"Anyone?" I said.

More silence.

My face was burning. I smiled desperately. "Bueller?"

Nothing.

I was just about to point to the back of the room, shout, "Fire!" then run out when they looked, when, finally, the chair of the department raised his hand.

He was an American.

Given these two extremes—the brand name and the humble brand—it's hard for a newcomer to know how to approach his audience. It's worth noting that this isn't an issue exclusive to Hong Kong: a colleague at a university in Thailand recently mentioned the difficulties visiting scholars often had at his school: "They know the information," he told me. "They just don't know how to deliver it."

Which would have made me feel better, I guess, but for the fact that knowing this didn't really help me function any better in Hong Kong. Three months into my stay, I had to give my first campus-wide talk on designing more effective writing assignments. This is a talk I've given a million times before, with a reasonable success. Now, though, I worried: would I come off as condescending? Would people respect my experience? I'd already attended one seminar where the speaker was eviscerated even before finishing his first slide. What if, when I was talking about Aristotle's rhetorics, some hot-shot professor—a real professor, mind you, not a phony like me—raised his hand and said, "Actually, new research has proven that Aristotle never existed"—and then rattled off some study I'd never heard of?

In the end, the workshop went fine. There were a few people there I knew, lots of people I didn't, and no one cried, not even me. I tried out William's advice and began each of the actively workshoppy moments with more of an invitation and less of a command. It felt a little gimmicky, but people spoke up a bit more and there were some really interesting assignments that emerged.

I still had two more of the briefings to do, however. Making things all the harder was the fact that one of the departmental chairs—a kind Singaporean who was a concert pianist in addition to being a (real!) professor—wanted me to not just give a briefing, but run a workshop. And, as I've mentioned, in the past the workshop elements of the briefing had always been the stickiest points.

One department member even told a colleague of mine that these active components were insulting. "We're not students," he said. "Don't treat us like we are."

Indeed, as the semester wore on, and despite my near-certainty that without active engagement, we were running a 90% risk that folks would simply forget what we told them, I had pretty much stripped all active learning out of the presentation.

Now, though, I dutifully went back to my slideshow and put some of these activities back in. I tinkered, though, with how I introduced the "work" part of "workshop," deleting titles like, "Which topics would make good GE courses?" and replacing them with titles like "And now, if you'd be so kind as to consider …"

And I changed what happened after these exercises. Rather than have the participants report to the group as a whole, I asked them to work in pairs. And then, rather than asking folks to offer their own results, I asked if anyone would like to volunteer the results of a colleague. After all, it may not be humble to mention your own ideas, but it can be entirely gracious to suggest that a friend of yours has achieved something noteworthy.

I also changed how I introduced myself. I'd struggled with this all year. Early on, I'd begun by talking about the Fulbright, how happy I was to be in Hong Kong, etc. etc. This felt stupid and artificial, even though it was true. Later, I talked about the philosophy behind the curricular revision and how I saw my role as a consultant. Also fake. By mid-semester, I'd taken to strolling into the room in a long black robe and hood, striking a single, tubular bell tuned to high "C," and chanting mournfully. And more recently, I'd given up on introducing myself or the project all together, simply walking in and glaring at everyone, daring them to challenge me. None of this seemed to work (though with the chanting, it's true, I at least had their attention).

What I did for my final talk with the art department, though, was begin by offering two confessions—one that I was going to have them do a little writing, and that I was doing this not because I wanted to make them feel like students, but because we really wanted proposals from their department and this was one way to ensure that we were all moving in the same direction. The other confession was that I myself had begun university as a music major.

When I said this, the group broke into applause. They seemed genuinely pleased to have among them yet another brilliant scholar-artist, just like themselves. I had to hold up my hand:

"The confession part, though, is that I was such a bad trumpet player that I had to switch and become an English professor."

They laughed and we launched into the workshop.

And it was wonderful. I knew this even before William told me so the next day: you could just tell by the faculty interaction, by the quality of the questions, by the wonderful ideas the participants came up with in just a few minutes. A lot of the success of this particular briefing, I know, was because of the chemistry of the department, their attitude toward general education, their willingness to take some risks in front of their colleagues.

Beyond that, I'm tempted to offer some insight about what all of this taught me about faculty development, about culture, about myself: how I finally found my true, humble self, for instance, or about how sometimes we have to go somewhere different to find who we really are. Or about how taking risks and exposing oneself is an essential part of saying anything that's truly meaningful. Or about how you can't expect anybody else to take risks if you're not going to.

I'd like to say all of those things, and much much more. Really I would.

But that wouldn't be humble.

What I'll do instead is tell you one more story:

Three weeks after the Fine Arts event, I bumped into the acting director of my program. "How is everything?" she said.

Wonderful, I told her. It was great to be done with the departmental briefings and move on to other, less repetitious stuff.

"These are very tough," she said. "Not much fun. People don't listen to what you're saying, then they want to know why their courses get turned down."

That was true, I said. "But even so, this last one with the art department went great."

I went on, explaining how engaged everyone had been, how active the conversation was. She listened, nodding politely, then put her hand on my arm.

"I know," she said. "But even so, after this event, one of the colleagues comes up to me and says, 'Who is this foreigner who comes to our department? Why does he waste all our time by talking about himself?'"

Stage Five
Cross-cultural Movements

Chapter 14

Seeing/Doing Chinese History from Two Sides: Hong Kong and the United States

David PONG

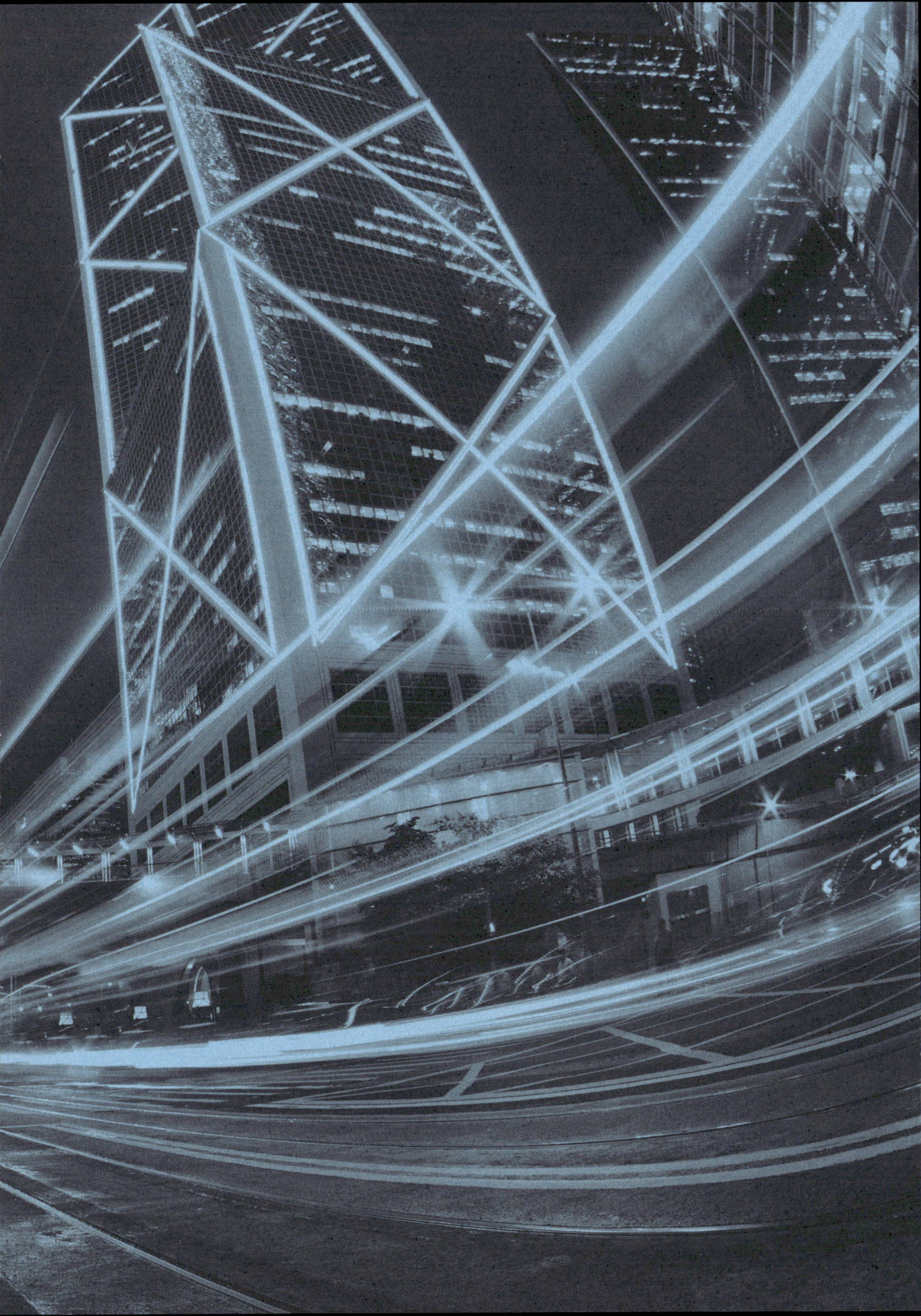

Bringing coal to Newcastle! This is exactly what it appears to be—an American scholar teaching Chinese history in Hong Kong, a place where Chinese history, at least in part, was made. Am I an imposter, or an imposer? Imposter in that I might be claiming to know more about China and its history than what can be offered by my colleagues in Hong Kong, that I actually have something to "teach"? Imposer because I am blatantly projecting my views of China and Chinese history on the local population—at least those who happened to cross my path?

Following the publication of the *Encyclopedia of Modern China* (Scribners & Sons, August 2009), of which I am the Editor-in-Chief, an interviewer quizzed me about the large number of contributors hailing from Hong Kong. The answer was easy—there are few other places in the world where one can find a denser concentration of China experts on a per capita basis. Do Beijing and Shanghai have more? Possibly, but I would not bet on it. What is certain, however, is that Hong Kong does have a high proportion of China experts schooled in modern research methods and possessing of a cosmopolitan outlook. There is truly a wealth of local talents. It begs the question, one more time, why bring coal to Newcastle?

I was born in Hong Kong, brought up partly in China (Guangzhou/Canton), but mainly in Hong Kong, where I finished high school, and went on to the School of Oriental and African Studies, University of London, to study "Far Eastern History." More than two-thirds of my life was spent outside of China and Hong Kong. My most formative years were split between Hong Kong and London. All my adult life was whiled away in the United States, with a three-year hiatus at the Australian National University at Canberra, Downunder, and more recently, a year as a Fulbright scholar-in-residence at the Chinese

14. Seeing/Doing Chinese History from Two Sides: Hong Kong and the United States

University of Hong Kong. An imposter or an imposer? Guilty as charged?

Let's begin from where it matters. My early years of schooling were nothing but chaotic, sometimes even traumatic. Following the end of the Pacific War, in the late 1940s and early 1950s, my father taught at Lingnan University, a private university in Guangzhou (Canton) established by American missionaries at the end of the 19th century. Given the political uncertainties at the time, my parents deemed it wise for my mother to hold on to a secure teaching job in neighboring Hong Kong, where their families had settled for generations. This arrangement, both awkward and inconvenient, was nonetheless a necessity in case we had to move back to Hong Kong at a moment's notice if things did not work out in Canton. Thus as a child, I was shunted between the two cities, hopping from school to school, sometimes repeating a year, other times skipping one, and in one case, dropping a year, all depended on when and where I could find an empty seat in a classroom in overcrowded Hong Kong! Because elementary schools in China did not teach much English, every time I found myself in Hong Kong, I could only be placed in a "Chinese" school, where Chinese was the language of instruction. In this British Crown Colony, it was a given that the Anglo-Chinese Schools, where English was the medium of instruction, were considered superior. Gaining admission to these schools was hard and certainly out of the reach of a peripatetic kid with no prior knowledge of the English language. Still, I am sure I learned something in the schools I attended, though what I actually did learn no longer resides in my memory. The highlights of these years, instead, consisted of wandering freely after school in the spacious and beautiful campus of Lingnan. For reasons that could not really

St. Paul's College is one of the oldest Anglo-Chinese schools in Hong Kong

be adequately grasped by a child in his tender age, some of my father's students at Lingnan seemed quite fond of me, and a couple of the teachers of the elementary school attached to the university also doted on me. But these were fuzzy feelings from even more fuzzy memories.

The moment of truth finally arrived when it came time for us, as a family, to make the hard choice—to settle in Hong Kong. It was decided that I should get into a good school, which meant my father's alma mater. St. Paul's College, one of the oldest schools, was also one of the best in this British Crown Colony. It was, of course, one of those Anglo-Chinese schools in which all subjects, except Chinese literature and history, were (and they still are) taught in English. To enter the school, one must pass an extremely competitive entrance examination, comprising in the first instance a test in English. "Dictation." In this exercise, the lector would read a piece of English prose at fairly normal pace, followed by a second reading, phrase by phrase, during which the young aspirants would try to write down the text. It concludes with a final reading, again at a normal pace, for the pupils to go over their piece and fill in what they might have missed. Those who passed (and many didn't) were then given tests in Chinese and mathematics the following week.

As noted, I had been studying in "Chinese" schools up to this point, and had only just begun to learn my first words of English before taking this grueling entrance exam at St. Paul's. My last days at Lingnan Elementary School at Canton consisted of lessons using flash cards with pictures of chair, table, and window. "This is a chair," "This is a table," are about the level at which I could function. My parents tried their best to prepare me for the St. Paul's entrance exam. But ignorance was bliss. I had no idea what was about to hit me.

On the day of the exam, hundreds of aspiring kids showed up—so many that they had to put the overflow into the Headmaster's office. I was among one of these fifteen to twenty kids. My father accompanied me to the room, and recognized the lector, a Mr. Lam, who was also an alumnus of St. Paul's, probably of my father's generation. The "Dictation" began. It took me no time to realize that my knowledge of the English language was not up to the challenge. I got my name right, and started writing, "The …", the rest went by me just like that. After an indeterminate amount of time, which, as one might imagine, felt like eternity, we had to submit our work. Then, all of a sudden, I totally lost control of my emotions and

The certificate of St. Paul's College in 1929

St. Paul's College
HONGKONG

This is to certify that *Pong Tak Ming* was a student in the College from *Sept., 1921* to *Nov., 1928*. On leaving he was in Class *I* and at his last examination was *1st* out of *18* boys.

He bore *a good* character

A. D. Stewart
Principal.

Date *Jan. 31st 1929*

burst out in tears. It must have been quite a commotion, as the Headmaster, who happened to pass by, inquired as to what was the matter. Mr. Lam told him, "That is James Pong's son …" I did not understand the rest, but anyone could have guessed what was said.

Days later, and they were very, very long days, my parents took me back to St. Paul's to see if my name was on the bulletin board— among those qualified to take the rest of the entrance examination. But how could that be since I handed in a blank? Well, because I was James Pong's son, I was given a chance! As I found out many years later, my father was well respected among the St. Paul's alumni—he was dux three years in a row, an unprecedented achievement! A dux was the head boy, later known as "Head Prefect." So, James Pong's son was given a second chance. He passed the tests in mathematics and Chinese and entered Primary 5.

I discovered on the first day of school that I was among the 81 new entrants, divided into two classes of 40 and 41, respectively. I was, as you might have guessed, in the class with 41 pupils. Everyone except me had passed the entrance examination, only I sneaked in through passing only the Chinese and the mathematics tests! James Pong's son did not stand in the way of a truly deserving pupil, however. As the 41st pupil in the class, I was not officially enrolled! To prevent schools from profiteering, no classrooms in Hong Kong were allowed to have more than 40 students. Inspectors from the Education Department would pay unheralded visits to schools to enforce the rule. To avoid being caught, I would sit next to the closet, and upon the school's janitor's signal I would shove my desk into the closet and take a leak. Attrition allowed me to become a legitimate pupil the second year when I was promoted to Primary 6. By that time, I had caught up somewhat, and was placed 21st in a class of 40.

The first semester was hard. I had no clue. Even mathematics was taught in English! In literature, we studied drama such as *Cinderella* or *Julius Caesar*. Even when rendered in simplified English, they were hard, and we had to memorize them, line by line! We would be called by name, stand up, given a role, and recite. "David Pong, you will play 'Stepmother' today; Desmond Yee, 'Stepsister,' Anthony Lee, 'The Prince,' and so on." Forget your line once, you remain standing. Forget twice, stand on the chair. Thrice, stand on the desk. I spent many hours on the desk!

I studied hard, but so did everyone else. There was tons of

homework. Studying till 10:00 p.m. or even 11:00 p.m. was common. Because everything (except Chinese literature and history) was taught in English, I really had to struggle. It did not take long before my Chinese and even mathematics—the two subjects which I passed on the entrance examination—began to fall behind. By the time I entered middle school, I had to have a tutor to help me in these subjects. I would go to her at the YWCA on Breezy Terrace for an hour or so on my way home. I would walk and save my 10 cents bus fare for a popsicle. It was my reward.

The curriculum was heavily academic, all geared towards the taking of the School Leaving Certificate Examinations at the end of the Fifth Form (after five years of middle/high school). It was not all work and no play, however. On a weekly basis, we had one 40-minute class each of art (mostly painting), woodwork, music (mainly singing), physical education, scripture (the Holy Bible in basic English) and chapel. Because of my childhood at Lingnan, where I spent a lot of time running around—my mother claimed that she could never find me before dinner time—I was somewhat athletic and had good ball sense. At St. Paul's, it took little for me to become a member of the school basketball team, table tennis team, tennis team, and track and field team! But our approach to these "competitive sports" was quite amateurish and laid back. Our 4 x 100 relay team practised passing the baton once before the annual inter-school competition. In tennis and table tennis, we were entirely on our own. It was only in basketball that the team practised together several times during the season.

With each passing year, the School Certificate Examinations loomed larger and larger. Rote learning was the time honored approach. Most of us felt that it was not really a smart way to go about it, but it was a safe approach. Besides, most of our teachers taught from the text books anyway. Because I was so poor in English to begin with, I spent a lot of time on grammar. By about Form Two or Three, I had it so well under my belt that Teacher Sung used to say, if anyone in the class could tell the page number in which past participles were discussed in the grammar book, David Pong was the one! The truth was, "Grammar King" Sung was truly an inspiring teacher, so much so that, decades later, one of our classmates spent his own money to order a reprint of the grammar book in his memory, as Sung did not author one of his own.

But how does one excel if everyone memorized the same stuff? My first breakthrough experience came in geography classes. Map reading and drawing liberated one from the text. How does one determine from an ordnance survey map that there was an escarpment in this or that part of Yorkshire? Yes, Yorkshire, England! It was an Anglo-Chinese school after all. Or, how does one draw a contour map of an imaginary volcanic region? (My geography teacher, Mrs. Christine Speak, will be jumping with joy when she reads this). My next revelation came from a rather unlikely source—our scripture classes, which were intended partly to impart the message of Christianity and partly to have just another lesson in English. Whatever the intentions, it was in reality our first ever opportunity to study an ancient text, and for me a kind of historical document, something that could be approached with a critical eye and subjected to interpretation. Somehow, our study of ancient Chinese texts never led us down the same line of inquiry. To this day, I still wonder whether this was indeed the case, or whether we, in the atmospherics of an Anglo-Chinese school, had imperceptibly developed a kind of Orientalist prejudice of our own. Or maybe we were too busy struggling to decipher the meaning of the texts and forgot what they might have told us about China's history and tradition. In any event, something was lost along the way.

It did help to have good teachers. Even the ones who taught us the basics and upheld the beacon of rote memorization were truly dedicated teachers. I owe them so much, and I salute them all. But perhaps the one who inspired me the most was Mrs. Audrey Faber. Maybe because she taught us history. Was it because I love history that I found her inspiring, or was it because she inspired me so much that I grew to love history? The intervening decades are playing tricks on my memory. Whichever was the case, I began to do well in the subject. But again, how does one excel if everyone just reads the same stuff? So a few of us began to exploit the resources at the British Council and the USIS (United States Information Service) libraries. To be seen or known to have regularly spent time at these vaunted places carried a certain cache among our peers. Besides, what better place was there to while away the hot summer than their quiet, air-conditioned reading rooms?

One hot summer day, weeks after the School Leaving Certificate Examinations, I was in the school playground, looking for a pick-up basketball game. I still loved to play even though I was no longer good enough or tall enough to make the A Division team. Colonel E. G. Stewart, the Headmaster, that very same gentleman who caught me crying in his office for handing in a blank at the "dictation" entrance examination seven years earlier, called me up to his office. There he told me that I had scored 96 points on my history examination—the highest score in all of Hong Kong not only for that year, but since the Pacific War! I do not recall how many thousands took that exam, but it didn't matter. Weeks later, before school began,

E. G. made me the Head Prefect for the next two years. I was not at the top of my class overall, but I was "James Pong's son," and that was good enough.

Forms Six and Seven (or Lower and Upper Six) were preparatory years for the two levels of examinations for entry into the University of Hong Kong—the lone university of the Crown Colony, as was the policy of the British government. The more adventurous among us also took the GCE (General Certificate of Education) examinations, which could lead to a place in a university in the United Kingdom. Having met the requirements at the end of the first year (Lower Six), I was ready to enter the School of Oriental & African Studies (SOAS) of the University of London, only to find that I had to wait a year as the passport application and the necessary medical examinations could not be completed in time.

The story, so far, gives us certain assurances that the old school system and even the old-style education could produce some positive results. But to look at it from a distance, it is clear that my stars were in the right places. I got into a great school through the side door. I have educated parents who nurtured me, and they did not mind spending extra money to hire tutors for me when they themselves had to skim on basic necessities. The old system could work for the few who enjoyed the "right" conditions. But as the next part of the story shows, this old-style education did have limitations.

The first year at SOAS was hard! This product of an Anglo-Chinese school in Hong Kong was just not good enough to understand his tutor, who rattled away in a heavy Scottish accent. But this was only a minor hurdle. The biggest shock was that this boy from Hong Kong could not score higher than a C or a B- in his history essays, no matter how hard he tried, whereas one of his classmates seemed to have done quite well without seemingly trying! So much for the record holder of the highest history score in postwar Hong Kong! Misery! Humiliation! After a year, I finally gathered enough courage to set aside my pride and begged this successful classmate to let me read his essays. This was truly a eureka moment. Finally, I began to understand the craft of history. (Thank you, Bob).

Armed with a BA in "Far Eastern History" or, in current, politically correct language, "East Asian History," and a doctorate in modern Chinese History, I thought I was ready to teach. And nine years of "experiential learning" in the great city of London shouldn't hurt either. So I thought to myself. But teaching in an American university presented its own challenge. It is commonly acknowledged in our profession that graduate students do not learn how to teach. The good instructors would teach the way they themselves had been taught; great teachers were simply born that way. Still, there were real adjustments to be made.

Class size was only a small consideration in the larger scheme of things. True, at SOAS, some of our classes were as small as 2 or 4, rarely 15 or more. Yet, in European and British history, we did attend lectures of 80 or 100. What was harder to adjust to was the fact that our college students did not come to my courses because they were interested in East Asian history. Some of them were, to be sure, but others enrolled for a multitude of reasons—to fulfill some sort of breadth requirements, or just to have a history course at the right time of day, definitely not a late Thursday or Friday morning class. Moreover, most of the students were not even history majors. And an even higher proportion was not accustomed to any form of discursive or analytical writing. This is the beauty of the American college system and of "liberal education" (however defined). It exposes students of all stripes to a field or a subject that they would otherwise not be interested in or have come across. I saw the wisdom of such a system but tremble at the thought of being able to address effectively the needs of such a diverse student body. I had great teachers at SOAS—William G. Beasley, Denis C. Twitchett, Michael Loewe, Jeremy Cowan, Bernard Lewis, to name just a few. But I knew I could not teach my students the way they taught me. I had to rethink and retool.

It is easier said than done. To put it charitably—if one could be charitable to oneself—it is still a "work in progress" after some forty years! Perhaps one could argue that there really is no perfect or near-perfect solution. Nor is there a foolproof method. Student interests change. They, perhaps more than us, the professoriat, are more sensitive to the shifting mood of the world around them. Their concerns became different. How to teach history, any history, to our students means becoming more attuned to the mood of the students and their concerns. In the United States, the Vietnam War generation or the baby boomers are some of the notable examples. In Hong Kong in recent years one talks about the post-80s generation for whom anti-colonialism, sustainable development, historical and cultural preservation are the main concerns. How does one teach Chinese history to this or that generation of students?

Students, however untutored they may be in the discipline of history, generally do bring with them the knowledge and methods of other disciplines. Their knowledge in other fields could be brought to bear on the study of history or the history of China. Over the years I have learned much from my students in this particular regard. I first heard about the concept of "soft power" from an International Relations major before I came across the term in my own readings some time later. It did not take long for me to discover how much more effective one could be if the history of China were taught with a degree of interdisciplinarity. History, after all, is a rather unique scholarly discipline in that it synthesizes the many fields within the humanities and the social sciences in an effort to understand human societies, past and present. It adapts easily to the use of data and approaches from many other disciplines in its delivery. I shall return to a more concrete discussion of this momentarily.

"The world is getting smaller," so goes a well-worn adage. It used to be, in studying the history of the United States, we seldom ventured abroad except when we were at war or engaged in "foreign affairs." It's an approach as intellectually satisfying as American exceptionalism is comfortable. This approach, thank goodness, is no longer fashionable. It goes against the grain of history. The study or teaching of Chinese history has been similarly subjected to a kind of Chinese exceptionalism. The Chinese call their own country "The Middle Kingdom" (*zhongguo*). The country was perceived as self sufficient, materially and culturally. In fact, China was civilization itself. Like American exceptionalism, however, this notion, too, is no longer tenable. China must be studied in a global context, and we must make a conscious effort to identify the context and relate it to China's historical development. Isn't it ironic that the scions of this Chinese exceptionalism so willingly accept "China" as universal reference when in fact it is a Western invention derived from the once-famous Qin [pronounced CHIN] dynasty (221–206 BC)? Frankly, the more we understand history, the more we realize how unexceptional we all are.

Continuing my quest for a better way to reach out to my American students, I turned more and more to the study of historical documents, "primary sources." The usual reasons given for the use of historical documents are enrichment, to provide illustrations and a flavor of how life was like, history was made, and society was viewed by its contemporaries. These are great reasons, but there are more. By reading these materials with my students, parsing each document, I sharpen their critical eyes and hone their analytical skills and judicious use of evidence. In half of the courses I teach, I have a discussion session after every three or four lectures, dedicated to the analysis of historical documents. Students seem to like it, as one emailed me, "Lastly, I just wanted to tell you, as this is our final discussion day, that I love the Cheng & Lestz book [of documents]. I honestly feel I've learned more from its documents... I wish all history classes had a similar accompanying book. I'm not going to be selling either of the books back because I know I'll return to them many times just for leisure reading." (Thank you, Jessica!)

As the call for "problem-based learning" (PBL) reached high decibel levels in the past decades, we, historians, were very much engaged in the discussion. Not everyone was ready to jump onto the bandwagon, to surrender part control of the classroom, to have students working in small collaborative groups and engage in open-ended investigations. Without being defensive, it can be genuinely argued that history, especially in the guise of essay writing, is indeed a form of problem-based learning without the trappings of the PBL methodology. After all, we do encourage and help students to formulate questions, conduct evidential research (first- or second-hand), and come up with a variety of well-argued responses. In the process, students acquire critical thinking skills, improve problem-solving capabilities, enhance writing skills, and reach conclusions that could be interpretive and invite further investigations. What is needed is care in the framing of the questions or problems, the guidance of the students' work, and the critique of the end product. A bonus, by the way, could well be a significant improvement in the students' ability to present a narrative or an argument in fine prose.

In September 2012, all of the eight institutions of higher education in Hong Kong will admit the last cohort of school-leavers who would have completed seven years of high school—the kind of schooling I underwent at St. Paul's—for a three-year curriculum in the university. Simultaneously, they will also admit the first cohort who would have had only six years of high school, to be followed by a four-year curriculum in the university. The structural change from a three- to a four-year curriculum is to facilitate a sea-change in the nature of higher education in the SAR, the Special Administrative Region, as Hong Kong is called since its retrocession to China in 1997. The "extra" year is to permit the introduction of general education in the curriculum. The goal is to produce university graduates who are strong in their specialties as if they had undergone the old, three-year system, but with the breadth of knowledge, problem-solving skills, critical and analytical thinking, as well as the creativity and adaptability that come with a more liberal, general education curriculum.

Each Hong Kong university has its own ideas and philosophy about how to reshape their curriculum, benefiting as well as being hampered by the history and tradition that gave each its distinctive character. But in one area they share a common concern: how to integrate the study of China, its history, culture, and civilization into the new, general education agenda. Hong Kong is part of China. Ninety-five per cent of its denizens are Chinese. Despite and because of the 156 years of British rule, it is at once Chinese and cosmopolitan. It makes eminent sense for all the university students in the new general education curriculum to have at least a one-time but truly university-level exposure to China's rich history and civilization, just as it makes sense for American students to study US History 101 upon entering college. If a student in former, colonial Hong Kong learned so much about metropolitan Britain in school, how much more so should post-1997 Hong Kong students know and understand China? But here's the rub.

I began this piece by stressing that there are plenty of great scholars and teachers of Chinese history and Chinese studies in the SAR. In a world that is flat (to borrow a concept from Thomas Friedman), China experts in Hong Kong are as well versed as colleagues elsewhere in the latest pedagogy and education theories. They benefit not just from our North American experience, but also from that coming out of the United Kingdom, Australia, and New Zealand. But, heretofore, the teaching about China in Hong Kong universities has resided in specialized disciplines. Historians of China teach Chinese history to history students, sociology to sociology students, and so forth. Now, from September 2012, Chinese history or culture will have to be taught to the general student body, many of whom will not take another course about China for the rest of their student life. Professors would have to create new courses or re-invent existing ones. For the first time as well, many students will enter university without a major, and quite possibly without any interest in history or culture. How does one introduce these students to the discipline of history and at the same time to have the students think consciously of themselves as living in a Chinese tradition? How does one design or deliver such a course?

As a discipline, history is situated in a rather privileged position.

It has been said that economics is the queen of the social sciences. If so, let me make a plug for history as the queen of the humanities and the social sciences. History deals with all facets of human life and experience. There is economic history, social history, gender history, historical geography, and even the history of history (historiography). A course on China can be anchored in history and yet be interdisciplinary and address the interests and needs of students who may never take another history course for the rest of their life. Although, if such a course is well taught, one wonders why they should not! Let this be a gateway course, one that opens the doors for further explorations.

So, in September 2012, professors and students will undergo a sea-change, in much the same way as I underwent my baptisms of fire when I made the transition from a Hong Kong high school to a university in the United Kingdom, and when I crossed the Atlantic and took my first teaching job in the United States. Over the past several years, my colleagues in Hong Kong have given a lot of thought to the teaching of Chinese history in the new milieu. They welcome the opportunities, and are well aware of the challenges.

China's is the longest living tradition in the world. The Chinese are rightly proud of their heritage. Against the backdrop of a rising China, many are doubly inclined to feel this pride. A similar self-perception was prevalent in the West when Europe and the United States took turns to lead the world. One by-product of this worldview was a distorted view of history, which, in the West, was largely built around the accomplishments of "the dead white male." There have been vast changes in the study of history since the 1950s, and my colleagues in Hong Kong are party to these changes. Instead of a Chinese version of the "dead white male" syndrome, a typical history department will have courses on social history, gender history, economic history, cultural history, and so forth. But these are courses for the history students. The task is to integrate these elements in a general education course or courses. Our outlook is that it (or they) will consist of many of the elements previously discussed. I shall mention a few here that I feel are sometimes given short shrift. They are presented below in no particular order:

Historical geography, underscoring the changing footprint of the Chinese empire and the major differences between predominantly Han Chinese dynasties and dynasties of conquests (notably the Mongols and the Manchus), disabusing the students' notion of a homogeneous or unchanging China.

A social history that is truly representative of the peoples of China, including the study of intellectual, economic and political elites as well as the under-classes. Demographically, this would include population growth and migration over time. I think students would be thrilled to note the internal dynamism of China's society throughout history. They would be thrilled to witness the evolution of China's rich civilization and note the nodal points where the march of China's history made its irreversible changes.

One could study the art of China along similar lines. China had produced great literati and court paintings, for example, but how should one view the Chinese equivalent of naïve painting in peasant art or revolutionary art?

China has serious ethnic problems, which are far more intractable than those found in the United States, as China's minorities are located in homelands that have been historically theirs, and as they speak different languages and follow distinctive religious faiths. Nothing in the United States is comparable to Tibet, Xinjiang, Inner Mongolia, and the numerous "autonomous" regions of minority groups found mainly in southwestern China. The Hakkas, too, deserve more than a passing glance. The Hakkas, in certain academic circles, are considered more comparable to ethnic minorities in the United States.

One could study China's place in the world. Here, the students' eyes should be open to a China that, despite conventional wisdom, was and is not isolationist, though it has a distinctive method of handling its foreign affairs as dictated by historical circumstances. Everybody knows that Buddhism is not native to China, but few think about it as only one of many foreign influences before modern times. When and from where did the Chinese acquire the habit of sitting on chairs? This example alone should open their eyes to the foreign origins of what has become a part of Chinese daily life. On the other hand, why are some of the most notable products of the creative and inventive mind not given proper attributions to the Chinese? Why is Chan Buddhism known to the world by its Japanese nomenclature, Zen? Similarly, why is the board game Go not called by its Chinese name, *weiqi*? How the Chinese present themselves in the world, and how the world perceives China are critical questions, not only for the intellectually curious, but also for business majors who might want to "sell" or "repackage" China!

The Chinese set great store by harmony, how do students understand the inextricable relationship between harmony and hierarchy in the country's social and political life? And in a world where one is expected to follow the dictates of harmonious living and observe hierarchical relationships, how does one express differences of opinion? What provisions are there for officials to remonstrate with their rulers, or officials to impeach other officials? What is the role of dissent? More importantly, what are the implications for the rule of law?

Over the ages, the Chinese excelled in many areas of science and technology. Sir Francis Bacon called printing, gunpowder, and the compass the three greatest inventions in the world, and they all came from China. What are the characteristics of Chinese science and technology? When did China lead the world, and when did it begin to lose that lead? What is the trajectory of China's modern transformation in these fields?

This short list already suggests a very rich and diverse China. The wonder is that it managed to hold together as a political and cultural entity for so long. Why didn't China become a Europe?

Hong Kong is a great place to study the history and culture of China. The place is itself a living museum. Weddings, funerals, parturition rites are grist for the mill in the study of social customs, religion, and human relationships. Sun Yat-sen's footprint is everywhere. The place is as much a classic example of Western colonialism as one of East-West cultural interaction, or a successful multi-ethnic city. It is the birthplace of China's first department stores. A short trip into the New Territories or nearby Mainland China and one will encounter living monuments of China's modern history, of lineage organization, out-migration, returned overseas Chinese, reform and revolution. If my students in the United States find reading historical documents exciting, how much more so it would be to study China's history in situ. This makes all of us in North America who must rely on texts and powerpoints feel rather dehydrated.

Still bringing coal to Newcastle? Not really. Helping to light a fire? Perhaps.

Postscript

How We Are Forever Changed …

Most cross-cultural journeys eventually come to an end. Contemplating the return to one's home culture initiates the final stage of cross-cultural experiences—that of reflection on the meaning of the experience and the long term impact of the journey. Whenever you live abroad, certain aspects of the host culture become integrated into your own personal lives—they have so influenced you that you can't leave them behind. Sometimes you acquire a phrase that is so perfect in its meaning that you keep using it. Other times it is a holiday or national emblem that now has meaning to you. On the surface these symbols don't appear to be profound, but I believe they represent a much deeper cross-cultural integration that has taken place.

Years ago I lived in southern Louisiana where they speak Cajun French. I still find myself saying "come see (ici)" rather than "come here." Having lived in New Zealand, my daughters and I hang out our New Zealand flag, support the All Blacks rugby team, and have a deeper understanding of the haka war dance that the All Blacks do prior to each game. We sometimes do our own version at home behind closed doors. And I continue to say, "no worries" and occasionally but less often, "good on you" (as in gudonyah), or ask for fizzy drink instead of soda or pop.

Each cross-cultural experience with its deep encounter with place contributes an additional richness to our lives. What did I think about as I moved toward closure in Hong Kong? The following is taken from my journal as I moved into this reflective stage:

> I find myself ending emails that acknowledge the receipt of something with "noted with thanks." During Chinese New Year I could not help myself from imitating others by ending emails with "Wishing you well in the Year of the Tiger." These phrases represent a beautiful sense of graciousness that I have grown to appreciate in Hong Kong. This week Karis came to school in the rain and a school guard insisted in holding the umbrella over her and then gave her the umbrella to keep. One of my colleagues brought me a cup of tea when she knew I had a headache. When I arrive at a meeting each place is set with a bottle of water, paper and pencil. When I have given a lecture, I am often given a small token of appreciation such as a pen with the university insignia on it. And you are never handed anything with one hand—for example you give your business card to people using both hands. I am to the point where I find myself feeling like I am quite rude when I hand money to a clerk with only one hand. I'm not sure I will ever be able to fully revert to the Western way of handing out or over items, and I think I am going to have to have a stash of gifts to give visitors or speakers.

Endless cultural gifts are given to each of us as we cross cultural boundaries throughout our lifetimes, whether within our own country's borders or without. We have attempted to describe our process of encountering, understanding, and accepting these gifts in

Postscript

this volume. I call these many encounters, that in the end change our lives forever, "lagniappe," using a Louisiana term—the little extra gift, a 13 piece dozen. And perhaps the greatest gift we receive is that we go home with greater understanding and insight into ourselves and our own culture. In learning to read another place and culture, we learn to read ourselves.

All these gifts are here noted with thanks.

Janel CURRY

Contributors

David A. CAMPION is the Dr. Robert B. Pamplin Jr. Associate Professor of History at Lewis & Clark College in Portland, Oregon, and was a Fulbright Scholar in General Education and Visiting Lecturer in History at the Hong Kong Baptist University in 2009–2010. He received a BA in History and English from Georgetown University and an MA and PhD in history from the University of Virginia. Campion's research and teaching focus on Modern Britain & Ireland, the British Empire, and Modern South Asia. He has held research fellowships in London, India and Washington DC and has led study abroad programs in East Africa and Australia.

Joseph CHANEY is Associate Professor of English at Indiana University South Bend, where he directs the Master of Liberal Studies Program. He was a Fulbright Fellow at the Chinese University of Hong Kong in 2009–2010. For many years he has written commentaries for the award-winning series Michiana Chronicles for WVPE Radio, an NPR affiliate. He also writes poetry, and his work has appeared in *The Nation, Yankee, Beloit Poetry Journal, Black Warrior Review*, and other magazines.

Janel CURRY has been serving as Provost of Gordon College in Massachusetts since 2012. Prior to going to Gordon College, she was Dean for Research and Scholarship and Professor of Geography and Environmental Studies at Calvin College, Grand Rapids,

Michigan. Curry was a Fulbright Scholar in General Education at City University of Hong Kong in 2010 and returned to continue her work with City University in 2012. She has also held a Fulbright Fellowship to Canada.

Christopher DENEEN started his career in education as an elementary and high school teacher. After earning his doctorate from Columbia University's Teacher's College, Chris spent several years living and working in New York City as an academic and as the Director of Assessment for Touro College's graduate divisions. Chris visited Hong Kong for the first time in 2004 and fell in love with the city. After visiting several times, he resettled there in 2009 and began working with the Hong Kong Institute of Education on the enhancement of assessment, teaching and learning as well as classroom technology integration. Chris is currently at the University of Hong Kong, as an Assistant Professor of Research. His principal field of interest is researching effective assessment practices in higher and teacher education. In August 2014, Chris will be joining The National Institute of Education in Singapore as an Assistant Professor with the Department of Curriculum, Teaching and Learning.

Patricia FLANAGAN has been exhibiting internationally since the mid 1990s and is represented in private and public collections in Australia, Ireland, Germany, Italy and China. She is the winner of four CASP funded Public Art commissions and a UGCTD Grant to develop PIPA; representative for Oceania at the Tournai Contemporary Textiles Biennial Belgium; recipient of the Australian Postgraduate Scholarship Award and winner of The Max Fabre Foundation Award for Environmental Awareness. She completed a Doctorate of Philosophy (Public Art) at University of Newcastle Australia; Master of Art (Visual

Art) at Bauhaus University Weimar; Bachelor of Arts (Fine Art) at University of Newcastle Australia and Associate Diploma awarded with honors (Fashion Design) at Hunter Institute of Technology NSW. Her research in human computer interaction is widely published and she holds a seat on the programming board for HCI–Design User Experience and Usability. Dr. Flanagan established the Wearables Lab at the Academy of Visual Art at HKBU in 2009 where she currently works as Assistant Professor.

Hedley FREAKE is Professor of Nutritional Sciences at the University of Connecticut and has been at that institution for more than 20 years. His research uses molecular approaches to investigate questions of nutritional significance and has focused on lipid metabolism as well as zinc homeostasis and action. He teaches several nutrition classes, ranging from large introductory general education courses ("Food Culture and Society") to advanced graduate courses ("Nutrition and Gene Expression"). His route to nutrition was via the kitchen. As well as having a life-long passion for food and cooking, he also worked as a chef for a number of years. He is the ultimate omnivore.

Susan GANO-PHILLIPS is an Interim Associate Dean in the College of Arts and Sciences and Professor of Psychology at the University of Michigan—Flint. She has been actively involved in the reform, implementation, and assessment of the general education program at UM-Flint since 2005. She has published on general education reform (*A Process Approach to GE Reform*, with R.W. Barnett, Atwood, 2010) as well as on leadership and organizational change in higher education. She completed a Fulbright Fellowship in General Education at City University of Hong Kong during the 2008–2009 academic year.

Paul HANSTEDT is Professor of English at Roanoke College and the author of two books: *Hong Konged*, a travel memoir, and *General Education Essentials*, a faculty introduction to current trends in liberal education.

Elizabeth HUEBNER is a movement specialist with a degree in dance performance and is a professional member of AmSAT. She has taught the Alexander Technique for over 30 years in London, Minnesota, Connecticut, and Hong Kong. She taught for 20 years at University of Connecticut and is currently reaching her own potential performing tap dance with the Mansfield Sparkettes.

David JAFFEE is Professor of Sociology at University of North Florida. He studies economic sociology, work and organizations, social and economic development, labor, and higher education. He received his PhD in sociology from the University of Massachusetts at Amherst. He was a Fulbright Fellow at City University of Hong Kong in 2010–2011.

Gray KOCHHAR-LINDGREN is Professor and Director of the Common Core at the University of Hong Kong. With degrees in philosophy, religious studies, and literature, and a PhD in Interdisciplinary Studies from Emory University, Gray is the author of *Narcissus Transformed, Starting Time, TechnoLogics, Night Café, Philosophy, Art, and the Specters of Jacques Derrida*, and, most recently, *Kant in Hong Kong: Walking, Thinking, and the City*. Gray has taught in Switzerland, Germany, and the United States, and, in 2009–10, served as a Fulbright Scholar in General Education at the University of Hong Kong and the Hong Kong American Center.

Jackie Jia LOU is Assistant Professor in the Department of English, City University of Hong Kong. She received her PhD in Linguistics from Georgetown University in 2009, with the dissertation titled "Situating Linguistic Landscape in Time and Space: A Multidimensional Study of the Discursive Construction of Washington, DC Chinatown." Lou's primary research interest lies in the discursive and semiotic construction of place and the ways in which cultural, economic, and political forces underpin such constructions.

David PONG 龐百騰 is Professor Emeritus in East Asian History at the University of Delaware, and has taught in England, Australia and Hong Kong. A graduate of St. Paul's College, Hong Kong, he earned both his BA (Hons.) and PhD in History at the School of Oriental and African Studies, University of London. His specialty is in modern Chinese history (late Qing). He has authored three books, edited three books, and published more than 30 journal articles and book chapters. He is the Editor-in-Chief of the four-volume *Encyclopedia of Modern China*, which received the Dartmouth Medal Honorable Mention for the best reference work published in 2009. He teaches courses on East Asian Civilizations and modern China. He founded and directed the East Asian Studies Program at Delaware (1989–2009) and has led many study abroad programs to China. He was a Fulbright Scholar-in-Residence at the Chinese University of Hong Kong for the academic year, 2009–2010. Since his contribution to this volume he has taken up an appointment as Foundation Master of Choi Kai Yau College in the newly established residential college system of the University of Macau.

Ivette VARGAS-O'BRYAN is Chair and Associate Professor in the Department of Religious Studies at Austin College in Sherman, Texas (USA). In the PRC, she was Visiting Associate Professor of Philosophy in the General Education Office at United International College in Zhuhai, China (2010–2011). Her specialization is on Indian and Tibetan Buddhist narratives and the interface of religion, disease and medicine. She is the co-editor and author of *Disease, Religion and Healing in Asia: Collaborations and Collisions* (Routledge 2014) and has two book projects with Brill Publications. She was a Fulbright Lecturer at City University of Hong Kong and assisted in the General Education Program in 2009. She also co-chaired "Health in Asia" in the Centre for Humanities and Medicine at HKU in 2009–10. She received her PhD at Harvard University.